Portable GUI Development with C++

Mark Watson

McGraw-Hill, Inc.

New York St. Louis San Francisco Blue Ridge Summit, Pa.
Auckland Bogotá Caracas Lisbon London Madrid
Mexico Milan Montreal New Delhi Paris San Juan
São Paulo Singapore Sydney Tokyo Toronto

FIRST EDITION
FIRST PRINTING

©1993 by **McGraw-Hill, Inc.**
Printed in the United States of America. All rights reserved.

Library of Congress Cataloging-in-Publication Data

Watson, Mark, 1951-
    Portable GUI development with C++ / by Mark Watson.
      p. cm.
    Includes bibliographical references and index.
    ISBN 0-07-068484-7 (paper)
    1. User interfaces (Computer systems)   2. C++ (Computer program language) 3. Computer graphics. I. Title.
    QA76.9.U83W38 1992
    005.4'2—dc20
                                                            92-22544
                                                                CIP

For information about other McGraw-Hill materials, call 1-800-2-MCGRAW in the U.S. In other countries call your nearest McGraw-Hill office.

Acquisitions Editor: Jeanne Glassor
Book Editor: Marianne Krcma
Supervising Editor: Joanne Slike
Director of Production: Katherine G. Brown

UNIX is a trademark of AT&T Bell Laboratories. BSD is a trademark of University of California, Berkeley. POSIX is a trademark of IEEE. The following are trademarks of Digital Equipment Corporation: DEC, UNIBUS, DEC/CMS, DEC/MMS, DECnet, PDP, VAX, VAXcluster, VMS, VT, XMI, VAXBI, ULTRIX, ALL-IN-1, Q-bus, MicroVAX, MASSBUS, DECwindows, DIGITAL, VAX RMS, ReGIS. IBM is a registered trademark of International Business Corporation. X Window System, Version 11 and its derivatives (X, X11, X Version 11, X Window system) are trademarks of the Massachussetts Institute of Technology.

Contents

Acknowledgments   ix

Introduction   xi

Part 1   Overview of Windows, Macintosh, and X Windows Programming Model and Design of an Abstract GUI C^{++} Class

Chapter 1. Portability   3

Chapter 2. Microsoft Windows   7

  2.1   Windows Application Interface to DOS   7
  2.2   Event Handling in Windows Applications   8
  2.3   Graphics Operations in Windows Applications   10
  2.4   Dialog Boxes in Windows Applications   11
  2.5   Creating a Document Window   13
  2.6   Creating an Application Environment   16
  2.7   Windows API Functions Used in Appendix B   17

Chapter 3. Apple Macintosh   25

  3.1   Macintosh Application Interface to the Operating System   26
  3.2   Event Handling in Macintosh Applications   27
  3.3   Graphics Operations in Macintosh Applications   28
  3.4   Resource Files for Building Macintosh Applications 29
  3.5   Dialog Boxes in Macintosh Applications   31
  3.6   Creating a Document Window   32
  3.7   Creating an Application Environment   32
  3.8   Macintosh Toolbox Functions Used in Appendix C   35

Chapter 4. X Windows   47

4.1 X Windows Application Interface to the Unix Operating System   48
4.2 Event Handling in X Windows Applications   48
4.3 Graphics Operations in X Windows Applications   50
4.4 Dialog Boxes in X Windows Applications   51
4.5 X Windows API Functions Used in Appendix D   53

Chapter 5. Abstract C++ GUI Class Library   61

5.1 Basic User Interface Components   61
5.2 Handling Background Processing   68
5.3 Sample Test Program Using the Abstract Class Library Design   70

Part 2   C++ Application Utility Classes

Chapter 6. Graphical Tree Browser Class   77

6.1 Design of the Tree Browser Class   77
6.2 Implementation of the Tree Browser Class   78
6.3 Using the Tree Browser Class   87

Chapter 7. Smart Persistent Data Object Classes   89

7.1 Rationale for Using Vector Classes   89
7.2 Interface for an Integer Smart Vector Class   91
7.3 Implementation of an Integer Vector Class   91

Chapter 8. File I/O   95

8.1 ASCII Text I/O   95
8.2 Binary I/O   96

Chapter 9. Curve Plotting Class   99

9.1 Design of the TPlotClass Curve Plotting Class   99
9.2 Interface to the TPlotClass Class   100
9.3 Implementation of the TPlotClass Class   101
9.4 Examples Using the TPlotClass   104

Chapter 10. Generic Pattern Matcher Class   109

10.1 Rationale for Using Neural Networks   109
10.2 Design of the TNeuralNet Class   110
10.3 Header File for the TNeuralNet Class   111
10.4 Source File for the TNeuralNet Class   114
10.5 Using the TNeuralNet Class   118

Chapter 11. Text Indexing Class   119

11.1 Requirements for the TextIndex Class   119

11.2 Design of the TextIndex Class · 120
11.3 Implementation of the TextIndex Class · · · · · · · · · · · 121
11.4 Using the TextIndex Class · 137

Part 3 Example Applications

Chapter 12. Hierarchical Information Browser · · · · · · 141

12.1 Example HIB Data · 141
12.2 HIB Functionality · 144
12.3 HIB Implementation · 148

Chapter 13. Handwriting Classifier · · · · · · · · · · · · · · · · 157

13.1 User Interface · 157
13.2 Implementation of the Handwriting Classifier · · · · · · 158

Chapter 14. Intelligent Text Browser · · · · · · · · · · · · · · 163

14.1 User Interface · 163
14.2 Implementation of the Text Browser Application · · · · 165

Chapter 15. 3D Chess · 171

15.1 Rules for 3D Chess · 171
15.2 User Interface Design for a 3D Chess Program · · · · · 172
15.3 C++ Classes to Play 3D Chess · · · · · · · · · · · · · · · · · · · 172
15.4 Complete Implementation of a 3D Chess Program · · 174

Appendix A. Generic GUI Class Reference · · · · · · · · · · · 203

Appendix B. Microsoft Windows Class Implementation · · · 205

B.1 Windows Resource Files · 205
B.2 Windows-Specific GUI Include Files · · · · · · · · · · · · · · · 211
B.3 Windows-Specific GUI C++ Source Files · · · · · · · · · · · 215
B.4 Windows-Specific Smart Vector Include Files · · · · · · · 225
B.5 Windows-Specific Smart Vector C++ Source Files · · · 228

Appendix C. Macintosh Class Implementation · · · · · · · · 235

C.1 Macintosh Resource Files · 235
C.2 Macintosh-Specific GUI Include Files · · · · · · · · · · · · · · 242
C.3 Macintosh-Specific GUI C++ Source Files · · · · · · · · · · 246
C.4 Macintosh-Specific Smart Vector Include Files · · · · · · 261
C.5 Macintosh-Specific Smart Vector C++ Source Files · · 263
C.6 Macintosh Makefiles · 270

Appendix D. X Windows Class Implementation   275

D.1 X Windows Menu Definition Include Files   275
D.2 X-Windows-Specific GUI Include Files   276
D.3 X-Windows-Specific GUI C++ Source Files   282
D.4 X-Windows-Specific Smart Vector Include Files   299
D.5 X-Windows-Specific Smart Vector C++ Source Files   301
D.6 X Windows Makefile   308

Bibliography   311
Index   313

Acknowledgments

I would like to thank my wife Carol for her encouragement while writing this book, Kemer Thomson at Sun Microsystems and John Hooker at Digital Equipment Corporation for making UNIX workstations available for the preparation of the X Windows software in this book, my father Ken Watson for the use of his laser printer, and my acquiring editor Jeanne Glasser for her help with this book project.

Introduction

There are either no standards for building graphic user interfaces (GUIs), or too many standards. Open software architectures like X Windows support portable GUIs, but most application development targets the IBM PC and Macintosh environments. This book provides a concise reference to the imaging and event-handling models used by Microsoft Windows, Macintosh Toolbox, X Windows, and X Toolkits (Athena and Motif). I abstract a common framework for handling events and graphical display objects, and develop an architecturally neutral design for implementing GUIs. I use C++ to implement this architecture for the common windowing toolkits. C++ is a standard language for software development because it combines backward compatibility to C with modern object-oriented programming methodology.

I do not attempt to provide an all-inclusive software toolkit supporting all windowing environments; instead, I provide a methodology to build software tools for specific applications that facilitate their portability. This book is designed for software developers producing custom in-house software applications and commercial software developers who want to maximize their investment in commercial product development. I cover practical problems facing C++ programmers of GUI-based applications, like implementing C "callback" event handlers for C++ libraries.

The following 10-line program implements the standard "hello world" program using the C++ GUI library developed in this book. This program has the standard behavior of a Macintosh, Microsoft Windows , and X Windows (Athena and Motif widget sets) application.

```
// File: hello.cp
#include "applib.h"
void TAppWindow::update_display()
{ plot_string(130, 90, "Hello World!"); }
void TAppWindow::mouse_down(int x, int y) { } // no mouse down action
                                             // required
```

```
void TAppWindow::mouse_up(int, int)        { } // no mouse up action
                                               // required
void TAppWindow::mouse_move(int, int)   { } // no mouse movement action
                                            // required
void TAppWindow::idle_proc()            { } // no background processing
                                            // required
void TAppWindow::do_menu_action(int item_number) // handle menu actions
{
    if (item_number==1) exit(0);   // exit program
}
INIT_PROGRAM        // Macro for machine dependent initialization
    // Application specific initialization is placed here
    RUN_PROGRAM;    // Macro for machine dependent event handling
}
```

This book provides many reusable C++ classes. I want to save you time and effort in your software development projects. As software developers, we must develop methodologies for code reuse to reduce programming costs and increase the functionality of the programs we write.

After designing an abstract windowing-environment independent class library, I develop several utility classes for machine-independent file I/O, browsing graphical tree displays, curve plotting for scientific and business applications, smart data objects that manage their own memory allocation and persistence, a generic (neural network) pattern matcher, and a text indexing class for rapid text retrieval. A short example program that is used for testing the GUI classes is seen in Fig. I.1. I finish this book with four complete applications: handwriting recognition, text browsing, information browser, and 3D chess. Figure I.2 shows the text-browser application developed in Chapter 14. Figure I.3 shows the 3D chess program developed in Chapter 15.

I have organized this book to give a brief introduction to portability in Chapter 1, followed by introductions to Microsoft Windows, Macintosh, and X Windows programming in Chapters 2, 3, and 4. The applications in chapters 12 through 15 use utility C++ classes developed in Chapters 6 through 11. C++ code should be reusable; I hide computational details in the implementation of these classes. If you're interested in neural network theory, smart data objects, and efficient text indexing, you can certainly study these utility classes. In general, however, these C++ classes should be used as off-the-shelf software components. Programmers can only build interesting, complex applications by either spending a great deal of time and money, or by intelligently using available software libraries.

Chapters in this book are ordered so that required background material is discussed before it is used. However, you might prefer to start with Chapter 5 on abstract GUI design, then work through the application chapter that most interests you (hierarchical data browser, handwriting recognition system, text browsing system, or the 3D chess program), using the machine-dependent material (Chapters 2, 3, and 4, and Appendices B, C and D) only for reference. Initially, treat the C⁺⁺ utility classes created in Chapters 6 through 11 as available, off-the-shelf components.

I welcome your comments about this book and my programs. I can be reached via electronic mail at CompuServe (75765,556) and BIX (wmark). You can also write to me in care of the publisher, or directly at the following address:

535 Mar Vista Drive
Solana Beach, CA 92075

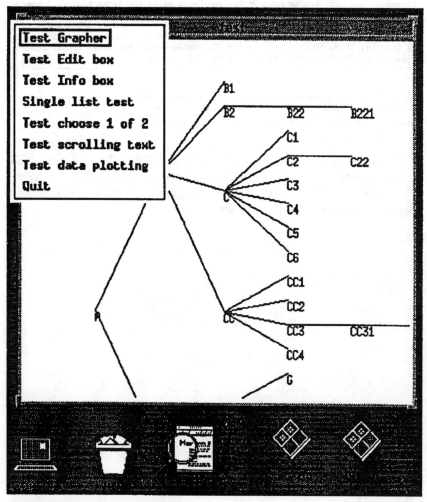

Figure I.1 Program for testing GUI classes.

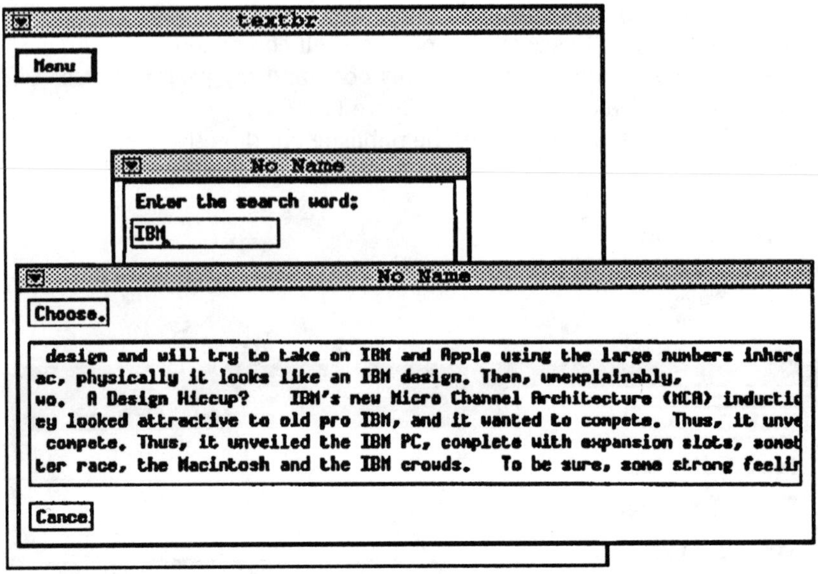

Figure I.2 Text browser application developed in chapter 14.

All source code in this book is available on an IBM PC and Macintosh format disk directly from me through the above address for $12. Either disk format contains all source listings presented in this book for the Macintosh, Microsoft Windows, and X Windows.

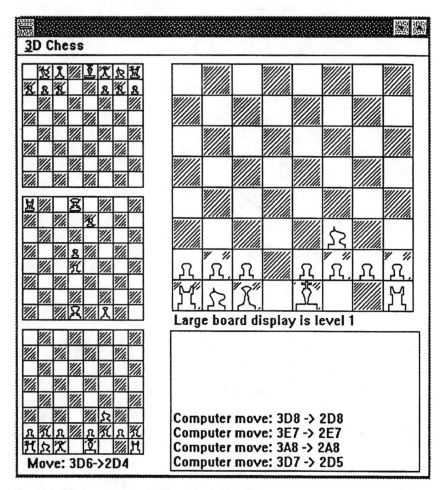

Figure I.3 3D chess program developed in chapter 15.

Overview of Windows, Macintosh, and X Windows Programming Model, and Design of an Abstract GUI C++ Class

Portability

Many programmers need to develop software for more than one type of computer and more than one windowing environment. This situation is both good and bad. The competition among the developers of operating systems and windowing environments improves technology. Unfortunately, many of us spend a fairly large percentage of our (professional) time porting applications among different computing environments.

When I started the project that evolved into this book, my intention was to develop a simple, but extensible, C++ class library for my own use in prototyping and developing relatively low-volume commercial applications. I have developed commercial applications for both the Macintosh and the Microsoft Windows environments. I have also developed custom X Windows applications. Even though I have designed the C++ utilities in this book for my own use, I feel certain that they will also be useful to other programmers.

The software contained in this book can be used without royalty fees of any kind under a few simple conditions: The software is presented "as is" with no warranties or proof of correctness, the software may only be distributed in compiled form, and I would appreciate written acknowledgment that you made use of my utilities.

I am writing this book on my Mac II using Microsoft Word 5.0 for word processing and document preparation and Apple's MPW C++ software development environment. I would like to thank both Digital Equipment Corporation and Sun Microsystems for the use of Unix workstations for X development. I use Sun's C++ compiler on SPARC machines, and DEC's C++ compiler on DEC RISC workstations. My Microsoft Windows development environment is Borland's C++ compiler (version 3.0) executing on my 386

PC clone. At work, I frequently use Interactive Unix with the Glockenspeil C++ compiler and recommend this combination for X development on Intel platforms.

When I have an idea for a new program, I like to be able to bring up a window-based graphical user interface (GUI) quickly. It only takes about ten lines of application code to bring up a simple application using the GUI libraries developed in this book. To whet your appetite, here is a very simple drawing program (this program is trivial; more interesting applications are developed in Chapters 12 through 15):

```
// File: draw.cp
//
// Description: Example Drawing program using the C++ GUI
//
// Copyright 1992 by Mark Watson Associates
//
//         No binary rights reserved: this software library may be used in
//         compiled form without restrictions.  All source rights
//         reserved: Source code to the GUI library can not be distributed
//         (on bulletin boards, or as part of shareware or commercial
//         products)
//         without written permission.
//

#include "applib.h"      // C++ GUI library include file
#include "int_vect.h"    // Use smart vector to store points

int nump = 0;            // count the number of points stored
int_vect points(99);     // stored as: (x, y, pen_up_or_down) triples

#define X(n)  (3*(n))
#define Y(n)  (3*(n)+1)
#define UP_OR_DOWN(n)  (3*(n)+2)

void TAppWindow::update_display() // draw all the saved points
{
    for (int i=0; i<nump - 1; i++) {
            if (points[UP_OR_DOWN(i)])
                plot_line(   points[X(i)], points[Y(i)],
                             points[X(i+1)], points[Y(i+1)]);
    }
}

void TAppWindow::mouse_down(int xp, int yp)
{
        points[X(nump)] = xp;   // smart vectors grow dynamically and
        points[Y(nump)] = yp;   // abort the program on insufficient memory
        points[UP_OR_DOWN(nump)] = 0;
        nump++;
}

void TAppWindow::mouse_up(int xp, int yp)  // AND mouse move logic
{
        points[X(nump)] = xp;   // smart vectors grow dynamically
        points[Y(nump)] = yp;   // and abort the program on insufficient
                                // memory
```

```
            points[UP_OR_DOWN(nump)] = 1;
            if (nump > 1)
                plot_line(points[X(nump-1)], points[Y(nump-1)],
                          points[X(nump)], points[Y(nump)]);
            nump++;
}

void TAppWindow::mouse_move(int xp, int yp)
{
            mouse_up(xp, yp);   // same functionality as mouse up event
}
void TAppWindow::idle_proc() { }   // no background processing necessary

void TAppWindow::do_menu_action(int item_number)
{   char buf[80], file_name[256];
        if (item_number == 1) {   // reset drawing
            nump = 0;
            clear_display();
        }
        if (item_number == 2) {   // save to a file
            if (choose_file_to_write("Save file (end in .drw)", file_name))
                Warning("Error opening file");
            else   points.save(file_name);
        }
        if (item_number == 3) {   // reload points from a file
            if (choose_file_to_read("Restore file", "drw", file_name))
                Warning("Error opening file");
            else  { points.restore(file_name);  nump = points.num_elements
/ 3; }
        }
}

INIT_PROGRAM

    // anything can go here for program initialization

    RUN_PROGRAM;
}
```

Figure 1.1 shows a drawing made with this short example program. This small program runs without source code modification on the Apple Macintosh, Microsoft Windows, and Unix computers supporting X Windows (using either Athena Widgets or Motif). All applications developed in this book are equally portable.

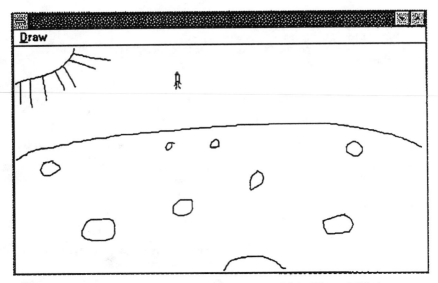

Figure 1.1 Tiny drawing program (50 lines of C++ source code) for Microsoft Windows.

2

Microsoft Windows

Chapter 1 shows how a drawing program can be implemented in about 50 lines of code using a GUI C++ class library. This chapter provides a brief introduction to Microsoft Windows programming. This introduction is useful both for understanding the program listings in Appendix B and in understanding the design of the GUI library in Chapter 5.

Many good programming tools are available for developing Windows applications. My personal preference is the Turbo C++ environment from Borland. Many of my Windows applications are partially derived from short example programs provided with the Borland programming environment. I want to express my personal gratitude to the engineers at Borland for both creating a fine compiler and environment, and for the small example programs that concisely demonstrate Windows programming with Borland Turbo C++.

2.1 Windows Application Interface to DOS

Figure 2.1 shows the interface between application programs and Windows, and between Windows and MS-DOS. Unlike the Macintosh operating system (Mac OS), the Windows environment sits on top of the MS-DOS OS. The main advantage of this layered approach (instead of rewriting MS-DOS) is the compatibility with old MS-DOS software and the huge installed base of IBM PC compatible machines. A minor disadvantage is the requirement for extra memory and disk space to support Windows. The Windows Kernel, GDI, and User modules interact with both the MS-DOS OS and the underlying ROM BIOS.

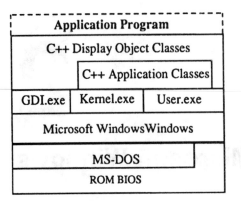

Figure 2.1 Microsoft Windows software architecture.

Microsoft has created a new operating system, New Technology (NT), which uses a Windows-style environment with a new preemptive multitasking operating system kernel that is POSIX call compatible. NT will be available on both Intel and RISC-based workstations. Application programs written for Windows will be very portable to NT.

2.2 Event Handling in Windows Applications

Microsoft Windows uses a very cleanly designed event-handling interface between Windows and Windows-based application programs, between one Windows-based application program and another one, and between a Windows-based application program and itself. All events are represented by messages. (In comparing Windows to the Mac OS and UNIX with X Windows, the word *message* is synonymous with event.)

All system messages (events) are stored in a global message queue. The Windows module User.exe is responsible for routing messages to the appropriate application program. The three valid message types are *user events* (mouse and keyboard), *environmental events* (such as window exposure/redraw), and *timer events*.

Application programs receive event messages through an application-specific callback function called a *window proc*. When Windows calls a window proc, it passes a message type identifier, a WORD parameter, and a LONG parameter. These parameters have different semantics for different message types. For example, for a menu event message (WM_COMMAND), the WORD parameter is the menu item number selected by the user, while in any mouse event message the LONG parameter is an encoding of the x-y position of a mouse click (low-order bits are the x position and high-order bits are the y position).

2.2.1 User events

The Windows system passes user event messages to an application when the program user interacts with the application by choosing a menu option, moving or clicking the mouse, or typing at the keyboard. The following user event messages are handled by the Windows version of the GUI Class Library in Appendix B: WM_COMMAND, WM_LBUTTONDOWN, WM_MOUSE_MOVE, and WM_LBUTTONUP.

The WM_COMMAND message is sent to an application when the user has selected a menu item. The WM_LBUTTONDOWN message is sent to an application when the user presses the left mouse button while in an application window. The WM_MOUSE_MOVE message is sent to an application when the mouse is moving in a window. The WM_LBUTTONUP message is sent to an application when the user releases the left mouse button while in an application window.

2.2.2 Environmental events

The primary environmental event processed by application programs involves redrawing a window. The Windows system sends an application program a WM_PAINT message when a window becomes exposed after being covered, is newly created, or the application program itself invalidates part or all of a window.

When a window is created, Windows programs need to handle an additional environmental event message, WM_CREATE. Any application-specific initialization is performed when this message is processed by the application program. The WM_DESTROY message is sent to an application when a window is destroyed.

2.2.3 Timer events

Unlike Macintosh and X Windows applications, which have a main program loop that polls for events, Windows does not support an application event loop. An application often has work that needs to be done periodically, even if no user events are generated and dispatched to the application program. A main event loop provides a convenient location to call an application-specific "work" function. For example, an application might have a clock display in an open window; periodically, the clock's time must be updated in the window.

Windows provides a Timer event that allows the application programmer to specify one or more functions that are called by Windows at specified time intervals. Windows sends an application program a WM_TIMER event when a specified time interval elapses. Due to the limitations of the 8259 timer chip used in PCs, Timer messages cannot be sent to an application program at a rate higher than 18.2 times per second (Petzold, 1990). Also, it is very important that a "work" function called when a Timer message is received completes its calculations quickly. Timer events are not asynchronous; WM_TIMER messages are placed in the application's event queue with all other messages. If other Windows applications are using the CPU, or if the application receiving the WM_TIMER message is busy performing another calculation, the application will not process the Timer event "on schedule."

In the abstract GUI C++ class library designed in chapter 5, the concept of user "work" functions are abstracted by allowing one application class method to be called periodically. As expected, the generic GUI class library, although far easier to use, lacks the complete flexibility of Windows Timer events.

2.3 Graphics Operations in Windows Applications

Windows provides a rich set of graphics primitives. The applications programming model for Micrsoft Windows is fundamentally different from those for the Macintosh or X Windows environments. The Macintosh applications programmer has a (relatively) fixed hardware target for which to program. The X Windows programmer writes to an abstract graphics server, the X Server. Windows programs, though, have to run on a large variety of video output devices (and printer output devices, which are handled much the same as video output).

Microsoft, in designing Windows, uses an abstract library, the *Graphics Device Interface* (GDI) library. GDI functions require access to a data structure called a *device context* (DC) which contains the attributes of the current graphics environment (such as font information, pen colors, pen thickness, and brush color). This is very similar to the use of DCs in the X Windows environment. In the following examples, a handle to the current DC is assumed to be defined in current_hDC:

```
MoveTo(HDC current_hDC, int x, int y);
LineTo(HDC current_hDC, int x, int y);
TextOut(current_hDHDC current_hDC, int x, int y, char *str, int len_str);
Rectangle(HDC current_hDC, int left, int top, int right, int bottom);
```

The MoveTo function moves the current drawing pen location to a new position. The LineTo function draws a line from the current pen location to a new location. The TextOut function draws characters in a Window. The Rectangle function fills a rectangle with the current brush.

Note that these graphics primitives are abstract; the actual drawing operations depend on the attributes stored in the DC data structure. For example, the pen thickness can be changed before calling LineTo to draw a line. There are six types of drawing "objects" supported by the GDI library: pens, brushes, bitmaps, regions, palettes, and fonts. Appendix B provides examples of the use of Windows objects. In these programs I restricted myself to "stock objects" that are provided automatically in the Windows environment.

In order for a C++ GUI library to be portable, you must restrict your use of graphics primitives to operations that are supported in all GUI environments. When you are developing Windows applications, start your development work using the Windows version of the C++ GUI library implemented in Appendix B. If your application requires non-portable graphics extensions, you can augment your program with additional non-portable GDI calls using a good Windows reference (refer to the bibliography for suggested reference books).

2.4 Dialog Boxes in Windows Applications

Microsoft Windows supports both *modal* and *modeless* dialog boxes. Modal dialog boxes capture all user input events while they are visible. Modeless dialog boxes only handle user events that are directed to them; users can type or click the mouse in one or more modeless dialog boxes and a main application window by changing the window focus. I prefer modal dialog boxes when I write applications for other users; users tend to get confused by modeless dialog boxes. However, when I write applications for myself or "power users," modeless dialog boxes allow users more flexibility in working with an application program. The abstract GUI class design in Chapter 5 supports only modal dialog boxes. Refer to a standard Windows reference for using modeless dialog boxes.

Creating and managing dialog boxes is fairly simple in Windows using the following steps:

- Create a resource file for the dialog box with a text editor or a graphics resource editor (supplied in both the Microsoft and Borland Windows development systems).
- Write an application-specific callback function that handles user event messages.
- Tell Windows which callback function to use for the dialog box.

For example, if you wanted to use a modal dialog box that allows the user to enter/modify a character string, you could use the following resource definition:

```
EditBox DIALOG 55, 51, 178, 92
STYLE WS_POPUP | WS_DLGFRAME
CAPTION " "
BEGIN
   EDITTEXT  102,   11, 8, 162, 42, ES_MULTILINE
```

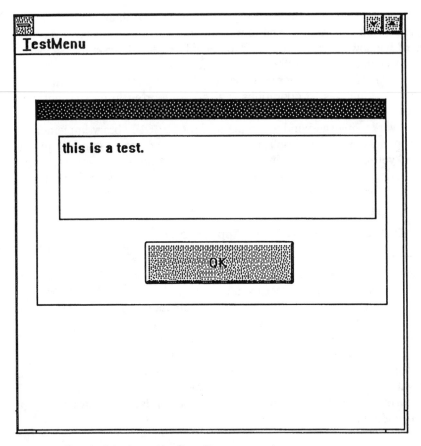

Figure 2.2 Sample dialog box with edit and button controls.

```
CONTROL "OK" 1002, "BUTTON", WS_CHILD | WS_VISIBLE | WS_TABSTOP, 55,
61, 76, 21
END
```

This short resource file defines a dialog box template with two controls: an edit field and an "OK" button. Figure 2.2 shows this dialog box popped up over a Windows application window. The following function serves as a callback to handle user-generated event messages for the dialog box in Fig. 2.2:

```
// Default Dialog Edit box:

static char FAR cpEdit[256]; // text from dialog edit filed will go here
```

```
int PASCAL DefaultEditBox(HWND hWnd, WORD iMessage, WORD wParam,
                LONG /* lParam */)
{
    switch (iMessage) {
      case WM_INITDIALOG:
          SetDlgItemText(hWnd, 102, cpEdit); // 102 is the edit control
                                             // index
          return TRUE;
      case WM_COMMAND:
          if (wParam == 1002) {  // OK button hit
              for (int i=0; i<256; i++)
                  cpEdit[i] = '\0';
                      GetDlgItemText(hWnd, 102, &(cpEdit[0]), 80);
                  EndDialog(hWnd, 0);
                  return TRUE;
          } else {
              return FALSE;
          }
      default:
          return FALSE;
    }
}
```

An application program can initialize the buffer cpEdit with text for the dialog box edit field. When this function is called with a WM_INITDIALOG message, this text is inserted into the edit field and the dialog box is made visible. When this function is called with a WM_COMMAND message, the message type is checked; if this message resulted from the OK button being clicked by the user, then the new text from the dialog box edit control is copied to the cpEdit buffer and the dialog box is made invisible.

The following code tells Windows to call this function to handle messages for the edit dialog box. This static data definition defines a FAR function pointer:

```
static FARPROC lpfnDefaultEditBox;
```

The following code is executed when a window is created to bind a C callback function to a dialog box:

```
case WM_CREATE:
    lpfnDefaultEditBox = MakeProcInstance((FARPROC)DefaultEditBox,
                            Application::hInstance);
```

These code fragments are taken from the complete GUI class library source listings in Appendix B.

2.5 Creating a Document Window

The GUI library designed in Chapter 5 provides a document window that it creates automatically. The following listing shows how to create a window in the Windows environment:

```
hWnd = CreateWindow( szClassName,
            szClassName,
            WS_OVERLAPPEDWINDOW,
            CW_USEDEFAULT,
            0,
            CW_USEDEFAULT,
            0,
            NULL,
            NULL,
            Application::hInstance,
            (LPSTR) this );
if ( ! hWnd )
    exit( FALSE );
```

The following listing shows how to register a window with the Windows kernel:

```
WNDCLASS wndclass;     // Structure used to register Windows class.
wndclass.style           = CS_HREDRAW | CS_VREDRAW;
wndclass.lpfnWndProc   = ::WndProc;
wndclass.cbClsExtra     = 0;
// Reserve extra bytes for each instance of the window;
// we will use these bytes to store a pointer to the C++
// (TAppWindow) object corresponding to the window.
// the size of a 'this' pointer depends on the memory model.
wndclass.cbWndExtra     = sizeof( TAppWindow * );
wndclass.hInstance      = Application::hInstance;
wndclass.hIcon            = LoadIcon( Application::hInstance, "whello"
);
wndclass.hCursor         = LoadCursor( NULL, IDC_ARROW );
wndclass.hbrBackground = GetStockObject( WHITE_BRUSH );
wndclass.lpszMenuName  = "MyMenu";
wndclass.lpszClassName = szClassName;

if ( ! RegisterClass( &wndclass ) )
    exit( FALSE );
```

The procedure ::WndProc is defined in the following listing. This code is derived from a C++/Windows example program supplied with the Borland C++ programming environment.

```
long FAR PASCAL _export WndProc( HWND hWnd, WORD iMessage, WORD wParam,
                            LONG lParam )
{
    // Pointer to the (C++ object that is the) window.
    TAppWindow *pWindow = GetPointer( hWnd );
    if ( pWindow == 0 )
    {
        if ( iMessage == WM_CREATE )
        {
            LPCREATESTRUCT lpcs;

            lpcs = (LPCREATESTRUCT) lParam;
```

```
                pWindow = (TAppWindow *) lpcs->lpCreateParams;

                // Store a pointer to this object in the window's extra
bytes;
                // this will enable to access this object (and its member
                // functions) in WndProc where we are
                // given only a handle to identify the window.
                SetPointer( hWnd, pWindow );

                // Now let the object perform whatever
                // initialization it needs for WM_CREATE in its own
                // WndProc.
                return pWindow->WndProc( iMessage, wParam, lParam );
        }
        else
            return DefWindowProc( hWnd, iMessage, wParam, lParam );
    }
    else
        return pWindow->WndProc( iMessage, wParam, lParam );
}
```

This C function also calls a C⁺⁺ method WndProc for class TAppWindow. The following listing shows the code for TAppWindow::WndProc:

```
long TAppWindow::WndProc( WORD iMessage, WORD wParam, LONG lParam)
{
    switch (iMessage) {
        // Menu item:
        case WM_COMMAND:
            do_menu_action(wParam);
            InvalidateRect(hWnd, NULL, TRUE);
            break;
        case WM_CREATE:
            // Set up a long pointer to a dialog box callback function:
lpfnDefaultAboutBox = MakeProcInstance((FARPROC)DefaultAboutBox
                            Application::hInstance]

        break;
        case WM_PAINT:
            Paint();
            break;
        case WM_LBUTTONDOWN:  // left button is down
            mouse_down_flag = 1;
            mouse_down(LOWORD(lParam), HIWORD(lParam));
            break;
        case WM_MOUSEMOVE:  // left button is down
            if (mouse_down_flag)
                mouse_move(LOWORD(lParam), HIWORD(lParam));
            break;
        case WM_LBUTTONUP:  // left button is down
            mouse_up(LOWORD(lParam), HIWORD(lParam));
            mouse_down_flag = 0;
            InvalidateRect(hWnd, NULL, TRUE);
            break;
        case WM_DESTROY:
        if (i_timer!=0)  KillTimer(NULL, i_timer);
        PostQuitMessage( 0 );
```

```
      break;
       default:
       return DefWindowProc( hWnd, iMessage, wParam, lParam );
}
return 0;
}
```

The Microsoft Windows environment requires every window to have a C callback window procedure. This function must be a C function, not a C++ method. Following the Borland example, I use a C callback procedure which then calls the C++ methodTAppWindow::WndProc. This C++ method then calls application specific methods like do_menu_action and mouse_up.

2.6 Creating an Application Environment

Creating an application environment and starting the execution of an applications program is a very different process in each of the three environments covered in this book. The file applib.h (listed in Appendix B) defines a macro definition for the symbol INIT_PROGRAM, which contains Windows-specific code to initialize an application program. The following listing shows this macro definition:

```
#define INIT_PROGRAM \
int PASCAL WinMain( HANDLE hInstance, HANDLE hPrevInstance, LPSTR
lpszCmdLine, \
          int nCmdShow ) \
{ \
    Application::hInstance = hInstance; \
    Application::hPrevInstance = hPrevInstance; \
    Application::nCmdShow = nCmdShow; \
    if ( ! Application::hPrevInstance ) { \
          TAppWindow::Register(); \
    } \
    TAppWindow MainWnd; \
    current_window = &MainWnd;
```

The C function WinMain is called by the Windows environment to start an application program. The method TAppWindow::Register( ), which was defined in the previous section, is called to register and set up a document window.

The C macro RUN_PROGRAM contains the Windows-specific code to run an application program and handle events (the file applib.h defines this macro):

```
#define RUN_PROGRAM \
    return Application::MessageLoop();
```

The following code fragment shows how method Application::MessageLoop( ) processes event messages from the Windows environment:

```
MSG msg;
while (GetMessage(&msg, NULL, 0, 0) )
{
    TranslateMessage(&msg);
    DispatchMessage(&msg);
}
```

2.7 Windows API Functions Used in Appendix B

Function BeginPaint returns a handle to the current display context after defining the current paint context:

```
PAINTSTRUCT ps;
 HDC hDC = BeginPaint(hWnd, // handle to window to set up for
                            // painting
                  &ps);     // paint structure information is
                            // returned
```

Function CreateWindow creates a new window based on a registered window class (function RegisterClass). A WM_CREATE message is passed to the applications window callback function which is responsible for initializing any application-specific data for the window. ö

```
hWnd = CreateWindow(windowName, // unique window class name
                    windowName, // window display name
                    WS_OVERLAPPEDWINDOW, // desired window style
                    CW_USEDEFAULT, // initial X window position
                    0, // initial Y window position
                    CW_USEDEFAULT, // initial window width
                    0,      // initial window height
                    NULL,   // parent window if this is a child
                            // window
                    NULL,   // menu specifyer (use class menu if
                            // NULL)
                    Application::instanceHandle, // application
                                                 // instance
                    (LPSTR) 0 ); // application specific data

if (hWnd == 0)    exit( FALSE );   // Failed to create a window!!
```

Function DefWindowProc is used to process all Windows message that your application ignores. DefWindowProc provides standard Windows-style behavior to applications:

```
long FAR PASCAL _export WndProc( HWND hWnd, WORD iMessage, WORD wParam,
                                 LONG lParam )
    switch (iMessage) {
    // Menu item:
    case WM_COMMAND:
        do_menu_action(wParam);
        InvalidateRect(hWnd, NULL, TRUE);
```

```
        break;
    case WM_CREATE:
        .
        .
        .
        break;
    case WM_PAINT:
        .
        .
        .
        break;
    case WM_LBUTTONDOWN:  // left button is down
        my_handle_mouse_down_function(LOWORD(lParam), HIWORD(lParam));
        break;
    case WM_DESTROY:
            PostQuitMessage( 0 );
              break;
    default:
                return DefWindowProc( hWnd, iMessage, wParam, lParam
);
    }
    return 0;
}
```

Function DialogBox is a utility for creating a modal dialog box. The DialogBox function passes responsibility for event handling to an application callback function DefaultAboutBox; this callback function should call EndDialog.

```
// Default Dialog About box:
int PASCAL DefaultAboutBox(HWND hWnd, WORD iMessage, WORD wParam,
             LONG /* lParam */)
{
    switch (iMessage) {
        case WM_INITDIALOG:
            return TRUE;
        case WM_COMMAND:
            if (wParam == 1002) {  // OK button hit
                EndDialog(hWnd, 0);
                return TRUE;
            } else {
                return FALSE;
            }
        default:
            return FALSE;
    }
}

static FARPROC lpfnDefaultAboutBox;


    .
    .
    .
    lpfnDefaultAboutBox = MakeProcInstance((FARPROC)DefaultAboutBox,
                                  Application::instanceHandle);
    .
    .
```

```
DialogBox(Application::instanceHandle,  "AboutBox",
          hWnd,lpfnDefaultAboutBox);
```

Function DlgDirList changes the contents of a dialog box list control to show the contents of a file directory:

```
DlgDirList(hWnd,        // dialog window handle
           "*.TXT", // file selection criteria string
           104,         // list box control ID
           105,         // static text control ID for showing file path
           0x4010); // desired DOS file types
```

Function DlgDirSelect returns the filename selected in a dialog list control:

```
DlgDirSelect(hWnd,         // dialog window handle
             szFileName,   // buffer with space for returned file
                           // name
             104);         // dialog list control ID
```

Function DispatchMessage calls Pascal application callback window function for the application. This window function processes window messages or ignores them.

```
MSG msg;
while (GetMessage(&msg,  // long pointer to a message structure
                  NULL,  // NULL for all application messages or a
                         // window
                         // handle to get messages for a specific
                         // window
                  0,     // lowest message number to retrieve, zero
                         // gets
                         // all messages
                  0)) {  // highest message number to retrieve, zero
                         // gets
                         // all messages
    TranslateMessage(&msg);
    DispatchMessage(&msg);
}
```

Function EndDialog is a utility for destroying a modal dialog box. The DialogBox function passes responsibility for event handling to an application callback function; this callback function should call EndDialog.

```
// Default Dialog About box:
int PASCAL DefaultAboutBox(HWND hWnd, WORD iMessage, WORD wParam,
               LONG /* lParam */)
{
    switch (iMessage) {
        case WM_INITDIALOG:
            return TRUE;
        case WM_COMMAND:
```

```
        if (wParam == 1002) {   // OK button hit
            EndDialog(hWnd,  0);
            return TRUE;
        } else {
            return FALSE;
        }
    default:
        return FALSE;
    }
}
```

Function EndPaint returns a handle to the current display context after defining the current paint context:

```
PAINTSTRUCT ps;
  HDC hDC = BeginPaint(hWnd,   // handle to window to set up for
                               // painting
                  &ps );  // paint structure information is returned
.
.
.
EndPaint(hWnd,  &ps);
```

Function FillRect fills in a rectangle with the current brush:

```
RECT r;
SetRect(&r, left, top, right, bottom);
FillRect(current_hDC,  &r,  GetStockObject(BLACK_BRUSH));
```

Function GetDlgItemText returns the text label of a dialog box control:

```
char buf[80];
GetDlgItemText(hWnd,  // window handle passed to the dialog box
                      // function
               102,   // dialog box item ID
               &(buf[0]), // address of buffer to copy text to
               80);   // text buffer size
```

Function GetMessage returns an application message from the application's message queue:

```
MSG msg;
while (GetMessage(&msg,   // long pointer to a message structure
                  NULL, // NULL for all application messages or a
                        // window
                        // handle to get messages for a specific
                        // window
                  0,        // lowest message number to retrieve,
                            // zero gets
                        // all messages
                  0)) {     // highest message number to retrieve,
                            // zero gets
                        // all messages
```

```
    // process message here...
  }
```

Function GetStockObject returns a handle to a predefined font, pen, or brush:

```
Handle black_brush = GetStockObject(BLACK_BRUSH);
```

Function InvalidateRect invalidates a specified area in a window; this causes Windows to send a WM_PAINT message to the window:

```
InvalidateRect(hWnd,    // Window to receive the WM_PAINT message
            NULL,       // Rectangle area (NULL for entire window
            0);         // 0 -> don't erase, 1-> erase background
```

Function KillTimer removes a Timer event specified by a window handle and a timer ID:

```
KillTimer(hWnd,          // window handle
        (int)1);         // integer timer ID
```

Function LineTo moves the current pen location while drawing a line:

```
static HDC current_hDC = ...;
.
.
  LineTo(current_hDC, 10, 20);  // move pen to x=10, y=20 in window
                                // coordinates while drawing with
                                // current pen
```

Function MakeProcInstance creates a procedure address object. In the following listing, function DefaultTimer and the current application instance are used to create a procedure address object:

```
FARPROC lpfnDefaultTimer = MakeProcInstance((FARPROC)DefaultTimer,
                        Application::instanceHandle);
```

Function MoveTo moves the current pen location without performing any draw operation:

```
static HDC current_hDC = ...;
.
.
  MoveTo(current_hDC, 10, 20);  // move pen to x=10, y=20
```

Function PostQuitMessage is used to ask Windows to send an application a WM_DESTROY message. Your application can call the C exit() function when it receives the WM_DESTROY message.

```
PostQuitMessage((int)0);   // argument passed with WM_DESTROY
                           // message
```

Function Rectangle is used to fill a rectangle with the current brush, and frame the rectangle using the current pen: ö

```
// erase a rectangle by selecting the appropriate draw objects:
SelectObject(current_hDC, backgroundBrush);
SelectObject(current_hDC, GetStockObject(NULL_PEN)); // zero pen
                                                     // width
Rectangle(current_hDC, left, top, right, bottom);
SelectObject(current_hDC, GetStockObject(BLACK_PEN));
```

Function RegisterClass registers a window class identified by a unique name. The following listing shows an example for setting up a new window class that can be used in a call to CreateWindow:

```
WNDCLASS wndclass;   // Structure used to register Windows class.
wndclass.style = CS_HREDRAW | CS_VREDRAW;
wndclass.lpfnWndProc = ::WndProc; // PASCAL type window callback proc
wndclass.cbClsExtra = 0;   // don't allocate extra bytes
wndclass.cbWndExtra = sizeof(TAppWindow *);
wndclass.hInstance  = Application::instanceHandle;
wndclass.hIcon  = LoadIcon( Application::instanceHandle, "GUIlib" );
wndclass.hCursor= LoadCursor( NULL, IDC_ARROW );
wndclass.hbrBackground = GetStockObject( WHITE_BRUSH );
wndclass.lpszMenuName  = "MyMenu"; // menu name
wndclass.lpszClassName = "aName";   // this name must be unique

if (RegisterClass(&wndclass) == 0) exit( FALSE ); // register
                                                  // failed
```

Function SelectObject is used to define the current default pen, brush, or font depending on the type of its input argument:

```
// erase a rectangle by selecting the appropriate draw objects:
SelectObject(current_hDC,  backgroundBrush);
SelectObject(current_hDC, GetStockObject(NULL_PEN)); // zero
                                                     // pen
                                                     // width
Rectangle(current_hDC, left, top, right, bottom);
SelectObject(current_hDC,  GetStockObject(BLACK_PEN));
```

Function SendDlgItemMessage sends a window message to a dialog box control:

```
SendDlgItemMessage(hWnd,       // dialog bow window handle
                   (int)101, // dialog box control ID
                   (WORD)EM_LIMITTEXT, // the message value
                     (WORD)80,  // extra message data (length of
                               // text field)
                   (DWORD)0L);  // extra message data (here:
                               // unused)
```

Function SendMessage sends a window message to an application's window:

```
SendMessage(hWnd,  // window handle (for window receiving this
                   // message)
           (WORD)WM_COMMAND,    // message to be sent
           1002,   // additional information: a button control ID
           (DWORD)0L);  // unused additional information
```

Function SetDlgItemText sets the text label of a dialog box control:

```
char *buf = {"New control title text"};
SetDlgItemText(hWnd, // window handle passed to the dialog box
                     // function
              102,  // dialog box item ID
              buf); // address of buffer to copy text from
```

Function SetRect fills in a rectangle's boundary data structure:

```
RECT r;
SetRect(&r, left, top, right, bottom);
FillRect(current_hDC, &r, backgroundBrush);
```

Function SetTimer registers procedure address objects for periodic execution:

```
FARPROC lpfnDefaultTimer = MakeProcInstance((FARPROC)DefaultTimer,
                                   Application::instanceHandle);
int i_timer=SetTimer(NULL,// Window. NULL for no window connected to
                          // timer
                    0,   // if window is not NULL, unique ID
                    300,  // time interval in milliseconds
                    lpfnDefaultTimer); // procedure address object
```

Function TextOut writes a character string to a display context:

```
static HDC current_hDC = ...;
.
.
  TextOut(current_hDC, // current display context
  10,              // x position
  20,              // y location
  (LPSTR)"Test",    // long pointer to a string
  4);              // string length
```

Function TranslateMessage translates virtual key messages:

```
MSG msg;
while (GetMessage(&msg, // long pointer to a message structure
                 NULL,  // NULL for all application messages or a
                        // window
                        // handle to get messages for a specific
```

```
                         // window
            0,           // lowest message number to retrieve, zero
                         // gets
                         // all messages
            0)) {        // highest message number to retrieve, zero
                         // gets
                         // all messages
    TranslateMessage(&msg);
    DispatchMessage(&msg);
}
```

3

Apple Macintosh

The Macintosh (Mac) System 7 window-based operating system (OS) sets the standard for usability and elegance. Apple Computer's insistence that software developers follow standard user interface design guidelines has yielded thousands of commercial applications with a similar look and feel. Mac users usually have an easy time learning new application software.

Developing Mac software is difficult, especially when programming without the benefit of one of the many fine object-oriented toolkits available for the Mac, like the Think C Class library or Apple's MacApp. The object-oriented GUI toolkit developed for the Mac in Appendix C is simpler than either MacApp or the Think C class library, but has the advantage that applications written with the GUI library are portable to Windows and Unix Motif platforms.

Many good programming tools are available for developing Macintosh applications. My personal preference is the MPW programming environment with the Apple port of the AT&T C++ translator. Apple Computer provides very good support to Macintosh software developers. Apple Macintosh Developer Technical Support provides a rich set of example programs demonstrating all aspects of Macintosh programming. These programs are available on public bulletin board services and through the Apple Program Developer's Association (APDA). The best resource for Macintosh programmers is the "develop" CD-ROM produced quarterly by Apple Developers Group. All of my Macintosh programs are partially derived from example programs developed by Apple Computer engineers, and I express my personal gratitude for the great work that they do.

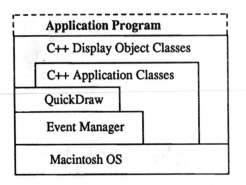

Figure 3.1 Macintosh software architecture.

3.1   Macintosh Application Interface to the Operating System

The Mac OS provides user event, file, display, and network services to application programs. Under release 7 of the Mac OS, applications can share files across a network as if the files resided on a local disk. Applications have several protocol layers for inter-application communication. The only significant weakness of the Mac OS is the cooperative multitasking environment; user interaction with a Mac will "hang" if an application program is not well-behaved (i.e., periodically relinquishes the CPU). Figure 3.1 shows how the GUI classes in Appendix C use the underlying Mac OS.

For complete portability using the C⁺⁺ GUI class library in Appendix C, your programs should only use calls to the GUI library and refrain from calling Macintosh Toolbox functions directly. A good strategy for maintaining portability is the addition of required Macintosh Toolbox functions to the

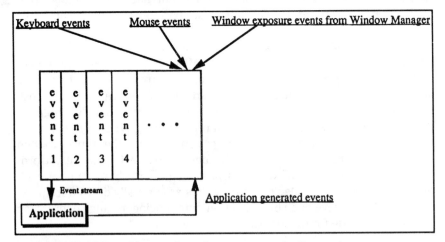

Figure 3.2 Mac OS Event Manager dispatches events to application event queue.

C++ GUI library. If your application program needs to be moved to either the Windows or X Windows environments, implement your extensions in the C++ GUI library implementations for those environments.

3.2 Event Handling in Macintosh Applications

Starting with release 7 of the Mac OS (and previous releases using the task-switcher MultiFinder), applications must be written to work cooperatively with both the Mac OS and other active applications. Figure 3.2 shows the general event dispatching mechanism of the Mac OS.

The following code sample shows a typical Macintosh application event loop:

```
while (fDone == false) {

    whichWindow = FrontWindow(); // first set up whichWindow
    SetPort(whichWindow);
    DoIdle();              // call idle time handler

    if (haveWaitNextEvent) {
        gotEvent = WaitNextEvent(everyEvent, &anEvent, (unsigned
long) 0,
                                 fMouseRgn);
    } else {
        SystemTask();
        gotEvent = GetNextEvent(everyEvent, &anEvent);
    }

    if (gotEvent) {  // if there is an available event to process:
        AdjustCursor();
        switch (anEvent.what) {
            case mouseDown :
                DoMouseDown();
                break;
            case mouseUp :
                DoMouseUp();
                break;
            case keyDown :
            case autoKey :
                DoKeyDown();
                break;
            case updateEvt :
                DoUpdateEvt();
                break;
            case diskEvt :
                DoDiskEvt();
                break;
            case activateEvt :
                DoActivateEvt();
                break;
            case kOsEvent :
                DoOSEvent();
                break;
            default :
                break;
```

```
      } // switch
    } // if
} // while
```

3.3 Graphics Operations in Macintosh Applications

The Macintosh Toolbox provides a rich set of graphics primitives. As with the X Windows and Microsoft Windows environments, graphics operations in a window are best done when the application receives an event message indicating that a window needs to be redrawn.

Before any graphics operations are performed as a result of a window-expose event, it is necessary to ensure that the graphics port is set to the current window. Assume that a global window pointer is available as follows:

```
WindowPtr aWindowPtr;
```

Then the following call sets the graphics port and draws a line from point (x1, y1) to point (x2, y2):

```
SetPort(aWindowPtr);
MoveTo(x1, y1);
LineTo(x2, y2);
```

WindowPtr is a pointer to a GrafPort data structure. GrafPort contains the information required by Quickdraw functions: a device identifier, a bitmap, an indirect pointer (handle) to a region of the window not covered by other windows, a clip region (used in Appendix C for clipping scrolling text), a background fill pattern, a foreground fill pattern, current drawing pen coordinates, current drawing mode (XOR, Copy, etc.), a pen-visible flag, current font, current font style, current text size, foreground and background colors, and an indirect pointer to a *Picture* data structure (a list of drawing commands). Application programmers do not directly set the variables in a GrafPort; Quickdraw functions like TextFont are available to set GrafPort internal parameters.

Given a character string, text can be drawn on the screen by converting the string to a "Pascal-type" string (i.e., the first byte contains the string length), and using the DrawString Toolbox function:

```
char *a_string; // assume that this gets initialized
.
.
.
char buf255[256];
sprintf(&(buf255[1]),"%s", a_string); // strlen(a_string) must be
                                       // <= 255
buf255[0] = strlen(a_string);
MoveTo(100,100);
DrawString((Str255)buf255);
```

Similar Mac Toolbox functions are used in Appendix C for drawing rectangles, ovals, etc. Note that the Quickdraw function DrawString requires a Pascal string which contains the string length in the first byte.

3.4 Resource Files for Building Macintosh Applications

Resource files make it fairly easy to design dialog boxes, menus, etc. My preference is to use the program ResEdit to graphically design an application's resources. Since I like to have "source code," I usually use the MPW tool *derez* to convert binary resource files into files that are (sort of) human readable. For the sample applications developed in this book, I use one base resource file (applib.r) for common resource definitions. The file applib.r is derived from the sample resource files provided with MPW, with changes to suit my own preferences. Each application program also uses its own resource file for specifying the menu item definitions (e.g., the application *chess3d* uses a resource file named *chess3d.r*).

The following listing comes from the file test.r in Appendix C:

```
/*
 *  File: test.r
 *
 *  Description: Resource definitons for program 'test'
 */


#include "SysTypes.r"
#include "Types.r"

#include "applibCommon.h"


resource 'WIND' (rDocWindow, preload, purgeable) {
      {64, 60, 520, 520},
      rDocProc, invisible,nogoaway, 0x0, "C++ GUI Library Test Program"
};

resource 'MENU' (mApp, preload) {
    mApp, textMenuProc,
    0b1111111111111111111111111111111,   /* enable everything */
      enabled, "Test App",
      {
        "Test Grapher Class", noIcon, "G", noMark, plain;
        "Test Edit Dialog", noIcon, "T", noMark, plain;
        "Test About box", noIcon, "A", noMark, plain;
        "Test Single List Selection", noIcon, "S", noMark, plain;
        "Test Multiple List Selection", noIcon, "M", noMark, plain;
        "Test choose one of 2 choices", noIcon, "D", noMark, plain;
        "Test scrolling text", noIcon, "F", noMark, plain;
        "Test data plotting", noIcon, "P", noMark, plain
      }
};
```

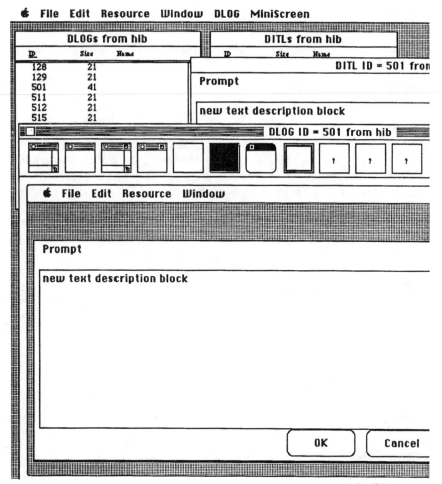

Figure 3.3 View of Macintosh screen while editing dialog box resources with ResEdit.

This code fragment is readable. The following code fragment for specifying the format of a dialog box from file applib.r was created by the MPW tool derez from a binary file created with ResEdit:

```
data 'DITL' (501, purgeable) {
    $"0002 0000 0000 00C8 012A 00E8 017D 0402"              /*
.......».*...}.. */
    $"4F4B 0000 0000 00C7 0192 00E7 01E9 0406"              /*
OK.....«.í...... */
    $"4361 6E63 656C 0000 0000 0005 0009 00C3"              /*
Cancel.......Δ.√ */
    $"01EA 101A 6E65 7720 7465 7874 2064 6573"        /* ....new text
des */
    $"6372 6970 7469 6F6E 2062 6C6F 636B"             /* cription
block */
};
```

```
data 'DLOG' (501, purgeable) {
    $"0042 0008 012E 01F6 0003 0100 0000 0000"               /*
.B............. */
    $"0000 01F5 1445 6E74 6572 206E 6577 206E"          /* .....Enter
new n */
    $"6F64 6520 7469 746C 65"                        /* ode title */
};
```

This may look ugly, but it is easy to change using ResEdit: simply use
ResEdit to edit any application that uses this dialog box, make the desired
changes, write the edited DITL and DLOG resources to a temporary file
(such as "temp.rsrc"), and use the MPW tool derez to convert the temporary file to ASCII text. Note that many Mac programmers just leave their resources in binary format, but I like to maintain ASCII source for all software
that I build. Figure 3.3 shows ResEdit editing these DITL and DLOG resources.

3.5 Dialog Boxes in Macintosh Applications

You saw the dialog box resources for a popup modal edit box in Section 3.4.
The following code fragment shows how to set up and handle events for this
edit box:

```
// Assume that char *text is the string to edit, and char *prompt is
// the
// string for a prompt:

    DialogPtr dLog;
    short itemHit = 0;
    GrafPort *savePort;
    char buf[257];
    *int itemType;*/  Handle itemH;  Rect r; int len;
    short itemType;
    GetPort (&savePort);

    dLog = GetNewDialog (501, (Ptr)0L, (WindowPtr) -1);

    InitCursor ();

    itemHit = 0;
    SetRect(&r,0,0,400,400);

    GetDItem(dLog, (short)4, &itemType, &itemH, &r);
    sprintf(&(buf[1]),"%s",prompt);  buf[0] = strlen(prompt);
    SetIText(itemH, (Str255)buf);

    GetDItem(dLog, (short)3, &itemType, &itemH, &r);
    sprintf(&(buf[1]),"%s",text);  buf[0] = strlen(text);
    SetIText(itemH, (Str255)buf);

    while ((itemHit != 2) && (itemHit != 1))
        ModalDialog(nil,&itemHit);
```

```
        if (itemHit == 1) {  // OK
            GetDItem(dLog, (short)3, &itemType, &itemH, &r);
            GetIText(itemH, (Str255)buf);
            if (TEXT_SIZE>buf[0]) len = buf[0];  else len = TEXT_SIZE - 1;
            for (int i=0; i<len; i++) text[i] = buf[i+1];
            text[len] = '\0';
    }

        DisposDialog (dLog);
        SetPort (savePort);
```

The function GetNewDialog returns a new dialog box created from resource number 501. The two calls to GetDItem and SetIText are used to set
the value of the prompt string and edit string field in the dialog box. The dialog item number of the prompt static text field is 4, and the dialog item
number of the edit field is 3. The Toolbox function ModalDialog is used to
handle all events until the user clicks either the OK button (dialog item 1)
or the Cancel button (dialog item 2). If the user clicks the OK button, then
the edited text is copied from the dialog box data structures to the original
string. The call to DisposDialog frees the memory allocated in the call to
GetNewDialog.

3.6   Creating a Document Window

The GUI library designed in Chapter 5 provides a document window. This
library creates the window automatically. This section shows how to create
a document window in the Macintosh environment.

The following listing shows how to create a window:

```
// Make a single document window for this application:
TAppWindow* appDoc;
appDoc = new TAppWindow(rDocWindow);
// Check for window allocation error:
if (appDoc == nil)
  Warning("Could not allocate a new document window");
```

This code fragment is executed in the TAppApp application class constructor listed in the following section.

3.7   Creating an Application Environment

Creating an application environment and starting the execution of an applications program is a very different process in each of the three environments covered in this book. The file applib.h (listed in Appendix C),
defines a macro definition for the symbol INIT_PROGRAM which contains
Macintosh OS-specific code to initialize an application program. The fol-

lowing listing shows this macro definition:

```
#define INIT_PROGRAM \
TAppApp *gTheApplication;\
int main(void)\
{ gTheApplication = new TAppApp;\
  if (gTheApplication == nil)\
      return 0;
```

The C function TAppApp constructor is called to start the application program. The following listing shows the TAppApp class constructor (this code
fragment was derived from a C++ example program supplied with the Apple
MPW programming environment):

```
TAppApp::TAppApp(void)
{
    SysEnvRec envRec;

    // initialize Mac Toolbox components
    InitGraf((Ptr) &qd.thePort);
    InitFonts();
    InitWindows();
    InitMenus();
    TEInit();
    InitDialogs((ResumeProcPtr) nil);
    InitCursor();

    (void) SysEnvirons(curSysEnvVers, &envRec);

    if (envRec.machineType < 0) {
            Warning("This machine does not have 128K ROMs!");
            exit(1);
    }

    MaxApplZone();  // create more zone space
    fHaveWaitNextEvent = TrapAvailable(_WaitNextEvent, ToolTrap);

    fWindow = nil;
    fWhichWindow = nil;
    fDone = false;
    fMouseRgn = nil;
    fInBackground = false;

    Handle menuBar;
    menuBar = GetNewMBar(rMenuBar);
    SetMenuBar(menuBar);
    DisposHandle(menuBar);
    AddResMenu(GetMHandle(mApple), 'DRVR');
    DrawMenuBar();
    fMouseRgn = NewRgn();

    // Make a single document window for this application:
    TAppWindow* tAppDoc;
    tAppDoc = new TAppWindow(rDocWindow);
}
```

The Toolbox function InitGraf is always called once at the beginning of a

Macintosh program to initialize the global variables used by Quickdraw. The Toolbox function InitFonts is called when Font Manager calls are used in an application. The Toolbox function TEInint initializes global data for using the TextEdit scrap area; this function is also necessary for the correct execution of Desk Accessories that use TextEdit functions. The Toolbox function InitDialogs sets up global data for the Dialog Manager. The Toolbox function InitCursor makes the cursor visible and sets the cursor to the standard system arrow cursor.

The Toolbox function SysEnvirons returns information on the Macintosh hardware information. The Toolbox function MaxApplZone increases the size of an application's heap. The function TrapAvailable is included with the sample programs provided with the Apple C++ compiler; this function is used in the C++ GUI library listed in Appendix C.

The Toolbox function GetNewMBar creates a new menu bar data structure using a menu template defined in a resource file. The Toolbox function SetMenubar installs a list of menu *handles* (indirect pointers) on the system menu bar. The Toolbox function AddResMenu adds the Desk Accessories to the system (Apple) menu. The function DrawMenuBar displays the menu across the top of the Macintosh desktop.

The C macro RUN_PROGRAM contains the Macintosh-specific code to run an application program and handle events. The file applib.h (listed in Appendix C) defines this macro:

```
#define RUN_PROGRAM \
    gTheApplication->EventLoop();\
    return 0
```

The following code fragment shows how method Application::EventLoop() processes event messages from the Macintosh environment:

```
int gotEvent;
EventRecord tEvt;

DoIdle();                 // do idle once

while (fDone == false) {
        // always set up fWhichWindow before doing anything
        fWhichWindow = FrontWindow();
        // make sure we always draw into correct window
        SetPort(fWhichWindow);

        DoIdle();         // call idle time handler

        if (fHaveWaitNextEvent) {
            gotEvent = WaitNextEvent(everyEvent, &tEvt,
                                (unsigned long)0, fMouseRgn);
        } else {
        SystemTask();
        gotEvent = GetNextEvent(everyEvent, &tEvt);
```

```
}
   fTheEvent = tEvt;

   // make sure we got a real event
   if ( gotEvent ) {
     switch (fTheEvent.what)
       {
         case mouseDown :
             DoMouseDown();       // calls TAppWindow do_mouse_down
                                  // method
             break;
         case mouseUp :
             DoMouseUp();         // calls TAppWindow do_mouse_up method
             break;
         case keyDown :
         case autoKey :
             DoKeyDown();
             break;
         case updateEvt :
             DoUpdateEvt();       // call TAppWindow update_display
                                  // method
             break;
         case diskEvt :
             DoDiskEvt();
             break;
         case activateEvt :
             DoActivateEvt();
             break;
         case kOsEvent :
             DoOSEvent();
             break;
         default :
             break;
       } // end switch (fTheEvent.what)
   }
}
```

The Toolbox function FrontWindow provides a window pointer to the top window on the desktop. The Toolbox functions WaitNextEvent and GetNextEvent wait for events to occur. WaitNextEvent also allows other programs to share the CPU with MultiFinder or the System 7 OS.

3.8 Macintosh Toolbox Functions Used in Appendix C

Function AddResMenu adds the Desk Accessories to the system (Apple) menu:

```
AddResMenu(GetMHandle(mApple), // handle to apple system menu
          'DRVR');       // Resource type (could also be 'FONT',
                         // etc.)
```

Function Alert brings up an alert dialog box. The format of this box is determined by an ALRT resource. An optional Pascal function can handle events in the Alert box:

```
Alert(1002, nil);  // use ALRT resource 1002, default event handler
```

Function BeginUpdate sets a windows-visible region to the part of the window that needs redrawing. You need to save a copy of the window's GrafPort before calling BeginUpdate, and restore the GrafPort after calling EndUpdate:

```
WindowPtr aWindow = ...;
GrafPrt savePort;
GetPort(&savePort);
SetPort(aWindow);
BeginUpdate(aWindow);
.
.
.
EndUpdate(aWindow);
SetPort(savePort);
```

Function ClipRect sets the valid drawing region for a GrafPort:

```
Rect r;  // clip rectangle boundaries
SetRect(&r, 10, 10, 100, 200); // left, top, right, bottom boundaries
ClipRect(&r);
```

Function DisposeRgn frees the storage for a region data structure:

```
RgnHandle h = NewRgn();  // create a new (empty) region
.
.
.
DisposeRgn(h);  // free region storage
```

Function DragWindow draws an outline of a window and moves this outline with mouse movement until the mouse button is released:

```
    EventRecord anEvent;
    WindowPtr mouseWindow;
    int windowCode;

    if (GetNextEvent(everyEvent, &anEvent)) {
        switch (anEvent.what) {
            case    mouseDown:
                windowCode = FindWindow(anEvent.where,  // mouse
                                                        // location
                                    &mouseWindow);
                if (windowCode == inDrag) {
                    DragWindow(mouseWindow,    // the window to drag
                            anEvent.where, // initial location
                            &qd.screenBits.bounds);
```

```
            }
            break;
        .
        .
    }
}
```

Function DrawMenuBar displays the menu across the top of the Macintosh desktop:

```
DrawMenuBar();
```

Function DrawString draws a string in the current GrafPort. The string must be a Pascal format string (the first byte is the length of the string):

```
static char *buf = {"A string"};
char pascal_buf[256];
sprintf(&(pascal_string[1]),"%s",buf);
pascal_string[0] = strlen(buf);
DrawString(pascal_string);
```

Function EndUpdate is called after updating the display contents of a window:

```
WindowPtr aWindow = ...;
GrafPrt savePort;
GetPort(&savePort);
SetPort(aWindow);
BeginUpdate(aWindow);
.
.
.
EndUpdate(aWindow);
SetPort(savePort);
```

Function EraseRect erases a specified rectangle in the current GrafPort:

```
Rect r;
SetRect(&r, 10, 10, 100, 100);   // left, top, right, bottom corners
EraseRect(&r);
```

Function FrameRect draws a border around a specified rectangle in the current GrafPort. The thickness of the border is determined by the pen width in the current GrafPort:

```
Rect r;
SetRect(&r, 10, 10, 100, 100);   // left, top, right, bottom corners
FrameRect(&r);
```

Function GetFontInfo retrieves font specifications from the current Graf-Port:

```
FontInfo fi;
GetFontInfo(&fi);
// fi.ascent, fi.descent, fi.leading, fi.widMax are available
```

Function GetNewMBar creates a new menu bar data structure using a menu template defined in a resource file:

```
Handle menuBar = GetNewMBar(rMenuBar);  // rMenuBar = menu bar
                                        // resource ID
SetMenuBar(menuBar);
DisposHandle(menuBar);
AddResMenu(GetMHandle(mApple), 'DRVR');
DrawMenuBar();
```

Function GetNextEvent copies the oldest event from the global event queue (see Fig. 3.2) and deletes the event entry from the global queue:

```
EventRecord anEvent;
if (GetNextEvent(everyEvent, &anEvent)) {
    switch (anEvent.what) {
        case   mouseDown:  ... break;
        .
        .
    }
}
```

Function GetPort retrieves the value of the current GrafPort. The constant everyEvent is defined in the Macintosh system include file Events.h. This constant indicates that all event types are requested from the global system event queue:

```
GrafPort savePort;
GetPort(&savePort);
```

Function FindWindow identifies which window on the Macintosh desktop contains a mouse click:

```
EventRecord anEvent;
WindowPtr mouseWindow;
int windowCode;

if (GetNextEvent(everyEvent, &anEvent)) {
    switch (anEvent.what) {
        case   mouseDown:
                windowCode = FindWindow(anEvent.where, //mouse
                                                       //location
```

```
                                    &mouseWindow);
        // windowCode will havew the value: inSysWindow,
        // inMenuBar,
        // inContent (application window), etc.
        break;
        .
        .
    }
}
```

Function GetDItem is a Dialog Manager function that returns information about a dialog item (such as an edit field, static text, or a button):

```
short itemType;
Handle itemHandle;
Rect r;
DialogPtr dPtr = GetNewDialog(515, (Ptr)0L, (WindowPtr)-1);
                                                // WindowPtr
GetDItem(dPtr, (short) 1, // dialog item number 1
         &itemType,       // returned dialog item type
         &itemH,          // returned handle ti dialog item
         &r);             // item location
if (itemHandle != 0) {
    char buf[256];
    sprintf(&(buf[1]),"New item title");
    buf[0] = 14; // length of new title
    SetCTitle((ControlHandle)itemHandle, (Str255)buf);
}
```

Function GetNewDialog is a Dialog Manager function that creates a new dialog box from a resource template:

```
DialogPtr dPtr = GetNewDialog(515,          // resource ID
                   (Ptr)nil,                // storage for
                                            // dialog
                   (WindowPtr)-1); // WindowPtr
```

Function GetNewWindow uses a window template defined in a resource file to create a new window:

```
WindowPtr newWindow =
   GetNewWindow(1202,  // resource ID for a window definition
                nil,   // pointer to storage. nil for automatic
                       // creation
                (WindowPtr)-1);  // bring window to front
```

Function HiliteMenu unhighlights any currently highlighted menu title, and highlights the title of a specified menu:

```
HiliteMenu(0);    // unhilight any hilited menu titles
HiliteMenu(101);  // Hilite title of menu with ID == 101
```

The Toolbox function InitCursor makes the cursor visible and sets the cursor to the standard system arrow cursor. The Toolbox function InitDialogs sets up global data for the Dialog Manager.

Function InitGraf is always called once at the beginning of a Macintosh program to initialize the global variables used by Quickdraw. Function InitFonts is called when Font Manager calls are used in an application:

```
// initialize Mac Toolbox components
InitGraf((Ptr)  &qd.thePort);
InitFonts();
InitWindows();
InitMenus();
TEInit();
InitDialogs((ResumeProcPtr)  nil);
InitCursor();
```

Function LineTo moves the current pen location in the active GrafPort while drawing a line:

```
MoveTo(100, 200);  // move pen location to x=100, y=200
```

Function LDispose is a List Manager utility for freeing the storage allocated to a list:

```
ListHandle myList = LNew(...);
.
.
.
LDispose(myList);
```

Function LNew is a List Manager utility for creating a new list:

```
char **list_items = {"item 1", "item 2", "item 3"};
Point cellLocation;
DialogPtr dLog = GetNewDialog(...);
Rect itemR = ...;  // rectangle for list item position in dialog box
Rect dataR;
SetRect(&dataR, 0, 0, 1, 3);  // 1 coloumn, 3 rows in list
ListHandle myList = LNew(&itemR, &dataR, cellSize, 0,
                         (WindowPtr)dLog,  false,  false,  true,
                         true);
```

Function LSetCell is a List Manager utility for changing the contents of a cell in a list:

```
char **list_items = {"item 1", "item 2", "item 3"};
Point cellLocation;
DialogPtr dLog = GetNewDialog(...);
Rect itemR = ...;
Rect dataR = ...;
ListHandle myList = LNew(&itemR, &dataR, cellSize, 0,
```

```
                         (WindowPtr)dLog, false, false, true, true);
for (int i=0; i<3; i++) {
    cellLocation.v = i;  // row 10
    cellLocation.h = 0;   // coloumn 0
    LSetCell(list_items[i], strlen(list_items[i]),
             cellLocation, myList);
}
```

Function MaxApplZone increases the size of an application's heap:

```
MaxApplZone();
```

Function ModalDialog is a Dialog Manager utility to automatically handle events for a modal dialog box. The first argument to ModalDialog is an optional Pascal event-handling function:

```
short itemHit = 0;
while (itemHit != 1)  // item 1 is the OK button
    ModalDialog(nil,  &itemHit);  // nil  ==  automatic event
                                  // handling
```

Function MoveTo changes the current pen location in the active GrafPort without performing any drawing operations:

```
MoveTo(100, 200);  // move pen location to x=100, y=200
```

Function NewRgn create a new region data structure:

```
RgnHandle h = NewRgn();  // create a new (empty) region
.
.
.
DisposeRgn(h);  // free region storage
```

Function ScrollRect scrolls a rectanglar area of the current GrafPort:

```
Rect r;  // clip rectangle boundaries
SetRect(&r, 10, 10, 100, 200); // left, top, right, bottom boundaries
ClipRect(&r);
RgnHandle h = NewRgn();  // create a new (empty) region
ScrollRect(&r, 10, -20, h);  // scroll right 10 pixels, up 20
                             // pixels
DisposeRgn(h);  // free region storage
```

Function SetCTitle is used to change the name (title) of a dialog item:

```
    short itemType;
    Handle itemHandle;
    Rect r;
```

```
DialogPtr dPtr = GetNewDialog(515, (Ptr)0L, (WindowPtr)-1); //
                        // WindowPtr
GetDItem(dPtr, (short) 1, // dialog item number 1
            &itemType,       // returned dialog item type
            &itemH,          // returned handle ti dialog item
            &r);             // item location
if (itemHandle != 0) {
    char buf[256];
    sprintf(&(buf[1]),"New item title");
    buf[0] = 14; // length of new title
    SetCTitle((ControlHandle)itemHandle,  (Str255)buf);
}
```

Function SetMenubar installs a list of menu handles on the system menu bar:

```
Handle menuBar = GetNewMBar(rMenuBar); // rMenuBar = menu bar
                                        // resource ID
SetMenuBar(menuBar);
DisposHandle(menuBar);
AddResMenu(GetMHandle(mApple), 'DRVR');
DrawMenuBar();
```

Function SetPort activates a GrafPort for Quickdraw graphics:

```
GrafPtr aPort = ...
SetPort(aPort);  // ready for Quickdraw operations
```

Function SetRect fills a rectangle data structure with the boundaries of the rectangle:

```
Rect r;
SetRect(&r, 10, 10, 100, 100);  // left, top, right, bottom
                                // corners
```

Function SFGetFile is a utility for selecting a Macintosh file for input. The fourth and fifth arguments to SFGetFile are the number of file types and a file type list; I usually use -1 for the number of specified file types and *nil* for the file type list to select all available files. I use a Pascal file filter function to determine which files in the current directory appear in the file selection box:

```
// File selection filter function:

pascal Boolean fileFilter(ParmBlkPtr paramBlock)
{
    int size2 = strlen(fileExtension);
    StringPtr sPtr = paramBlock->fileParam.ioNamePtr;
    char * fileName = (char *)sPtr;
    int size = fileName[0];
    char buf[257];
    for (int i=0; i<size; i++) buf[i] = fileName[i+1];
```

```
    buf[size] = '\0';

    // 'buf' now conatins a C string value of the current file name. Your
    // program
    // needs to decide if this file should appear in the file selection
    // box:
    .
    .
    // Choose:

    return true; // skip this file name
    .
    .
    // Or:

    return false; // put this file name in the selection box
}
    .
    .
    .

    // Get a file for input:

    SFReply sf;
    Point p; p.h = 100; p.v = 100;
    SFGetFile(p,  (Str255)"",  (FileFilterProcPtr)fileFilter,  -1,
             (SFTypeList)nil,  (DlgHookProcPtr)nil,  &sf);

    // Convert the retuned file name a C string:

    int size = sf.fName[0];
    if (sf.good == 0)  size = 0;
    for (int i=0; i<size; i++)  returned_filename[i] = sf.fName[i+1];
    returned_filename[size] = '\0';
    .
    .
    .
```

Function SFPutFile is a utility for choosing an output file. The first argument is the position of the standard file selection box on the Macintosh desktop. The second argument is a Pascal type prompt string. The third argument is a Pascal string containing the default filename. The fourth argument is an optional event-handling function. The last argument is a SFReply data structure:

```
SFReply sf;
Point p; p.h = 100; p.v = 100;
SFPutFile(p,  (Str255)"",  (Str255)"",  (DlgHookProcPtr)nil,
&sf);
    // Convert the returned file name to a C string:
    int size = sf.fName[0];
    for (int i=0; i<size; i++)
        returned_filename[i] = sf.fName[i+1];
    returned_filename[size] = '\0';
```

Function ShowWindow makes a window visible. Note that ShowWindow does not change the window stacking order on the desktop:

```
ShowWindow((WindowPtr)aWindow);
```

Function SysEnvirons returns information on the Macintosh hardware:

```
SysEnvRec envRec;
(void) SysEnvirons(curSysEnvVers, &envRec);

if (envRec.machineType < 0) {
    Warning("This machine does not have 128K ROMs!");
    exit(1);
}
```

Function TEInint initializes global data for using the TextEdit scrap area; this function is also necessary for the correct execution of Desk Accessories that use TextEdit functions:

```
// initialize Mac Toolbox components
InitGraf((Ptr) &qd.thePort);
InitFonts();
InitWindows();
InitMenus();
TEInit();
InitDialogs((ResumeProcPtr) nil);
InitCursor();
```

Function TextFont sets the font for a GrafPort:

```
SetFont(4);   // non-proportional monaco font
```

Some common font values include the following:

0	systemFont (usually Chicago font)
1	applFont (usually Geneva font)
3	geneva
4	monaco
5	venice
20	times
21	helvetica

Function WaitNextEvent copies the oldest event from the global event queue (see Fig. 3.2) and deletes the event entry from the global queue. If the WaitNextEvent trap is not in the current Macintosh ROM, use the GetNextEvent trap:

```
EventRecord anEvent;
static Region fMouseRgn = nil;
if (fMouseRgn == nil) fmouseRgn = NewRgn(); // allocate Region only
                                            // one time

if (WaitNextEvent(everyEvent,
                  &anEvent,
                  (unsigned long)0,
                  fMouseRgn)) {
    switch (anEvent.what) {
        case    mouseDown:   ... break;
          .
          .
    }
}
```

4

X Windows

X Windows was designed to work in a networked environment. Application programs executing on one machine can open windows on remote display servers. I have executed application programs on computers in Europe while directing the output to an X Windows display in my office in San Diego. There are huge benefits to remote access (including full use of graphics) rather than physically traveling to remote locations.

The X Windows programming environment provides an elegant and complete set of graphics and windowing utilities to the application programmer. The source code for the X Windows version of the GUI library in Appendix D is set up to work with both Athena and Motif widget sets and with both X11R3 and X11R4.

There are three levels of X Windows programming support: low-level XLib calls, the X Intrinsic toolkit, and high-level *widget* display objects as provided by the Athena, Motif, and Andrew toolkits. Writing X applications in pure XLib is tedious; most X applications are written with one of the higher-level widget-based toolkits. I prefer using the Motif toolkit, but I have chosen to implement the X Windows version of the GUI class library using both Motif and the public-domain Athena widget toolkit, since most X Windows systems include the Athena widget set.

The Unix "makefile" is set up to build the GUI library for both Athena and Motif. The source files for the GUI library use #ifdefs to set off Motif-and Athena-dependent parts of the source code. The conversion to Sun Microsystems OpenWindows widget toolkit is straightforward.

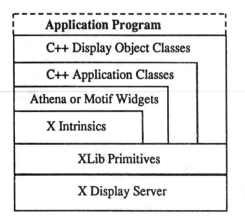

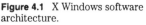

Figure 4.1 X Windows software architecture.

4.1 X Windows Application Interface to the Unix Operating System

Figure 4.1 shows the software architecture that supports the C++ GUI class library. X Windows applications are typically written using calls to both a widget library (e.g., Athena or Motif) and to the low-level XLib library. For complete portability using the C++ GUI class library listed in Appendix D, your programs should only use calls to the GUI library, and refrain from calling XLib functions directly. A good strategy for maintaining portability is the addition of required XLib operations to the C++ GUI library. If your application program needs to be moved to either the Macintosh or Windows environments, then implement your extensions to the C++ GUI library implementations for those environments.

4.2 Event Handling in X Windows Applications

Event handling in X Windows is divided between the X Server software and application programs. The X Server maintains a global event queue containing events for all applications using one of the X Server's displays. The X Server dispatches global events to the appropriate applications, as seen in Fig. 4.2.

The sample main event loop for an X Windows application is simple to implement:

```
while (1) {
    XEvent an_event;
    XtNextEvent(&an_event);
    XtDispatchEvent(&an_event);
}
```

The function XtNextEvent waits for an available X event on the application event queue. The function XtDispatchEvent calls user-defined callback functions. Application programs define callback functions which are called when events occur. For example, here is a callback function to execute whenever a Command Button widget (or PushButton in Motif) is pressed with the mouse pointer:

```
void do_hello_button(w, data1, data2)   /* arg data2 is unused here */
Widget w;
int * data1;
caddr_t data2;
{
    /* argument data1 could be used here */
        printf("hello\n");
}
```

When you create a Command Button widget, you can specify that function do_hello_button is called when the button is pressed:

```
Widget hello_button
   XtCreateManagedWidget ("Hello",commandWidgetClass,form,args,n);
static int ibuf[200];
```

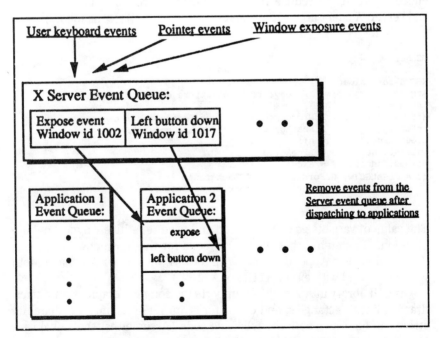

Figure 4.2 X Server dispatches events to application event queues.

```
XtAddCallback(hello_button,XtNcallback,
      (XtCallbackProc)do_hello_button,
          (XtPointer)ibuf);
```

Here a block of data defined in *ibuf* is passed to the callback function do_hello_button.

The C++ GUI library supports several types of dialog boxes that are implemented in the file applib.cxx in Appendix D. This example code for setting up event callbacks is used for controlling user interaction with command buttons, menus, and lists of items.

4.3 Graphics Operations in X Windows Applications

GUI-based programs should usually not draw graphics in a window unless the application receives an expose event. This is true for X Windows, Macintosh, and Microsoft Windows programs. The graphics primitives described in this section are usually used inside a callback function that is called when an application receives an expose event for one of its windows.

An application program usually creates one or more *graphics contexts* (GCs) used to specify drawing parameters like line thickness, foreground and background colors, and fonts. GCs are stored in the X Server and referenced indirectly to reduce the communications required between client and server. A client application can create a GC for X11R3 as follows:

```
GC gc;

XGCValues values;
Arg        args[5];   // Leave room for future code modifications
int n = 0;
XtSetArg(args[n], XtNforeground, &values.foreground); n++;
XtSetArg(args[2], XtNbackground, &values.background); n++;
XtGetValues(w, args,n);
values.line_style = LineSolid;
values.function    = GXcopy
gc = XtGetGC(w, GCForeground | GCBackground |
          GCFunction | GCLineStyle, &values);
```

The value of variable gc can be stored and used repetitively by a client application. (Remember that the source code for the X Windows version of the GUI library in Appendix D is set up to work with either Athena or Motif widget sets and with either X11R3 or X11R4.)

The GUI library in Appendix D supports the common graphics primitives: drawing lines, rectangles, and character strings. For example, a character string can be drawn with the following code (Assume that the global variable global_gc of type GC is already defined.):

```
extern GC global_gc
   .
   .
   .

   Display *disp;
   Window *win;
   GC gc;
   int x, y;
   char *string;
      .
      .
      .

   XDrawString(disp, win, global_gc, x, y, string, strlen(string));
```

Here is a complete example showing how a Widget's expose callback function can draw "Hello" in the Widget:

```
extern GC global_gc

void  draw_in_widget_callback(w, dummy1, dummy2)
Widget w;
caddr_t dummy1, dummy2; /* not used */
{
       XDrawString(XtDisplay(w), XtWindow(w), global_gc, 20, 20, "Hello",
       5);
}
```

4.4 Dialog Boxes in X Windows Applications

The GUI library in Appendix D provides a few simple types of dialog boxes that are designed in Chapter 5. The following simple example shows how to create and handle the events for a simple dialog box. This example can be made to work as a modal or modeless dialog box by changing one line of code for trapping the pointer inside the dialog box.

```
static int done_show_info;
static void show_info_ok(Widget, Widget, caddr_t)
{
    done_show_info = 1;
}

void show_info(char * prompt)
{   Arg args[5];

    int n = 0;
    XtSetArg(args[n], XtNlabel, "Popup"); n++;
        Widget  p_show_info  =  XtCreatePopupShell("show_info",
        shellWidgetClass, global_form, args, n);

#ifndef MOTIF
    Widget form =
XtCreateManagedWidget("form",formWidgetClass,p_show_info,
                          NULL, 0);  /* ATHENA */
```

```
#else
    Widget form = XtCreateManagedWidget("form", xmFormWidgetClass,
                                p_show_info, NULL, 0);   /* MOTIF
*/
#endif

    n = 0;
    XtSetArg(args[n], XtNy, 2); n++;
    XtSetArg(args[n], XtNlabel, prompt); n++;

#ifdef MOTIF
    Widget label = XtCreateManagedWidget(prompt,xmLabelWidgetClass,

                                    form, args, n);
#else
    Widget label = XtCreateManagedWidget(prompt,labelWidgetClass,

form, args, n);
#endif

#ifdef MOTIF
    n = 0;
    XtSetArg(args[n], XmNy, 40); n++;
Widget ok_button =
XtCreateManagedWidget("OK",xmPushButtonWidgetClass,form, args, n);

#else
    n = 0;
    XtSetArg(args[n], XtNy, 110); n++;
    XtSetArg(args[n], XtNfromVert, label); n++;
    XtSetArg(args[n], XtNvertDistance, 20); n++;
    Widget ok_button = XtCreateManagedWidget("OK",commandWidgetClass,
                                    form, args, n);
#endif
    XtAddCallback(ok_button,XtNcallback, (XtCallbackProc)show_info_ok,
                (XtPointer)NULL);

    XtManageChild(p_show_info);

    /* Warp pointer to edit field */
    XWarpPointer(XtDisplay(ok_button),None,XtWindow(ok_button),
                0, 0, 0, 0, 10, 10);

    /* For MODAL dialog boxes: constrain the pointer here to 'form' */

    done_show_info = 0;
    while (done_show_info == 0) {
        XEvent an_event;
        XtNextEvent(&an_event);
        XtDispatchEvent(&an_event);
    }
    XtPopdown(p_show_info);
    XtDestroyWidget(p_show_info);
    popup_active = 0;
}
```

If you want to use modal dialogs, you do not have to take over event handling in the above *while* loop; use the callback function show_info_ok to popdown widget p_show_info. Note that this example code uses a Unix environment variable MOTIF as a compiler flag to generate either Athena- or Motif-dependent code.

4.5 X Windows API Functions Used in Appendix D

The following list of API functions includes XLib (XCreateFontCursor and XClearArea), X Toolkit (XtCreateWidget and XtAddWorkProc), and Motif (XmCreateMenubar and XmStringCreate) functions. The naming conventions are as follows:

- Functions starting with Xt are X Toolkit functions.
- Functions starting with Xm are Motif functions.
- All other functions starting with X are low-level XLib functions.

Function XClearArea clears a specified rectangle in a widget. The last argument to XClearArea is a flag indicating whether an expose (redraw) event is generated:

```
Widget dWidget = ...;
XClearArea(XtDisplay(dWidget), // X display for widget 'dWidget'
           XtWindow(dWidget),  // X Window for widget 'dWidget'
           0,     // left boundary to clear
           0,     // top boundary to clear
           1024,   // right boundary to clear
           1024,   // bottom boundary to clear
           0);  // flag: 0-> do no generate expose event, 1->
                 // generate
                 // an expose event
```

Function XCreateFontCursor creates a new cursor for the X Server specified by a Display pointer:

```
Font crosshair_cursor =
   XCreateFontCursor(XtDisplay(dWidget), // Display pointer
                     XC_crosshair);   // constant defined in X
                                       // Toolkit
```

Function XDrawLine draws a line between two specified points:

```
Widget dWidget = ...;
XDrawLine(XtDisplay(dWidget),  // X display for widget 'dWidget'
          XtWindow(dWidget),   // X Window for widget 'dWidget'
          current_GC,          // current graphics context
```

```
10,          // first x coordinates
15,          // first y coordinate
110,         // second x coordinate
125);        // second y coordinate
```

Function XDrawString draws a C string at a specified location in a widget. The font is determined by the current graphics context:

```
Widget dWidget = ...;
XDrawString(XtDisplay(dWidget),     // X  display  for  widget
                                    // 'dWidget'
           XtWindow(dWidget),       // X  Window  for  widget
                                    // 'dWidget'
```

Function XmCreateMenubar is a Motif convenience function that creates an unmanaged menu bar widget:

```
Widget control_area =
   XtCreateManagedWidget("controls",
                   xmBulletinBoardWidgetClass,
                   global_form,NULL,0);
Widget menubar;
Arg args[5];
n = 0;
menubar = XmCreateMenuBar(control_area,    // parent Widget
                 "menubar",         // Widget name
                 args,              // Arg array
                 n);                // # entries in Arg array
```

Function XmCreatePulldownMenu is a Motif convenience function that creates a pulldown menu widget:

```
Widget the_menu =
   XmCreatePulldownMenu(parent,     // parent Widget
                   "Menu1",         // Widget name
                   NULL,            // Arg array (or NULL)
                   0);              // # elements in Arg array
             current_GC,            // current graphics context
             10,                    // x coordinates
             15,                    // y coordinate
             (char *)str,           // C string
             strlen(str));          // length of C string
```

Function XmTextGetString returns a *(char *)* pointer to a new block of text containing the contents of a Motif text widget. (Your application program is responsible for freeing this storage.)

```
char * cp = XmTextGetString((Widget)dialog);

// Use the text:
   .
   .
   .

// Free the storage allocated by XmTextGetString:
free(cp);
```

Function XmStringCreate creates Motif-style 16-bit characters from 8-bit ASCII text:

```
static char **list_items = {"item1", "item number 2"};
int number_of_items = 2;
XmString *string_MOTIF = (XmString *)XtMalloc(sizeof(XmString)
                                       *(number_of_items +
1));
    for (int k=0; k<number_of_items; k++)
        string_MOTIF[k] = XmStringCreate(list_items[k],
                                XmSTRING_DEFAULT_CHARSET);

    // Use the Motif strings:
    .
    .
    .

    // Free the storage allocated for the Motif strings:
    for (k=0; k<number_of_items; k++)
        XmStringFree(string_MOTIF[k]);
    free((char *)string_MOTIF);
```

Function XtAddCallback adds a callback function to a widget. The last argument to XtAddCallback is a pointer to a block of storage that is passed to the callback function (see section 4.2):

```
XtAddCallback(menu,         // Widget receiving new callback
                            // function
              XtNcallback,  // X Toolkit constant
              (XtCallbackProc)do_make_menu, // a C callback
                                       // function
              (XtPointer)NULL); // auxiliary data if required
```

Function XtAddEventHandler binds an event callback function to a widget.

```
XtAddEventHandler(dWidget,      // Widget receiving a new event
                                // handler
                  ExposureMask, // event mask for event types
                                // processed
                  1,            // nonmaskable event flag
                  (XtEventHandler)draw_screen,   // callback
                                         // function
                  (XtPointer)NULL);  // auxiliary data if
                                     // required
```

Function XtAddWorkProc specifies a work function which is called periodically:

```
XtAddWorkProc(do_work,   // add a work function to application
              NULL);   // auxiliary data if required
```

Function XtCreatePopupShell creates a popup shell widget and adds it to a parent widget's popup list. Use XtPopup to display a popup and

XtPopdown to hide a popup shell:

```
Arg args[5];

int n = 0;
XtSetArg(args[n], XtNlabel, "Popup"); n++;
Widget p_do_edit =
    XtCreatePopupShell("do_edit",              // Shell name
                    shellWidgetClass,      // Widget class
                    global_form,        // parent Widget
                    args,               // Arg array
                    n);                 // # elements in Arg array
```

Function XtCreateManagedWidget creates a widget and then manages it:

```
Widget control_area =
    XtCreateManagedWidget("controls",
                        xmBulletinBoardWidgetClass,
                    global_form,
                    NULL,
                    0);
```

Function XtCreateWidget creates a new widget:

```
Widget form =
    XtCreateWidget("form",      // Widget name
        xmFormWidgetClass,      // Widget class
        parent,      // parent of new Widget
        NULL,        // Arg array
        0);          // # elements in Arg array
```

Function XtDestroyWidget destroys a widget and all children widgets contained in the widget:

```
XtDestroyWidget(form);    // form is the Widget being destroyed
```

Function XtDispatchEvent processes an event by looking up the application callback function associated with the event and calling the callback function:

```
while (1) {    // run forever, or until a callback exit the
               // application
    XEvent an_event;
    XtNextEvent(&an_event);
     XtDispatchEvent(&an_event);
}
```

Function XtDisplay is a toolkit macro which returns the Display component of a widget data structure:

```
XClearArea(XtDisplay(dWidget),
           XtWindow(dWidget), 0, 0, 1024, 1024, 1);
```

Function XtGetGC returns a graphics context (GC) for drawing in a widget:

```
XGCValues values;
values.foreground = 3;
values.background = 1;
values.line_style = LineSolid;
values.function   = GXcopy;  // or use GXor
gc = XtGetGC((Widget)w,
             GCForeground | GCBackground |
             GCFunction | GCLineStyle,
             &values);
```

Function XtGetValues returns the values of X resources named in an Arg array:

```
XGCValues values;
Arg       args[5];
int n = 0;
XtSetArg(args[n], XtNforeground, &values.foreground); n++;
XtSetArg(args[n], XtNbackground, &values.background); n++;
 XtGetValues(w, args,n);
```

Function XtInitialize initializes the X Toolkit intrinsics by making a connection with the X Server (which may be executing on a different machine than the application program), loading default X resources, and processing command line arguments:

```
main(int argc, char **argv)
{
  Widget toplevel, menu;
  Arg args[10];
  int n = 0;
  toplevel = XtInitialize(argv[0], "main", args, i,
                          (Cardinal *)&argc, argv);
```

Function XtListShowCurrent is an Athena widget list function that returns a list data structure. The following code shows how to detect which list item has been selected:

```
#ifndef MOTIF
static void list_cb(Widget this_list, int, caddr_t)          // ATHENA
{
    XtListReturnStruct *list_struct = XtListShowCurrent(this_list);
#ifdef X11R3
    done_list_choose = 1 + list_struct->index; // fetch list item
selected
#endif
#ifdef X11R4
    done_list_choose = 1 + list_struct->list_index; // fetch list item
```

```
selected
#endif
    free((char *)list_struct); // we need to give back this storage
}
#else
static void list_cb(Widget, int, XmListCallbackStruct *list)    // MOTIF
{
    done_list_choose = 1 + list->item_position;
}

#endif
```

Function XtManageChild manages a widget by adding it to its parent's managed-widget list:

```
XtPopup(p_do_edit);  // p_do_edit is the popup Widget to make
                     // visible
```

Function XtManageChildren manages a list of widgets by adding this list to a parent's managed-widgets list:

```
// Add command buttons to a menu list:
for(int i=0;i<num_items;i++) {
    menu_buttons[i] = XtCreateWidget(item_names[i],
                                xmPushButtonWidgetClass,
                                the_menu, NULL, 0);
    XtAddCallback(menu_buttons[i], XmNactivateCallback,
                    (XtCallbackProc)do_menu,i); // pass i=menu item
                                                // number
}
 XtManageChildren(menu_buttons,      // Parent Widget
                num_items);  // an array of Widgets to manage
```

Function XtNextEvent waits for an available event which is returned through its XEvent argument:

```
 while (1) {    // run forever, or until a callback exit the
                // application
    XEvent an_event;
     XtNextEvent(&an_event);
    XtDispatchEvent(&an_event);
}
```

Function XtPopdown hides a widget made visible with XtPopup:

```
XtPopdown(p_do_edit); // p_do_edit is the popup Widget to hide
```

Function XtPopup makes a popup widget visible:

```
XtManageChild(buttonWidget);    // buttonWidget is the child
                                // Widget
```

Function XtRealizeWidget realizes a widget by creating a display window for it:

```
Widget toplevel = ...
// Intialization:
  .
  .
  .
XtRealizeWidget(toplevel);
```

Function XtWindow is an X Toolkit macro that returns the window component of a widget data structure:

```
XClearArea(XtDisplay(dWidget),
    XtWindow(dWidget),      // fetch the window component of a Widget
    0, 0, 1024, 1024, 0);
```

Abstract C⁺⁺ GUI Class Library

What are the basic user interface components to use in your programs? How do GUI components interface with the data structures and algorithms that comprise applications? How do you design user interface components that are abstract enough to deal with a wide variety of windowing systems? These questions are answered in this chapter.

5.1 Basic User Interface Components

The design of the base set of user interface components is the most critical design decision in this book. The basic set of components must be simple enough to implement on a wide variety of windowing systems, be sufficiently general to support most applications, and be extensible. The core GUI components that I have designed and implemented are an application class, menus, a document window with methods for all standard graphics operations (including text display), and a small set of modal dialog boxes (for entering single values, selecting from a list, selecting files, and entering and modifying text).

I have also developed a set of application utility classes designed to make custom software development easier and faster. These utilities provide a graphic tree browser, dialog box support for opening files, smart data types with *object persistence* (structured C⁺⁺ data objects that handle their own memory management and can save and restore themselves from disk files), a generic (neural network) pattern matcher that can be easily embedded in application programs, and curve plotting for business and scientific applications.

The goal here is not to design a complete GUI toolkit that supports all GUI functionality of applications like Microsoft Excel or Word. Rather, the goal is to build a framework that supports rapid custom program development. An easy-to-use, portable toolkit is of great practical value for programmers who need to rapidly prototype applications.

The look and feel of the applications you develop with this toolkit will depend on the underlying windowing system; the functionality of the applications will be identical.

5.1.1   Application class

The application C++ class provides basic interaction with the host operating system and windowing environment. This class must handle program initialization and termination. Different operating and windowing systems require very different code for program initialization. C++ macros are used for standard initialization to provide portability.

The application class is not used directly in application programs that use the C++ GUI library. The C++ constructor call for the application class is hidden in a C macro named INIT_PROGRAM which you have already seen in the sample drawing program listed in Chapter 1.

5.1.2   Application menu

Both the Microsoft Windows and the Macintosh programming environments provide tools for using a data file to specify menus and menu item names. Our toolkit needs to call application-specific functions when a menu item is selected. X Windows applications using the toolkit will use a text data file to specify menu item names for complete C++ application source-code compatibility with Windows and the Macintosh.

Application programs are notified of user interaction with a menu through the method do_menu_action in class TAppWindow defined in section 5.1.3. For easy portability across different windowing systems, the C++ GUI class library is limited to using one menu with any number of menu items. System menu options are supported differently in each operating system. In Microsoft Windows, a system menu can be used to kill a program, iconify a program, etc. With the Macintosh, the Apple Menu is active for using "Desk Accessories." In X Windows, standard Athena Universal Window Manager and Motif Window operations are available for killing a program, iconifying a program, moving a window, etc.

5.1.3   TAppWindow document window

A generic document window comes "free" with our C++ toolkit; it is hard to imagine an application that does not require a window, so the C++ GUI library creates one automatically. The standard behavior of the application class is to create a generic window during program initialization. The document window class provides methods for all standard graphics operations. Additionally, the document window class provides methods for all standard input events; application programs can simply override these methods to intercept user events.

The external behavior of the document window class for dealing with events is controlled by five methods:

```
void TAppWindow::update_display()
```

is defined in your application program to update the contents of the current document window.

```
void TAppWindow::mouse_down(int x, int y)
```

is defined in your application program and is called with the x-y location of a mouse-down event in the current document window.

```
void TAppWindow::mouse_up(int x, int y)
```

is defined in your application program and is called with the x-y location of a mouse-up event in the current document window.

```
void TAppWindow::mouse_move(int x, int y)
```

is defined in your application program and is called with the x-y location of a mouse motion event in the current document window.

```
void TAppWindow::do_menu_action(int menu_item_number)
```

is defined in your application program to perform actions when a user selects a menu item.

Three methods are provided for use in drawing in a document window:

```
void TAppWindow::plot_line(int x1, int y1, int x2, int y2)
```

for drawing lines.

```
void TAppWindow::plot_string(int x, int y, char *str)
```

for drawing text.

```
void TAppWindow::plot_rect(int top, int right, int bottom, int left)
```

for drawing a rectangle.

The document class also supports scrolling text display; the display area can be the entire window or a specified rectangle. Two methods initialize internal data structures to support scrolling text output:

```
void TAppWindow::init_scrolling_text(int top, int right, int
bottom, int left)

void TAppWindow::init_scrolling_text()
```

The method used to write out a line of text is:

```
void TAppWindow::put_scrolling_text(char *buf)
```

The method that erases all text in a scrolling text field is:

```
void TAppWindow::reset_scrolling_text()
```

The following methods can be used to get information about a document window:

```
int TAppWindow::string_height(char *str)
```

returns the number of pixels needed to plot a string vertically.

```
int TAppWindow::string_width(char *str)
```

returns the number of pixels needed to plot a string horizontally.

5.1.4 Modal dialog boxes

Typically, modal dialog boxes are implemented as a window subclass. However, I decided to provide dialog boxes as utility methods to the document window class. This allows a single line of code to pop up a dialog box, allow editing of desired value(s), and return these values to the application program.

To display values to a user and allow values to be edited, use the following method:

```
void TAppWindow::do_edit(char *prompt, char *buf)
```

This method displays the characters in *buf* in a large multiline edit field. The user can modify the character data in place. A nonzero return value indicates that the user hit the OK button to stop the editing; a zero return value indicates that the user hit the Cancel button. Figure 5.1 shows this dialog box. The appearance is different under Microsoft Windows, Mac OS, and X Windows, but the functionality is identical. The screen dump in Fig. 5.2 shows a TAppWindow::do_edit dialog box in Windows.

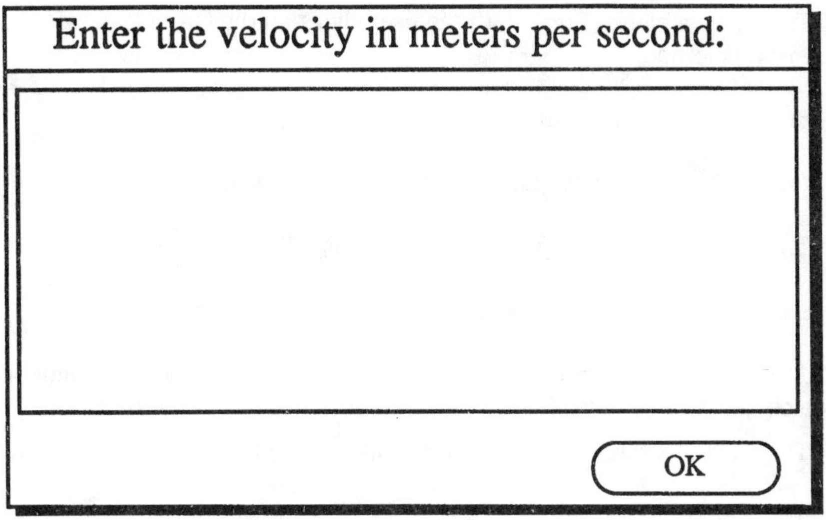

Enter the velocity in meters per second:
OK

Figure 5.1 Generic dialog box to prompt the user for a text string.

Mark test
TestMenu
this is a test.
OK

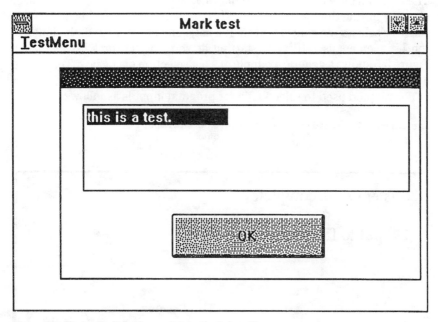

Figure 5.2 Text edit dialog box using method do_edit.

To display a block of text until the user clicks on the OK button, use the following method:

```
void TAppWindow::show_info(char *info_buf)
```

Figure 5.3 shows an example of this type of dialog box.

The method to display two text strings is as follows:

```
int TAppWindow::choose_one(char *prompt1, char *prompt2)
```

The user can select either string; the method returns 0 or 1 depending on the choice made. Figure 5.4 shows an example call to this method.

The method to show a scrolling list of items is as follows:

```
int TAppWindow::choose_one_from_list(char *prompt,
                               char
                               **list_items,
                               int number_of_items)
```

The user can either choose one item from the list by clicking on the item, or abort by hitting the Cancel button. This method returns a value of –1 when the user selects the cancel button. If a list element is selected, the index of the list element is returned (starting at zero for the first list element). Figure 5.5 shows a generic example of a list selection dialog box. The screen dump in Fig. 5.6 shows a list selection dialog box in Windows.

The method used to select a file for program input is as follows:

```
int TAppWindow::choose_file_to_read(char *prompt,
                                char
```

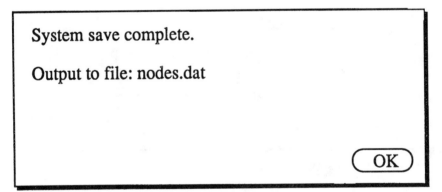

Figure 5.3 Generic dialog box to show the user a text string.

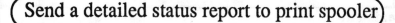

Figure 5.4 Dialog box for choosing one option from two choices.

```
                              *extension,
                         char
                         *returned_filename):
```

The buffer extension holds a file extension for matching files to show in the file selection list (for example, an extension string "txt" will match all files ending in ".txt"). The buffer returned_filename must be allocated by the calling program and must be large enough to hold any legal filename. The screen dump in Fig. 5.7 shows a file selection dialog box in the Macintosh OS. The method choose_file_to_read( ) has the same functionality under Microsoft Windows and X Windows.

To select a file for program output, use the following method:

```
int TAppWindow::choose_file_to_write(char *prompt,
                              char *returned_filename):
```

The buffer returned_filename must be allocated by the calling program, and must be large enough to hold any legal filename. The screen dump in Fig. 5.8

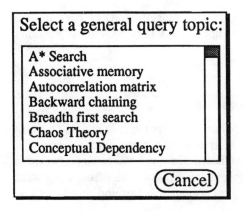

Figure 5.5 Dialog box for choosing one item from a list.

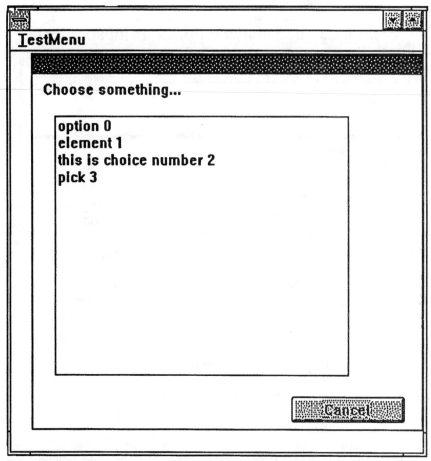

Figure 5.6   List selection dialog box using method choose_one_from_list.

shows a file selection dialog box in the Macintosh OS. The method
choose_file_to_write( ) has the same functionality under Microsoft Windows
and X Windows.

5.2   Handling Background Processing

The basic model for a GUI-based application waits for user events to cause
calculations to be performed. The user selects a menu option, clicks the
mouse in a window, or types at the keyboard. However, this model is not quite
general enough to handle many applications. Programmers frequently want
their GUI-based applications to perform periodic background processing. As

discussed in chapters 2, 3, and 4, the Windows, Macintosh, and X Windows programming environments all provide the means to write "work" functions that are executed periodically even when there are no user events.

The method **void TAppWindow::idle_proc()** is called periodically by the underlying windowing system or operating system to perform any necessary periodic calculations in an application. This method should perform its processing and terminate quickly (i.e., in less than 100 milliseconds), otherwise, interaction with the application program will be slow. Logically, this method could belong to the Application class, but I prefer a static class method for TAppWindow since applications are likely to be written by subclassing TAppWindow.

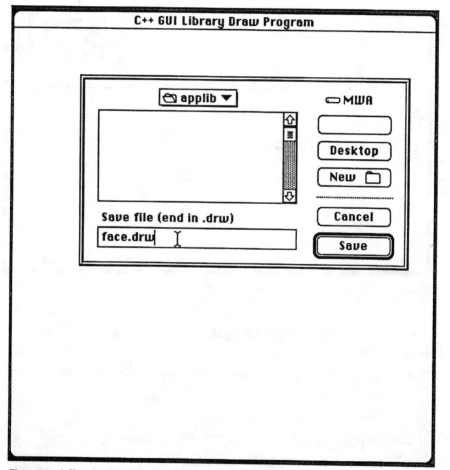

Figure 5.7 A file selection dialog box implemented on a Macintosh using choose_file_to_read( ).

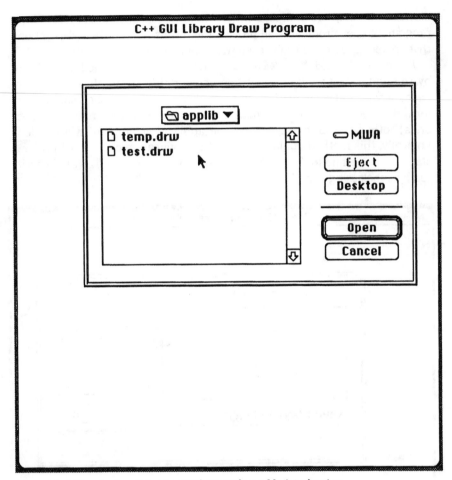

Figure 5.8 A file selection dialog box implemented on a Macintosh using choose_file_to_write( ).

5.3. Sample Test Program Using the Abstract Class Library Design

The following listing shows a program written to test the components of the C++ GUI library.

```
// File: test.cp
//
// Description: This file tests the GUI utility classes
//
// Copyright 1992 by Mark Watson Associates
//
//       No binary rights reserved: this software library may be used in
//       compiled form without restrictions.  All source rights
//       reserved: Source code to the GUI library can not be distributed
```

```
//        (on bulletin boards, or as part of shareware or commercial
//        products)
//        without written permission.

//        This software is provided "as is". The user accepts all
//        responsibility for its use.
//

#include "applib.h"
#include "Grapher.h"
#include "tplot.h"

//  USER DEFINED CALLBACK(S):

// for testing:

static int nump = 0;
static int xx[10], yy[10];

static TGraph *my_graph = (TGraph *)NULL;
static TPlotClass *tp = (TPlotClass *) NULL;
static TPlotClass *tp2 = (TPlotClass *) NULL;

static char my_text[100];

void TAppWindow::update_display()
{
//  clear_display(); // this bombs on the PC
    if (my_graph != (TGraph *)NULL)
        my_graph->Draw();
    if (tp != (TPlotClass *)NULL)
        tp->plot();
    if (tp2 != (TPlotClass *)NULL)
        tp2->plot();
    for (int i=0; i<nump; i++) {
        plot_line(xx[i], yy[i], xx[i]+10, yy[i]+10);
        char buf[22];
        sprintf(buf,"%d",i);
        plot_string(xx[i], yy[i] - 15, buf);
    }
    plot_string(30, 30, my_text);
}

void TAppWindow::mouse_down(int x, int y)
{
    if (nump < 9) {
        xx[nump] = x;
        yy[nump] = y;
        nump++;
    }
}

void TAppWindow::mouse_up(int, int)
{
}

void TAppWindow::mouse_move(int, int)
{
}
```

```
void TAppWindow::idle_proc()
{
}

void TAppWindow::do_menu_action(int item_number)
{
    if (item_number == 1) {
        nump = 0;
        my_graph = new TGraph(this, "A");
        my_graph->test();
        clear_display();
        update_display();
    }
    if (item_number == 2) {
        sprintf(my_text,"this is\n\n\na test.\n");
        do_edit("Prompt:", my_text);
    }
    if (item_number == 3)
        show_info("This is a test application for the C++ GUI Library");
    if (item_number == 4)  {
        static char *sel_list[] = {"option 0", "element 1",
                                   "this is choice number 2", "pick 3"};
        // Use a Modal dialog box to choose from a list:
        int ii = choose_one_from_list("Choose something...",sel_list,4);
        char buf2[255];
        sprintf(buf2,"item selected = %d", ii);
        Warning(buf2);
    }
    if (item_number == 5)  {
        // Use a Modal dialog box to choose one of two choices:
        int ii = choose_one("0", "1");
        char buf2[255];
        sprintf(buf2,"item selected = %d", ii);
        Warning(buf2);
    }
    if (item_number == 6)  {
        static int need_to_init_text = 1;
        if (need_to_init_text) {
            need_to_init_text = 0;
//          init_scrolling_text(20, 180, 180, 33);  // small scrolling
                                                     // text field
            init_scrolling_text(); // use entire window for scrolling text
        }
        static int countit = 0;
        static char buf2[256];
        sprintf(buf2,"This is a test %d
1234567890123456789012345678901234567890123456789012345678901234567890",c
ountit++);
        put_scrolling_text(buf2);
    }
    if (item_number == 7)  {  Uses the Plot library from chapter 9
        static double xp[30];
        static double yp[30];
        for (int i=0; i<30; i++) {
            double x = i - 12;
            double y = 0.2*x*x*x*x*x-4.0 * x*x*x*x + 11.0 * x*x*x -
5.0*x*x - 7;
            xp[i] = x;
            yp[i] = y;
```

```
        }
                    tp = new TPlotClass(current_window, "A
title",xp,yp,30,40,390,170,55);

    static double xp2[30];
    static double **yp2 = new double *[6];
    for (int l=0; l<6; l++)  yp2[l] = new double[30];
    for (int j=0; j<6; j++) {
        for (i=0; i<30; i++) {
            double x = i - 12 - j;
            double y = 0.001*j*x*x*x*x*x - 4.0 * x*x*x*x + 11.0 *
                        x*x*x - 5.0*x*x -
                        7 + 100* x * x * j;
            xp2[i] = x;
            yp2[j][i] = y;
        }
    }
    tp2 = new TPlotClass(current_window,"Second title",xp2,yp2,6,30,
                    200,390,420,55);
    clear_display();
    update_display();
    }
}


INIT_PROGRAM

    // anything can go here

    RUN_PROGRAM;
}
```

C++ Application Utility Classes

6

Graphical Tree Browser Class

Tree browsers are frequently seen in artificial intelligence (AI) applications written in LISP. In this chapter you'll see a C++ class that implements a flexible tree browser, and is easily used in applications. This TGraph class is written to be used with the TAppWindow class. It uses graphics callbacks to an instance of a TAppWindow to display itself. The TGraph class supports mouse interaction with a tree; an instance of a TGraph knows which, if any, node has been selected by a user.

Figure 6.1 shows an example use of a TGraph inside a TAppWindow. Note that a selected node will be highlighted; this behavior is automatic whenever a user clicks on a node. All event handling is internal to the TGraph, TAppWindow, and TAppApp classes.

The algorithm for laying out a tree diagram was designed by Gabriel Robins (refer to ISI/TM0-88-197). Robins' algorithm is very efficient, since the required execution time is linear with the number of nodes in the tree.

6.1 Design of the Tree Browser Class

There are several requirements for a tree browser C++ class:

- The tree layout calculations are efficient.
- A tree display is simple to create in a TAppWindow.
- Nodes in the tree are defined and can later be accessed by a unique name.
- Event handling for user interaction with a tree is automatic and does not add to the complexity of an application program.

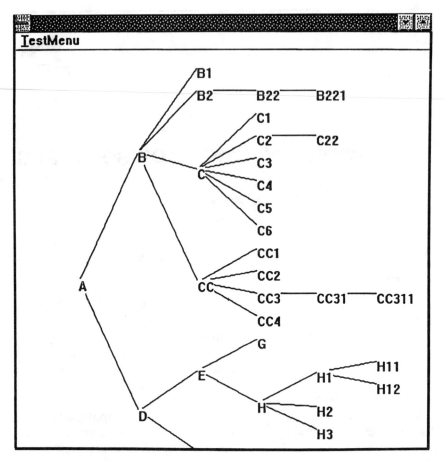

Figure 6.1 Sample TGraph plot in a Microsoft Windows window.

The TGraph C++ Class maintains a single tree data structure with all necessary internal data to perform the layout calculations. A tree data structure contains a fixed block of node data structures, and a count of the number of nodes currently being used. A node data structure contains a name, a relative x-y position, the node's display size in pixels, the index of its parent node in the tree, a flag used during the layout calculations, and a flag telling the application program whether the user has selected the node using the mouse.

6.2 Implementation of the Tree Browser Class

The following listing shows the data structure definitions for the tree browser class:

```
// File: Grapher.h
//
// Description:  Grapher utility include file
//
// Copyright 1992 by Mark Watson Associates
//
//        No binary rights reserved: this software library may be used in
//        compiled form without restrictions.  All source rights
//        reserved: Source code to the GUI library can not be distributed
//        (on bulletin boards, or as part of shareware or commercial
//        products)
//        without written permission.


#ifndef Grapher_Defs
#define Grapher_Defs

#include "applib.h"

#define MAX_NODES 40

#define TEXT_SIZE 20

typedef struct _node {
    char name[20];
    int x, y;
    int parent_id;
    int plot_node;        // used for sub-tree displays
    char *private_data;   // used for application data
    int selectionFlag;    // 0=not selected, 1=a child node is selected,
} node;                   //   2=this node selected, 3=a parent node is
                          //   selected
typedef struct _tree {
    node nodes[MAX_NODES];
    int num;
    int parent_node;
} tree;

class TGraph {
  public:
    TGraph(TAppWindow * myWind, char * root_name);
    void add_child(char *name, char * parent);
    int name_to_id(char *name);
    void do_layout();
    void do_layout(int new_parent_node);
    void test();
    void Draw();

    TAppWindow *myWindow;

    void setSelection(int node_id); // node_id=-1 for clear whole graph
    int closestNode(int x, int y);
    int TGraph::getSelectedNode();
    tree t;
  private:
    int last_y;
    void init_tree(char *root_name);
    int get_children(char *name, int *child_list, int buf_size);
```

```
        void Y_layout(int node_id, int level);
        void X_layout(int node_id, int level);
        void set_selection_children(int node_id);
        void set_selection_parent(int node_id);
};
```

```
#endif Grapher_Defs
```

The *node* structure definition defines the data items for each node in the display tree: a node name, an x-y screen position, the node's parent node index, a flag defining whether an active node should be drawn (used for subtree displays), a pointer to private node data (so application programs can associate arbitrary data with each tree node), and a node display selection flag to control the highlighting of nodes on the display.

The *tree* structure definition defines the data items for a complete tree structure: a static block of nodes, the number of active nodes, and the index of the tree root node.

The *class TGraph* integrates the tree and node data structures with both the data and procedural code (methods) required to lay out trees, draw trees in a TAppWindow, and facilitate user interaction with the graphical tree display.

The following listing shows the implementation of the TGraph class. The constructor TGraph::TGraph has two required arguments: a pointer to a TAppWindow containing the TGraph instance, and the name of the root tree node. The constructor calls the private method TGraph::init_tree to set up the data structures for laying out the tree:

```
// File: Grapher.cp
//
// Description: This file implements the Grapher utility class
//
// Copyright 1992 by Mark Watson Associates
//
//        No binary rights reserved: this software library may be used in
//        compiled form without restrictions.  All source rights
//        reserved: Source code to the GUI library can not be distributed
//        (on bulletin boards, or as part of shareware or commercial
//         products)
//        without written permission.
//
//        This software is provided "as is". The user accepts all
//        responsibility for its use.
//
#include "Grapher.h"
#include <String.h>

#define X_OFF 5
#define Y_OFF 3


TGraph::TGraph(TAppWindow * myWind, char * root_name)
{
```

```
    myWindow = myWind;
    init_tree(root_name);
    t.nodes[0] .private_data = new char[strlen(root_name)+1];
    sprintf(t.nodes[0] .private_data,"Data for root %s", root_name);

    // layout the nodes:
    do_layout();
}

void TGraph::do_layout()
{
    t.parent_node = 0;
    for (int i=0; i<t.num; i++) {
        t.nodes[i].x = 0;
        t.nodes[i].y = 0;
        t.nodes[i].plot_node = 0;
    }
    last_y = 0;
    Y_layout(0, 0);
    X_layout(0, 0);
    for (i=0; i<t.num; i++) {
        t.nodes[i].selectionFlag = 0;
        t.nodes[i].x += X_OFF;
        t.nodes[i].y += Y_OFF;
    }
}

void TGraph::do_layout(int new_parent_node)
{
    t.parent_node = new_parent_node;
    for (int i=0; i<t.num; i++) {
        t.nodes[i].x = 0;
        t.nodes[i].y = 0;
        t.nodes[i].plot_node = 0;
    }
    last_y = 0;
    Y_layout(t.parent_node, 0);
    X_layout(t.parent_node, 0);
    for (i=0; i<t.num; i++) {
        t.nodes[i].selectionFlag = 0;
        t.nodes[i].x += X_OFF;
        t.nodes[i].y += Y_OFF;
    }
}

void TGraph::test()
{
    // add a few test nodes:
    add_child("B", "A");
    add_child("B1", "B");
    do_layout();
    add_child("B2", "B");
    add_child("B22", "B2");
    add_child("B221", "B22");
    add_child("D", "A");
    add_child("E", "D");
    do_layout();
    add_child("F", "D");
    do_layout();
    add_child("C", "B");
```

```
        do_layout();
        add_child("C1", "C");
        add_child("C2", "C");
        do_layout();
        add_child("C3", "C");
        do_layout();
        add_child("C4", "C");
        do_layout();
        add_child("C5", "C");
        add_child("C6", "C");
        do_layout();
        add_child("CC", "B");
        do_layout();
        add_child("CC1", "CC");
        do_layout();
        add_child("CC2", "CC");
        add_child("CC3", "CC");
        do_layout();
        add_child("CC4", "CC");
        add_child("CC31", "CC3");
        do_layout();
        add_child("CC311", "CC31");
        do_layout();
        add_child("F11", "F");
        do_layout();
        add_child("C22", "C2");
        do_layout();
        add_child("G", "E");
        do_layout();
        add_child("H", "E");
        do_layout();
        add_child("H1", "H");
        do_layout();
        add_child("H2", "H");
        add_child("H3", "H");
        do_layout();
        add_child("H11", "H1");
        do_layout();
        add_child("H12", "H1");
        do_layout();
}

#define Y_SPACING 20

void TGraph::Draw()
{   int i, parent;
    char buf[80];

    myWindow->erase_rect(0,1024,1024,0);

    for (i=0; i<t.num; i++)  {
        if (t.nodes[i].parent_id > -1)  { /* plot a line between this node
        and parent */
            parent = t.nodes[i].parent_id;
            if (t.nodes[parent].plot_node == 1)
                myWindow->plot_line(t.nodes[parent].x,
                            t.nodes[parent].y - (TEXT_SIZE / 2)+3,
                                t.nodes[i].x, t.nodes[i].y - (TEXT_SIZE /
2)+3);
        }
```

```
        }
    for (i=0; i<t.num; i++)  {
        if (t.nodes[i].plot_node == 1) {
            if (t.nodes[i].selectionFlag == 1)
                sprintf(buf,"<%s>",t.nodes[i].name);
            else if (t.nodes[i].selectionFlag == 2)
                sprintf(buf,"** %s **",t.nodes[i].name);
            else if (t.nodes[i].selectionFlag == 3)
                sprintf(buf,"[%s]",t.nodes[i].name);
            else
                sprintf(buf,"%s",t.nodes[i].name);
            myWindow->plot_string(t.nodes[i].x, t.nodes[i].y - 4, buf);
        }
    }
}

void TGraph::init_tree(char *root_name)
{   int i;
    for (i=0; i<MAX_NODES; i++) {
        t.nodes[i].name[0] = '\0';
        t.nodes[i].private_data = (char *)NULL;
    }
    sprintf(t.nodes[0].name,"%s",root_name);
    t.num = 1;
    t.nodes[0].parent_id = -1;   /* special for root node */
    t.nodes[0].x = t.nodes[0].y =  0;
}

void TGraph::add_child(char *name, char *parent)
{   int parent_index, i;
    if (t.num < (MAX_NODES - 1)) {
        parent_index = -1000;
        for (i=0; i<t.num; i++)
            if (strcmp((char *)parent,(char *)t.nodes[i].name) == 0) {
                t.nodes[t.num].parent_id = i;
                sprintf(t.nodes[t.num].name,"%s",name);
                t.nodes[t.num].x = t.nodes[t.num].y = 0;
                t.num++;
                break;
            }
    }
}

int TGraph::name_to_id(char *name)
{   int i;
    for (i=0; i<t.num; i++)
        if (strcmp((char *)name, (char *)t.nodes[i].name) == 0)
            return i;
    return -1;
}

int TGraph::get_children(char *name, int *child_list, int buf_size)
{   int i, count, node_id;
    count = 0;
    node_id = name_to_id(name);
    if (node_id > -1) {
        for (i=0; i<t.num; i++)
            if (node_id == t.nodes[i].parent_id)
                if (count < (buf_size - 1))
                    child_list[count++] = i;
```

```
    }
    return count;
}

void TGraph::Y_layout(int node_id, int level)
{   int i, nc, clist[50], average_y;
    t.nodes[node_id].plot_node = 1;
    if (t.nodes[node_id].y == 0) {  /* not yet laid out */
        nc = get_children(t.nodes[node_id].name, clist, 50);
        if (nc > 0) { /* unlaid out children to process */
            for (i=0; i<nc; i++)
                Y_layout(clist[i], level+1);
            average_y = 0;
            for (i=0; i<nc; i++) average_y += t.nodes[clist[i]].y;
            average_y = average_y / nc;
            t.nodes[node_id].y = average_y;
        } else {   /* no children */
            t.nodes[node_id].y = last_y + Y_SPACING;
            last_y = t.nodes[node_id].y;
        }

        t.nodes[node_id].x = 0;
    }
}

void TGraph::X_layout(int node_id, int level)
{   int clist[50];
    if (level == 0) {
        t.nodes[node_id].x = 12;
        int nc = get_children(t.nodes[node_id].name, clist, 50);
        if (nc > 0) { /* unlaid out children to process */
            for (int i=0; i<nc; i++)
                X_layout(clist[i], level+1);
        }
    } else {
        // calculate x spacing based on length of parent node's name:
        int len = strlen(t.nodes[t.nodes[node_id].parent_id].name);
        t.nodes[node_id].x = t.nodes[t.nodes[node_id].parent_id].x  +
            12 + myWindow->string_width("A") * len;
        int nc = get_children(t.nodes[node_id].name, clist, 50);
        if (nc > 0) { /* unlaid out children to process */
            for (int i=0; i<nc; i++)
                X_layout(clist[i], level+1);
        }
    }
}


void TGraph::set_selection_children(int node_id)
{   int i, nc, clist[20];
    t.nodes[node_id].selectionFlag = 1;
    // set selection flag child nodes = 1:
    nc = get_children(t.nodes[node_id].name, clist, 20);
    for (i=0; i<nc; i++)
        set_selection_children(clist[i]);
}

void TGraph::set_selection_parent(int node_id)
{
```

```
        t.nodes[node_id].selectionFlag = 3;
        if (t.nodes[node_id].parent_id >= 0)
            set_selection_parent(t.nodes[node_id].parent_id);
}

void TGraph::setSelection(int node_id)
{   int i, nc;  int clist[20];
    // clear all selection flags:
    for (i=0; i<t.num; i++) t.nodes[i].selectionFlag = 0;
    if (node_id < 0)  return;
    // set selection flag child nodes = 1:
    nc = get_children(t.nodes[node_id].name, clist, 20);
    for (i=0; i<nc; i++)
        set_selection_children(clist[i]);
    // set selection flag of parent nodes = 3:
    if (t.nodes[node_id].parent_id >= 0)
        set_selection_parent(t.nodes[node_id].parent_id);
    // set this node's selection flag = 2:
    t.nodes[node_id].selectionFlag = 2;
}

int TGraph::getSelectedNode()
{
    for (int i=0; i<t.num; i++)
        if (t.nodes[i].selectionFlag == 2)  return i;
    return -1;
}

int TGraph::closestNode(int x, int y)
{
    int distX, distY;
    for (int i=0; i<t.num; i++)  {
        distX = (x  - 15) - (t.nodes[i].x - X_OFF); // offset for node-
                                                    // center
        distY = y - (t.nodes[i].y - Y_OFF);
        distX = distX * distX / 3; // allow a larger error in x-direction
        distY = distY * distY;
        if ((distX + distY) < 60)  return i;
    }
    return -1;
}
```

The public method TGraph::do_layout() lays out the current tree. This layout process requires that each tree node be assigned an x-y display position inside the TAppWindow containing the tree. The public method TGraph::do_layout(int new_parent_node) lays out a subset of the tree contained in the TGraph's internal data structures. This is useful if an application program wants to display part of a tree.

The public method TGraph::test() is used for testing the TGraph class. I find it convenient to keep debug code available; this method can be removed from the class to save space.

The method TGraph:draw() uses callbacks to its TAppWindow to draw itself. A TGraph has an instance variable (my_window) that points to its TAppWindow. Graphics operations simply use this pointer as shown in this code fragment:

```
char buf[256];
sprintf(buf," %s ",t.nodes[i].name);
myWindow->plot_string(t.nodes[i].x, t.nodes[i].y - 4, buf);
```

The private method TGraph::init_tree(char *root_name) initializes the static block of tree nodes. Note that a tree is limited to MAX_NODES nodes. Tree nodes each require about 50 bytes of data (depending on the hardware word size for int and char * data types). Allocating a static block of nodes is convenient and simple to implement. If your application requires hundreds or thousands of tree nodes, you can change the method TGraph:add_child (char *name, char *parent) to allocate more node storage if the current number of nodes exceeds MAX_NODES. Method TGraph:add_child(char *name, char *parent) creates a new node and links it to a parent node.

The method TGraph::name_to_id(char *name) is a utility method for finding the tree node index of a node given its name.

The method TGraph::get_children(char *name, int *child_list, int buf_size) is a utility for finding all child nodes of a given named node. This method is necessary since the tree nodes are singly linked: a child node knows its parent, but a parent node does not maintain a list of child nodes. In practice, searching for all children of a node is fast since it is simply a linear search through the block of active nodes. For applications with thousands of nodes, it might be preferable to add a list of child pointers to node data structure, trading additional memory for faster tree calculations.

The method TGraph::Y_layout(int node_id, int level) performs the recursive calculations necessary to calculate the y-locations of the nodes. This method is short, yet due to its recursive nature has interesting computational properties. The runtime behavior is complex enough to require additional explanation: method TGraph::Y_layout is called both with a node index and a tree level counter. If a node has children, TGraph::Y_layout calls itself once for each child node (passing the child node index and its own level counter incremented by one). A node's y-location is taken to be the average of the y-locations of all of its child nodes. These TGraph::Y_layout calls proceed recursively down to the lowest parts of the tree (where nodes have no child nodes) before this average y-location is calculated.

The x-locations of a tree's nodes are simply calculated in method TGraph::X_layout(int node_id, int level) from the parent node's x-location and the parent's name width.

The utility method TGraph::set_selection_children(int node_id) marks all children of a specified node. Note the use of recursion.

The utility method TGraph::set_selection_parent, int node_id) marks all parents of a specified node. Note the use of recursion.

The utility method TGraph::set_selection(int node_id) marks a node as selected and calls Graph::set_selection_children(int node_id) and TGraph:: set_selection_parent(int node_id) to mark child and parents of the indicated node.

The utility method TGraph::getSelectedNode() returns the node index of the currently selected node. A value of −1 is returned if the user has not selected a node using the mouse.

The utility TGraph::closestNode(int x, int y) finds the closest node to a mouse click at a given x-y position.

6.3 Using the Tree Browser Class

The following code fragment shows how to create a tree display in a TAppWindow. After the tree is created, nodes can be added to the tree. We assume that the current application has a TAppWindow visible and that the variable current_window points to the TAppWindow object.

```
TGraph tg(current_window, "root_name");
tg.add_child("child node 1", "root_node);
tg.add_child("child node 2", "root_node");
tg.add_child("sub-child  1", "child node 1");
tg.do_layout();
```

The method do_layout recalculates the displayed tree layout. The TGraph class contains a method test which creates a sample tree.

Figure 6.1 shows the generic test program listed in Chapter 5. The first menu option has been chosen to draw a sample TGraph using the TGraph method test.

7

Smart Persistent
Data Object Classes

The C++ classes developed in this chapter are independent of any GUI software. They are included in this book because their use greatly simplifies the design and implementation of most applications. These classes support vectors of several common base types. These vectors perform runtime index checking (which can be turned off), and grow dynamically when their current index is greater than the current size of the vector. These vector classes also have methods for saving themselves to a named disk file and reloading themselves from a disk file.

Implementations are provided for integer- and character string smart vector classes. An equivalent smart vector class for float or double data types can be produced simply by copying the source files for integer vectors and globally changing "int" to "float" or "double." Frame data structures used in artificial intelligence are easily implemented as new classes with smart vectors as elements.

7.1 Rationale for Using Vector Classes

Many C programmers will read the code for implementing smart vectors and complain that they can write more efficient code using pointers and do custom file input/output (I/O) using primitives that are specific to the current operating system that they are using. These complaints might be technically valid, but the philosophy behind this entire book involves trading some efficiency for ease of software development, maintenance, and portability between machine and windowing architectures. Sections 7.1.1

bility between machine and windowing architectures. Sections 7.1.1 through 7.1.4 explore the advantages of using higher-level data structures.

7.1.1 Use of existing software

The use of smart vectors makes use of available software. You will not repetitively re-create custom memory management and file I/O utilities. You will not introduce new software bugs. And you will spend less time writing your applications.

7.1.2 Faster software testing

It is impossible to overrun an array index using a smart vector. Out-of-bounds (positive) array indices simply cause a smart vector to grow larger. Very large array indices will terminate your program cleanly after a warning. Negative indices are also checked at runtime.

The runtime array (vector) index checking is accomplished by overloading the C++ operators: []. Consider the following code fragment:

```
test2()
{
    int_vect v2(128);  // allocate space for 128 integers
    foo(&v2);
    ......
}

foo(int_vect &v)
{
    v[300] = 1; // illegal array reference causes this smart vector to
                // grow
    ......
}
```

This type of runtime bounds checking certainly requires extra processing time. It can be turned off (at the expense of not having smart vectors grow dynamically) for time-critical applications after they have been debugged.

7.1.3 Increase the readability of application programs

Shorter programs are easier to read. Using appropriate C++ classes like smart vectors drastically reduces the length of application programs, making them much easier to read and understand.

7.1.4 Portability for special memory limitations

Both Unix and Macintosh programming environments allow large blocks of memory to be allocated either directly with the standard C library function *malloc* or indirectly using malloc via the C++ *new* operator. Microsoft

Windows, however, requires well-behaved programs (Petzold 1990) to allocate memory in relocatable blocks which need to be "locked in place" before use and "unlocked" after use. The smart vector classes can handle this
unlocking automatically with some performance penalty.

7.2   Interface for an Integer Smart Vector Class

You have already seen smart vectors used in Section 7.1.2 and in the example drawing program listed in the introduction. The following is the C++
header file for an integer smart vector class:

```
// File: int_vect.h
//
// Description:  smart int vector
//
// Copyright 1992 by Mark Watson Associates
//
//         No binary rights reserved: this software library may be used in
//         compiled form without restrictions.  All source rights
//         reserved: Source code to the GUI library can not be distributed
//         (on bulletin boards, or as part of shareware or commercial
//         products)
//         without written permission.


#ifndef __int_vect
#define __int_vect

#include "applib.h"

class int_vect {
    int *p;
    int size;
    void grow(int new_size);
        int ub() { return (size - 1); }
  public:
    int num_elements;
    int_vect(void);
    int_vect (int n);
    int_vect(int_vect &v);
    int_vect(int a[], int n);
    ~int_vect() { delete p; }
    int & operator [] (int i);   // range check safeguards
    void save(char *filename);
    void restore(char *filename);
};

#endif
```

7.3   Implementation of an Integer Vector Class

This section contains the C++ implementation file for an integer smart vector class. This class contains four constructors seen in the following exam-

ple code fragment:

```
int_vect iv1;      // default: smart vector with 10 elements
int_vect iv2(100);    // create a smart vector with 100 elements
int *buf = {0, 1, 2, 3, 4, 5, 6, 7, 8, 9};
int_vect iv3(buf,10); // copy existing int array into the new smart
int_vect
int_vect iv4(iv3);    // make an exact copy of an exiting int_vect
```

The [] operator is defined for the smart int_vect class in order to provide both protection from illegal array references and dynamic resizing. The method int_vect::grow(int new_size) increases the size of an int_vect. The methods int_vect::save(char *file_name) and int_vect::restore(char *file_ name) save and restore the values in an int_vect to named disk files.

The following listing shows a generic implementation of a smart vector for systems which have nonsegmented memory architectures:

```
// File: int_vect.cp
//
// Description: This file implements the int smart vector class
//
// Copyright 1992 by Mark Watson Associates
//
//         No binary rights reserved: this software library may be used in
//         compiled form without restrictions.  All source rights
//         reserved: Source code to the GUI library can not be distributed
//         (on bulletin boards, or as part of shareware or commercial
//         products)
//         without written permission.
//
//         This software is provided "as is". The user accepts all
//         responsibility for its use.


#include "int_vect.h"

extern "C" { void exit(int); };

extern void Warning(char *);

// Define constants for the dynamic grow rate for int_vect data types and
// the maximum number of elements that a smart int_vect can have:

const int GROW_RATE = 1;
const int MAX_SIZE = 5000;

int_vect::int_vect(void)
{
    num_elements = 0;
    size = 10;
    p = new int[size];
}

int_vect::int_vect(int n)
{
    if (n<= 0) {
```

```
        Warning("illegal size for a int_vect");
        exit(1);
    }
    num_elements = 0;
    size = n;
    p = new int[size];
}

int_vect::int_vect(int a[], int n)
{
    if (n<= 0) {
        Warning("illegal size for a int_vect");
        exit(1);
    }
    num_elements = size = n;
    p = new int[size];
    for (int i=0; i<size; i++)  p[i] = a[i];
}

int_vect::int_vect(int_vect &v)
{
    size = v.size;
    p = new int[size];
    for (int i=0; i<size; i++)  p[i] = v.p[i];
    num_elements = size;
}

int & int_vect::operator [] (int i)
{
    if (i < 0) {
        Warning("illegal index for int_vect");
        exit(1);
    }
    if (i > ub()) {
        grow(i);
    }
    if ((i + 1) > num_elements)  num_elements = i+1;
    return (p[i]);
}

void int_vect::grow(int new_size)
{
    if ((new_size + GROW_RATE) >= MAX_SIZE) {
        Warning("error in dynamic resizing of a smart int_vect");
        exit(1);
    }
    int *np = new int[(new_size + GROW_RATE)];
    for (int i=0; i<size; i++)  np[i] = p[i];
    delete p;
    size = (new_size + GROW_RATE);
    p = np;
}

void int_vect::save(char *file_name)
{
    filebuf out_file;
    if (out_file.open(file_name, output)==0) {
        Warning("Could not open output file for int vect save");
        exit(1);
    }
```

```
    ostream out_stream(&out_file);
    out_stream << num_elements << "\n";
    for (int i=0; i<num_elements; i++)
        out_stream << p[i] << "\n";
    out_file.close();
}

void int_vect::restore(char *file_name)
{
    filebuf in_file;
    if (in_file.open(file_name, input)==0) {
        Warning("Could not open input file for int vect restore");
        exit(1);
    }
    istream in_stream(&in_file);
    in_stream >> size;
    num_elements = size;

    if (size > ub()-1)  grow(size);
    for (int i=0; i<num_elements; i++)
        in_stream >> p[i];
    in_file.close();
}

#if 0

// test code:

main()
{
    cerr << "Start of int_vect test:\n\n";
    int_vect vv(10);
    vv[2] = 2;
    vv[220] = vv[2];   // illegal index !!
    cerr << "Done with test.\n";
}

#endif
```

The implementation of smart vectors is more complex for systems like Microsoft Windows (see Appendix B for complete smart vector implementations for Windows).

8

File I/O

The example applications in this book use the standard C⁺⁺ stream I/O libraries designed originally at AT&T's Bell Labs and implemented in all commercial C⁺⁺ compiler products. This chapter serves as a short review of using streams in C⁺⁺, and as a short reference for understanding how file I/O is handled in the example programs in this book.

8.1   ASCII Text I/O

The following short listing shows how to open, write to, and close a text file using streams:

```
#include <stream.h>
    .
    .
    .
    filebuf out_file;
    if (out_file.open("test.dat", output)==0) {
        Warning("Could not open output file");
        exit(1);
    }
    int input_size, hidden_size, output_size;
    input_size = hidden_size = output_size = 16;
    ostream out_stream(&out_file); // output stream constructor
    // Write out some data to the file::
    out_stream << input_size << "\n";
    out_stream << hidden_size << "\n";
    out_stream << output_size << "\n";
    out_file.close();
```

In this example, the data written to file test.dat could have been float, double, int, long, or char * data. The << operator for streams is overridden to work with all standard C++ data types.

The following code sample shows how to read file test.dat:

```
#include <stream.h>
    .
    .
    .
    filebuf in_file;
    if (in_file.open("test.dat", input)==0) {
        Warning("Could not open input file");
        exit(1);
}
int f_input_size, f_hidden_size, f_output_size;
istream in_stream(&in_file);
// Read data from file "test.dat":
in_stream >> f_input_size;
in_stream >> f_hidden_size;
in_stream >> f_output_size;
in_file.close();
```

In this example, the data read from file test.dat could have been float, double, int, long, or char * data. The >> operator for streams is overridden to work with all standard C++ data types.

8.2 Binary I/O

The following short listing shows how to open, write to, and close a binary file using streams:

```
#include <stream.h>
    .
    .
    .
    filebuf out_file;
    if (out_file.open("bin.dat", output)==0) {
        char buf5[256];
        sprintf(buf5,"Could not open output file %s","bin.dat");
        Warning(buf5);
        exit(1);
    }

    char buf[1024];
    .
    .
    .
    ostream out_stream(&out_file);
    out_stream.write((unsigned char *)buf, 1024);
    out_file.close();
```

The following code sample shows how to read file bin.dat:

```
#include <stream.h>
    .
    .
    .
    filebuf in_file;
    if (in_file.open("bin.dat", input)==0) {
        char buf5[256];
        sprintf(buf5,"Could not open input file %s", "bin.dat");
        Warning(buf5);
        exit(1);
    }

    char buf[1024];
    .
    .
    .
    istream in_stream(&in_file);
    in_stream.read((unsigned char *)buf, 1024);
    in_file.close();
```

9

Curve Plotting Class

The C++ class TPlotClass designed and implemented in this chapter will greatly facilitate adding scientific and business plots to your applications. This class contains methods for plotting arrays of floating point numbers.

9.1 Design of the TPlotClass Curve Plotting Class

The curve plotting class requires the following design goals:

- A one-line C++ constructor creates a plot.
- Plots can be sized and placed anywhere in a TAppWindow.
- Window refresh (on window expose events) is handled in TAppWindow:: update_display( ).
- Manual refresh of plot is done via a method call when the data changes.

The rationale for the first design goal is simple: application programmers, given data to plot, must to be able to add a plot to a TAppWindow with a single line of code. For flexibility, the plots can be scaled and placed anywhere in a window. The redrawing of a TPlotClass object can be done simply by calling a TPlotClass::plot( ) method in a TAppWindow update_display method. Manual refreshing of a TPlotClass object is necessary when data changes and the applications programmer wants to immediately update the display.

9.2 Interface to the TPlotClass Class

The TPlotClass class supports multiple plots on one set of axes. The instance variable x_coord points to a copy of the x-coordinates, and the table y_coords holds one or more sets of y-coordinates.

```
// File: tplot.h
//
// Description: This File contains the data structure/class definition
//        for the TPlotClass.
//
//
// Copyright 1992 by Mark Watson Associates
//
//        No binary rights reserved: this software library may be used in
//        compiled form without restrictions.  All source rights
//        reserved: Source code to the GUI library can not be distributed
//        (on bulletin boards, or as part of shareware or commercial
//         products)
//        without written permission.
//

#include "applib.h"

const int MAX_PLOTS = 8;

class TPlotClass {
    // Pointer to the X coordinate data:
    double *x_coord;
    // Pointers to the Y Coordinates for the plot(s):
    double *y_coords[MAX_PLOTS];
    // The number of points to plot:
    int num_points;
    // The number of active plots:
    int num_plots;  // To a maximum of MAX_PLOTS.
    char *my_title;
    // Store the value of the pointer to the TAppWindow containing this
    // plot:
    TAppWindow *my_window;
    // Private plot data:
    int top, right, bottom, left;
    int x_org, y_org;
    double x_scale;  // x_value * x_scale + x_org = x coordinate in
                     // my_window
    double y_scale;  // y_value * y_scale + y_org = y coordinate in
                     // my_window
    double x_min, y_min, x_max, y_max;
    // Calculate private scaling data:
    void calc_data(double x_min, double x_max, double y_min, double
y_max);

public:
    TPlotClass(TAppWindow *window, char *plot_title, double *x, double
*y,
                int np,  int in_top, int in_right, int in_bottom, int
in_left);
    TPlotClass(TAppWindow *window, char *plot_title,
                double *x, double **y, int number_of_plots,
```

```
                      int np, int in_top, int in_right, int in_bottom, int
in_left);
     ~TPlotClass();
     void rescale();
     void plot();
};
```

9.3 Implementation of the TPlotClass Class

The following listing shows the implementation of the TPlotClass class:

```
// File: tplot.cp
//
// Description: This File contains the methods for the TPlotClass.
//
// Copyright 1992 by Mark Watson Associates
//
//        No binary rights reserved: this software library may be used in
//        compiled form without restrictions.  All source rights
//        reserved: Source code to the GUI library can not be distributed
//        (on bulletin boards, or as part of shareware or commercial
//        products)
//        without written permission.
//
//        This software is provided "as is". The user accepts all
//        responsibility for its use.


#include "tplot.h"


// Public methods:

void TPlotClass::calc_data(double x_min, double x_max, double y_min,
double y_max)
{
    x_scale = 0.999 * ((double)(right - left )) / (x_max - x_min);
    y_scale = ((double)(bottom - top))/ (y_max - y_min);
    x_org = left;
    y_org = top;
}


TPlotClass::TPlotClass(TAppWindow *window, char *plot_title,
                       double *x, double *y, int np, int in_top,
                       int in_right, int in_bottom, int in_left)
{
    // Copy the plot boundaries:
    top = in_top + 22;       right = in_right-3;
    bottom = in_bottom - 10;    left = in_left + 30;

    // Calculate the scaling data and plot origin:
    double MinX = 9999999.9;
    double MaxX = -MinX;
    for (int i=0; i<np; i++) {
        if (x[i] < MinX)  MinX  = x[i];
        if (x[i] > MaxX)  MaxX = x[i];
    }
    double MinY = 9999999.9;
```

```
    double MaxY = -MinY;
    for (i=0; i<np; i++) {
        if (y[i] < MinY)  MinY = y[i];
        if (y[i] > MaxY)  MaxY = y[i];
    }
    x_min = MinX;   y_min = MinY; x_max = MaxX; y_max = MaxY;
//  strcpy(my_title, plot_title);

        my_title = new char[strlen(plot_title)+1];
            for (int k=0; k<strlen(plot_title); k++) my_title[k] =
plot_title[k];
        my_title[strlen(plot_title)] = '\0';
    calc_data(MinX, MaxX, MinY, MaxY);
    x_coord = x;
    y_coords[0] = y;
    num_plots = 1;
    num_points = np;
    my_window = window;
}


void TPlotClass::rescale()
{
        double MinX = 9999999.9;
        double MaxX = -MinX;
        for (int i=0; i<num_points; i++) {
                if (x_coord[i] < MinX)  MinX = x_coord[i];
                if (x_coord[i] > MaxX)  MaxX = x_coord[i];
        }
        double MinY = 9999999.9;
        double MaxY = -MinY;
        for (int k=0; k<num_plots; k++) {
            for (i=0; i<num_points; i++) {
                if (y_coords[k][i] < MinY)  MinY = y_coords[k][i];
                if (y_coords[k][i] > MaxY)  MaxY = y_coords[k][i];
            }
        }
        x_min = MinX;   y_min = MinY; x_max = MaxX; y_max = MaxY;
        calc_data(MinX, MaxX, MinY, MaxY);
}


TPlotClass::TPlotClass(TAppWindow *window, char *plot_title,
                       double *x, double **y, int number_of_plots,
                       int np,
                            int in_top, int in_right, int in_bottom, int
in_left)
{
    // Copy the plot boundaries:
    top = in_top + 22;      right = in_right-3;
    bottom = in_bottom - 10;    left = in_left + 30;

    // Calculate the scaling data and plot origin:
    double MinX = 9999999.9;
    double MaxX = -MinX;
    for (int i=0; i<np; i++) {
        if (x[i] < MinX)  MinX = x[i];
        if (x[i] > MaxX)  MaxX = x[i];
    }
    double MinY = 9999999.9;
    double MaxY = -MinY;
```

```
    x_coord = x;
    for (int k=0; k<number_of_plots; k++) {
        y_coords[k] = y[k];
        for (i=0; i<np; i++) {
            if (y[k][i] < MinY)  MinY = y[k][i];
            if (y[k][i] > MaxY)  MaxY = y[k][i];
        }
    }
    x_min = MinX;  y_min = MinY; x_max = MaxX; y_max = MaxY;
//  strcpy(my_title, plot_title);

    my_title = new char[strlen(plot_title)+1];
    for (k=0; k<strlen(plot_title); k++) my_title[k] = plot_title[k];
    my_title[strlen(plot_title)] = '\0';
    calc_data(MinX, MaxX, MinY, MaxY);
    num_plots = number_of_plots;
    num_points = np;
    my_window = window;
}


TPlotClass::~TPlotClass()
{
    delete my_title;
}


void TPlotClass::plot()
{
    my_window->erase_rect(top-20, right+10, bottom+24, left-30);
    // Frame the Plot:
    my_window->plot_rect(top, right, bottom, left);

    for (int k=0; k<num_plots; k++) {
        double old_value_of_x = x_org + (x_coord[0]  - x_min)* x_scale;
        double old_value_of_y = bottom - (y_coords[k][0]   - y_min)*
y_scale;
        for (int i=1; i<num_points; i++) {
            double x = x_org + (x_coord[i]  - x_min)* x_scale;
            double y = bottom - (y_coords[k][i]  - y_min)* y_scale;
            my_window->plot_line((int)old_value_of_x, (int)old_value_of_y,
(int)x, (int)y);
            old_value_of_x = x;
            old_value_of_y = y;
        }
    }
    my_window->plot_line(left, bottom, left, bottom+4);
    my_window->plot_line(right, bottom, right, bottom+4);
    my_window->plot_line(left, bottom, left-4, bottom);
    my_window->plot_line(left, top, left - 4, top);
    char buf[32];
    sprintf(buf,"%6.1f",x_min);
    my_window->plot_string(left - (my_window->string_width(buf) / 2),
                           bottom + 19, buf);
    sprintf(buf,"%6.1f",x_max);
    my_window->plot_string(right - (my_window->string_width(buf) / 2),
                           bottom + 19, buf);
    sprintf(buf,"%6.1f",y_min);
    my_window->plot_string(left -  my_window->string_width(buf) - 4,
                           bottom + 5, buf);
    sprintf(buf,"%6.1f",y_max);
```

```
    my_window->plot_string(left -  my_window->string_width(buf) - 4,
                           top + 5, buf);
    int pixel_len = my_window->string_width(my_title);
    int mid_x_pos = (left + right) / 2;
    int x_start = mid_x_pos - (pixel_len / 2);
    my_window->plot_string(x_start, top - my_window->string_height(" ") -
2, my_title);
}
```

The method TPlotClass::calc_data() calculates plot scaling from the data range and desired plot size. The constructor that produces a single plot is:

```
TPlotClass::TPlotClass(TAppWindow   *window,    char    *plot_title,
                       double *x, double *y, int np, int in_top,
                       int in_right, int in_bottom, int  in_left)
```

The constructor that produces multiple plots on one set of axes is:

```
TPlotClass::TPlotClass(TAppWindow *window, char *plot_title,
                       double *x, double **y, int number_of_plots,
    int np,
                       int in_top, int in_right, int in_bottom, int
    in_left)
```

The method TPlotClass::rescale() determines the range of the plot data. The destructor ~TPlotClass::TPlotClass() frees the storage for the plot title. The method TPlotClass:plot() draws the plot in the TAppWindow that is pointed to by the instance variable my_window.

9.4   Examples Using the TPlotClass

The screen dump in Fig. 9.1 shows two TPlotClass graphs in a Microsoft Windows window. The same plot data is used for each curve.

The following listing shows how the two plots in Fig. 9.1 were made:

```
static TPlotClass *tp = (TPlotClass *)NULL;
static TPlotClass *tp2= (TPlotClass *)NULL;

void TAppWindow::update_display()   // callback to draw display
{
    if (tp != (TPlotClass *)NULL)
        tp->plot();
    if (tp2!= (TPlotClass *)NULL)
        tp2->plot();
}
void TAppWindow::do_menu_action(int item_number)
{
        .
        .
        .
```

```
if (item_number == 8) {
    static double xp[30];
    static double yp[30];
    for (int i=0; i<30; i++) {
        double x = i - 10;
        double y = 0.2*x*x*x*x*x*x - 4.0 * x*x*x*x + 11.0 * x*x*x -
5.0*x*x - 7;
        xp[i] = x;
        yp[i] = y;
    }
    tp = new TPlotClass(current_window,"Little plot",xp,yp,30,
                            50,280,130,45);
    tp2= new TPlotClass(current_window,"BIG plot",xp,yp,30,
                    170,350,350,90);
    clear_display();
    update_display();
}
;
```

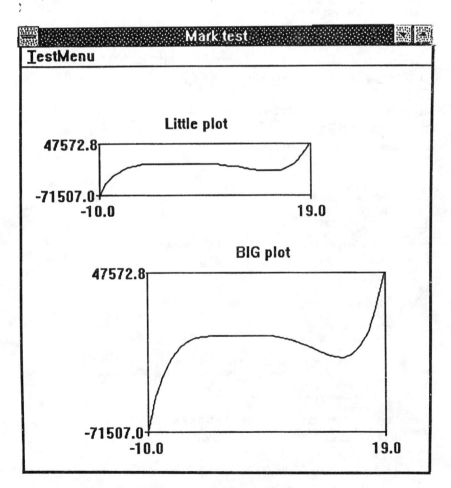

Figure 9.1   Two sample TPlotClass objects in a TAppWindow.

Note that you allocate the storage for the points to be plotted as static data. This is very important since the TPlotClass does not copy the data points passed to the constructor. If you allocated the data dynamically, as

```
double xp[30];
double yp[30];
```

then the storage for xp and yp would be on a stack frame which is released when the do_menu_action method returns. Later, when the update_display method is called, the address for the points to be plotted no longer contains valid data. Allocating static data as

```
static double xp[30];
static double yp[30];
```

prevents this error.

The two plots shown in Fig. 9.2 use different data. The lower plot shows six curves on one set of axes. The following listing produces Fig. 9.2:

```
static TPlotClass *tp = (TPlotClass *) NULL;
static TPlotClass *tp2 = (TPlotClass *) NULL;

void TAppWindow::update_display()
{
    if (tp != (TPlotClass *)NULL)
        tp->plot();
    if (tp2 != (TPlotClass *)NULL)
        tp2->plot();
}

void TAppWindow::do_menu_action(int item_number)
{
    .
    .
    .
    if (item_number == 8)  { // test TPlotClass:
        static double xp[30];
        static double yp[30];
        for (int i=0; i<30; i++) {
            double x = i - 12;
            double y = 0.2*x*x*x*x*x - 4.0 * x*x*x*x + 11.0 * x*x*x
                       - 5.0*x*x - 7;
            xp[i] = x;
            yp[i] = y;
        }
        tp = new TPlotClass(current_window, "A
title",xp,yp,30,40,390,170,55);

        static double xp2[30];
        static double **yp2 = new double *[6];          // allocate
                                                        // pointers
        for (int l=0; l<6; l++)  yp2[l] = new double[30];   // allocate
                                                        // data
```

```
for (int j=0; j<6; j++) {
    for (i=0; i<30; i++) {
        double x = i - 12 - j;
        double y = 0.001*j*x*x*x*x*x*x - 4.0 * x*x*x*x + 11.0 * x*x*x
                           - 5.0*x*x - 7 + 100* x * x * j;
        xp2[i] = x;
        yp2[j][i] = y;
    }
}
tp2 = new TPlotClass(current_window,"Second title",xp2,yp2,6,30,
              200,390,420,55);

clear_display();
update_display();
}
}
```

** File Test App**

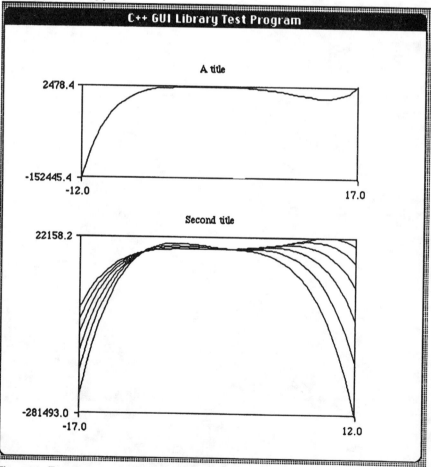

Figure 9.2 Two plots; the bottom plot shows six curves on one set of axes.

Note how the double ** variable yp2 is allocated in this code fragment. To get six curves, you first allocate six pointers to doubles with this code:

```
static double **yp2 = new double *[6];                // allocate
                                                      // pointers
```

Then you allocate a block of 30 doubles for each double pointer:

```
for (int l=0; l<6; l++)  yp2[l] = new double[30];    // allocate data
```

## Chapter 10

Generic Pattern Matcher Class

The TNeuralNet C++ class designed and implemented in this chapter is useful for adding pattern-matching capabilities to your applications. It is used in Chapter 13 to write an application program that enables you to draw letters and numbers in a TAppWindow using the mouse. These hand-drawn characters are identified and displayed on the screen.

10.1 Rationale for Using Neural Networks

Neural networks are now a standard technology for performing pattern matching operations like speech recognition and hand writing recognition (Watson 1991). Neural networks are trained by collecting data samples of patterns to be recognized with corresponding classifications. In Chapter 13 you will see how to train a neural network to recognize hand-drawn characters by providing many training examples.

Neural networks can be easily retrained with new data to improve system performance. For example, if an application programmer is writing a pen-based application and the system initially confuses the hand-drawn characters Q and O, system performance can be enhanced by providing additional training data for these two letters and retraining the neural network. No software modifications are necessary to improve the system.

The TNeuralNet class is presented here with little neural network theory. The use of this C++ class is not dependent on an understanding of the underlying technology.

10.2 Design of the TNeuralNet Class

The primary design requirement for the TNeuralNet class is ease of both training and integration into larger C++ programs. There are two functional components in this class: a training module and a runtime module. The training module accepts training data either in memory or on disk, and calculates the appropriate internal state for a neural network to provide the required pattern-matching capability. This internal state can be saved to an external disk file for later use, or kept in memory for immediate use.

10.2.1 Theoretical Model for the TNeuralNet Class

A neural network contains two principle components: *neurons* and *connections* between the neurons. A neuron has one or more inputs, one output, and an internal state commonly called its *activation energy*. A neuron calculates its activation energy by adding the input(s), calculating the value of a transfer function, and then making this output activation energy available as input to other neurons with which it is connected.

Connections are characterized by a *weight*, a numeric value which scales the output value of the activation energy of a connected neuron. Figure 10.1 shows a three-neuron network; the calculation of neuron M's activation energy depends on the activation energies of neurons A and B, and on the connection weights connecting neurons A and B to neuron M.

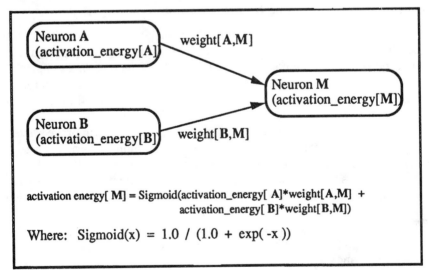

activation energy[M] = Sigmoid(activation_energy[A]*weight[A,M] +
activation_energy[B]*weight[B,M])

Where: Sigmoid(x) = 1.0 / (1.0 + exp(-x))

Figure 10.1 Basic neural network model.

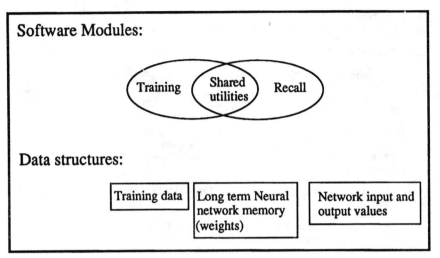

Figure 10.2 General design of the TNeuralNet class.

10.2.2 Required data structures and software modules

Figure 10.2 shows the basic design for the required software modules in this class, and the data flow between these modules. There are four constructors for the TNeuralNet class: two for training and two for recall.

10.3 Header File for the TNeuralNet Class

The following listing shows the include file for defining the TNeuralNet class:

```
// File: TNeural.h
//
// Description: This is the header file for the TNeuralNet C++ class.
//              This class provides both back propagation training and
//              runtime modules.
//
// Copyright 1992 by Mark Watson Associates
//
//         No binary rights reserved: this software library may be used in
//         compiled form without restrictions.  All source rights
//         reserved: Source code to the GUI library can not be distributed
//         (on bulletin boards, or as part of shareware or commercial
//         products)
//         without written permission.
//
#ifndef __TNeuralNet
#define __TNeuralNet
```

```
#include "applib.h"
extern "C" { void exit(int); };

class TNeuralNet {

    // Storage to hold the size of a neural net instance:
    int input_size;
    int hidden_size;
    int output_size;

    // Pointers to storage for activation energies:
    double *input_activations;   // input values
    double *hidden_activations; // hidden neuron calculated activation
    values

    // Pointers to temporary storage for calculating sum-of-product terms
    // for
    // hidden and output neurons:
    double *hidden_sums;
    double *output_sums;

    // Pointers to storage for weights connecting the input to hidden
    // neurons
    // and the hidden to output neurons:
    double *w1; // logically dimensioned [input_size][hidden_size]
    double *w2; // logically dimensioned [hidden_size][output_size]

    // Pointers to storage for accumulated errors
    double *hidden_errors;
    double *output_errors;

    // Number of training examples stored in memory:
    int num_training_examples;

    // Pointers to "packed" input and output training data:
    // (e.g., if num_train_examples is 100, and input_size is 10 neurons,
    // then
    // there will be 100*10=1000 input training examples)
    double *input_samples;
    double *output_samples;

  public:
    double *output_activations; // output neuron calculated activation
                                // values

    // Utility methods and Runtime utilities:

    void forward_pass(double *inputs);
    void backwards_error_pass(double *inputs, double *target_outputs);
    // Constructor for a net with a 1 dimensional input:
    TNeuralNet(int input_size, int hidden_size, int output_size);

    // Constructor for a net with a 2 dimensional input: use a 1 D neural
    // net
    // and linearize the 2 D input vector.

    // Utilities for training:
    double auto_train(int max_iterations,int num_samples,
               double *packed_inputs, double *packed_outputs);
```

```
    ~TNeuralNet();
    void save(char *filename);
    void restore(char *filename);
};

#endif
```

10.4 Source File for the TNeuralNet Class

The following listing shows the implementation of the TNeuralNet class:

```
// File: TNeural.cp
//
// Description: This is the source file for the TNeuralNet C++ class.
//              This class provides both back propagation training and
//              runtime modules.
//
// Copyright 1992 by Mark Watson Associates
//
//         No binary rights reserved: this software library may be used in
//         compiled form without restrictions.  All source rights
//         reserved: Source code to the GUI library can not be distributed
//           (on bulletin boards, or as part of shareware or commercial
//           products)
//         without written permission.
//
//         This software is provided "as is". The user accepts all
//         responsibility for its use.
//

#include "iostream.h"
#include "TNeural.h"
#include "math.h"

static long seed = 123456789;

void Warning(char *);

static double random(double lower, double upper)
{
    seed = (seed * (long)13) / (long)11;
    long ival = seed % 1000;
    double x = (double)ival;
    return ((x * 0.001 * (upper - lower)) - lower);
}

static double sigmoid(double x)
{
    return (1.0 / (1.0 + exp(-x)));
}

static double sigmoidP(double x)
{
    double y = sigmoid(x);
    return (y * (1.0 - y));
}
```

```
static void check_allocation(char *prompt, double *p)
{
    if (p == (double *)NULL) {
        char buf[100];
        sprintf(buf,"Failed memory allocation for %s", prompt);
        Warning(buf);
        exit(1);
    }
}

TNeuralNet::TNeuralNet(int a_input_size, int a_hidden_size, int
a_output_size)
{
    input_size = a_input_size;
    hidden_size = a_hidden_size;
    output_size = a_output_size;

    check_allocation("input a",
        (input_activations = new double[input_size]) );
    check_allocation("hidden a",
        (hidden_activations = new double[hidden_size]) );
    check_allocation("output a",
        (output_activations = new double[output_size]) );

    check_allocation("hidden sums",
        (hidden_sums = new double[hidden_size]) );
    check_allocation("output sums",
        (output_sums = new double[output_size]) );

    check_allocation("hidden errors",
        (hidden_errors = new double[hidden_size]) );
    check_allocation("output errors",
        (output_errors = new double[output_size]) );

    check_allocation("w1", (w1 = new double[input_size*hidden_size]) );
    check_allocation("w2", (w2 = new double[hidden_size*output_size]) );
    for (int h=0; h<hidden_size; h++) {
        for (int i=0; i<input_size; i++)
            w1[i*hidden_size + h] = random(-0.2,0.2);
        for (int o=0; o<output_size; o++)
            w2[h*output_size + o] = random(-0.2,0.2);
    }
    input_samples = 0;
    output_samples = 0;
}

double TNeuralNet::auto_train(int max_iterations,int num_samples,
                        double *packed_inputs, double *packed_outputs)
{   double error = 0;
    for (int i=0; i<max_iterations; i++) {
        for (int s=0; s<num_samples; s++) {
            backwards_error_pass(&(packed_inputs[s*input_size]),
                            &(packed_outputs[s*output_size]));
            for (int j=0; j<output_size; j++)
                error += output_errors[j] * output_errors[j];
        }
    }
    return error;
}
```

```
TNeuralNet::~TNeuralNet()
{
    delete input_activations;
    delete hidden_activations;
    delete output_activations;
    delete hidden_sums;
    delete output_sums;
    delete w1;
    delete w2;
    if (input_samples != 0)   delete input_samples;
    if (output_samples!= 0)   delete output_samples;
}

void TNeuralNet::save(char *filename)
{
    filebuf out_file;
    if (out_file.open(filename, output)==0) {
        Warning("Could not open output file");
        exit(1);
    }
    ostream out_stream(&out_file);
    // Read in header information from file to get the size of this
neural network:
    out_stream << input_size << "\n";
    out_stream << hidden_size << "\n";
    out_stream << output_size << "\n";

    for (int i=0; i<input_size; i++)
        for (int j=0; j<hidden_size; j++)
            out_stream << w1[i*hidden_size+j] << "\n";
    for (i=0; i<hidden_size; i++)
        for (j=0; j<output_size; j++)
            out_stream << w2[i*output_size+j] << "\n";

    out_file.close();

}

void TNeuralNet::restore(char *filename)
{   int f_input_size, f_hidden_size, f_output_size;
    filebuf in_file;
    if (in_file.open(filename, input)==0) {
        Warning("Could not open input file");
        exit(1);
    }
    istream in_stream(&in_file);
    // Read in header information from file to get
    // the size of this neural network:
    in_stream >> f_input_size;
    in_stream >> f_hidden_size;
    in_stream >> f_output_size;
    if (f_input_size != input_size ||
        f_hidden_size != hidden_size ||
        f_output_size != output_size) {
        Warning("Mismatch between current network size and training
file.");
        exit(1);
    }
```

```cpp
    for (int i=0; i<input_size; i++)
        for (int j=0; j<hidden_size; j++) {
            in_stream >> w1[i*hidden_size+j];
        }

    for (i=0; i<hidden_size; i++)
        for (j=0; j<output_size; j++) {
            in_stream >> w2[i*output_size+j];
        }

    in_file.close();
}

void TNeuralNet::forward_pass(double *inputs)
{
    for (int i=0; i<input_size; i++)
        input_activations[i] = inputs[i];
    for (int h=0; h<hidden_size; h++) {
        hidden_sums[h] = 0.0;
        for (i=0; i<input_size; i++)
            hidden_sums[h] += input_activations[i] * w1[i*hidden_size +
h];
    }
    for (h=0; h<hidden_size; h++)
        hidden_activations[h] = sigmoid(hidden_sums[h]);
    for (int o=0; o<output_size; o++) {
        output_sums[o] = 0.0;
        for (h=0; h<hidden_size; h++)
            output_sums[o] += hidden_activations[h] * w2[h*output_size +
o];
    }
    for (o=0; o<output_size; o++)
        output_activations[o] = sigmoid(output_sums[o]);
}

void  TNeuralNet::backwards_error_pass(double  *inputs,  double
*target_outputs)
{
    forward_pass(inputs);
    for (int o=0; o<output_size; o++)
        output_errors[o]=(target_outputs[o]-
output_activations[o])*sigmoidP(output_sums[o]);
    for (int h=0; h<hidden_size; h++) {
        hidden_errors[h] = 0.0;
        for (o=0; o<output_size; o++)
            hidden_errors[h] += output_errors[o] * w2[h*output_size+o];
    }
    for (h=0; h<hidden_size; h++)
        hidden_errors[h] = hidden_errors[h] * sigmoidP(hidden_sums[h]);
    for (o=0; o<output_size; o++)
        for (h=0; h<hidden_size; h++)
            w2[h*output_size+o]                          +=
0.4*output_errors[o]*hidden_activations[h];
    for (h=0; h<hidden_size; h++)
        for (int i=0; i<input_size; i++)
            w1[i*hidden_size+h]                          +=
0.4*hidden_errors[h]*input_activations[i];
}
```

The function sigmoid calculates a nonlinear transfer function for a neuron's output energy. The function sigmoidP is the derivative of the function calculated by function sigmoid. The function check_allocation checks memory allocations and terminates the program with an error message if a memory request failed.

The constructor that initializes a new neural network object is:

```
TNeuralNet::TNeuralNet(int a_input_size,  inta_output_size)
                       int a_hidden_size,
```

The method that trains a neural network object with a set of training cases is:

```
double  TNeuralNet::auto_train(int  max_iterations,int  num_samples,
double *packed_inputs, double *packed_outputs)
```

This method returns the root-mean-square error comparing network output with the training data output; call this method repetitively until this error decreases to an acceptable level. The methods TNeuralNet::save and TNeuralNet:restore save and restore a neural net object to named disk files.

The method used both internally to train a network object and at runtime when using a trained neural network in an application is:

```
void TNeuralNet::forward_pass(double *inputs)
```

The method used internally to train a neural network is:

```
void TNeuralNet::backwards_error_pass(double *inputs, double
*target_outputs)
```

You do not need to call this method in your application programs.

The following code fragment (from the handwriting recognition application in Chapter 13) shows how to use a trained neural network:

```
int in_vect[10]; // 10 input neurons
// fill input neuron with values:
.
.
.
// run the network:
nnet.forward_pass(in_vect);

// Find the largest output activation of the 10 output neurons:
double max_act = -9999.0;
int max_index = 0;
```

```
for (int i=1; i<10; i++)
   if(nnet.output_activations[i]>nnet.output_activations[max_index])
      max_index = i;
recall_value = max_index;    // index of the output neuron
                             // with the largest value
```

10.5   Using the TNeuralNet Class

The following short example program shows how to use the TNeuralNet
class in your programs:

```
// Test code for the TNeuralNet Class:

#include <stdio.h>
#include <stdlib.h>

void Warning(char *w) // Define a Warning callback
{
    cerr << w << "\n";
}
double Sinputs[9] = {0.9,0.1,0.1, 0.1,0.9,0.1, 0.1,0.1,0.9};  // input
                                                              // data
double Soutputs[9]= {0.1,0.9,0.1, 0.1,0.1,0.9, 0.9,0.1,0.1};  // output
                                                              // data

void main()
{
    cerr << "Starting test.\n";
    TNeuralNet nn(3,3,3); // constructor defines the network size
//  nn.restore("test.dat");  // uncomment this line to restore
                             // a saved network.
    for (int j=0; j<20; j++) {
        double error = nn.auto_train(30,3,Sinputs,Soutputs);
        cerr << "Error: " << error << "\n";
    }
    nn.save("test.dat");
    cerr << "Done with test.\n";

}
```

Chapter

11

Text Indexing Class

The TextIndex C⁺⁺ class operates on disk files or on text buffers in memory containing ASCII text. The class has methods for both building efficient index links and retrieving text indexed by one or more keywords. Class TextIndex supports a single word index over multiple disk files.

Fully indexed text databases are a great source of quick information. Commercial products using fully indexed text databases include CD-ROM encyclopedias and complete copies of newspapers. For years, I have kept a large on-line text database of *BYTE* magazine articles; I download the articles from BIX (Byte Information Exchange, where I am the "neural network" moderator) and build the indexes to browse for required information.

11.1 Requirements for the TextIndex Class

The TextIndex class must meet the following design requirements:

- Provide rapid access to text databases.
- Make index files as compact as possible.
- Allow a single word index to include more than one text file.
- Be relatively easy to implement.

The design limitations of the class require it to perform index-building in memory and load index structures for a text database into memory for browsing. These limitations are severe for computers with limited memory, but they make the implementation of class TextIndex fairly simple.

Figure 11.1 shows the use of indices to access raw text. As you can see in this figure, the theory of indexing text is simple: a list of unique words is created, each with a pointer to a list of file-pointer/file-byte indices that allow a program to quickly find the word's location(s) in indexed files. (The actual data structures used in this chapter are slightly more compact than those in Fig. 11.1.)

11.2 Design of the TextIndex Class

The TextIndex class data structures for holding the text indices are fairly compact, at the expense of slightly increasing CPU and disk requirements when browsing text. To reduce the amount of storage used to store the word keys in an index, characters are mapped into uppercase and defined as their own character set with 0 being a null character, 1 being the character A, 2 being the character B, etc. In this way, you can store a character in only five bits—this savings is important.

A maximum of eight characters is stored per word index: words starting with the same eight characters are simply indexed together. To save more index data space, the file pointer structure shown in Fig. 11.1 is limited to 16 bits: one bit for an end-of-list flag (0 for end of list, 1 for next pointer valid for current word), three bits for a file index (allowing eight text files to be indexed in one index structure), and twelve bits for a file block pointer.

File blocks are defined to be 4096 bytes, so the largest single file that can be indexed is 4,194,304 bytes (four megabytes). One instance of an IndexClass object can thus hold eight files, for a total of 32 megabytes of raw text. These limitations can be changed by editing the constant definitions at the top of the TextIndex include file.

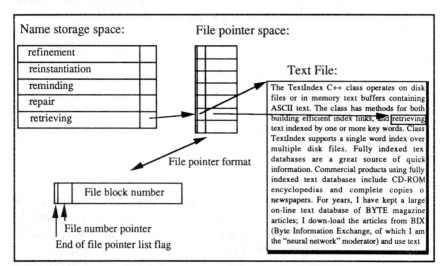

Figure 11.1 Logical data structures used to index text in multiple files.

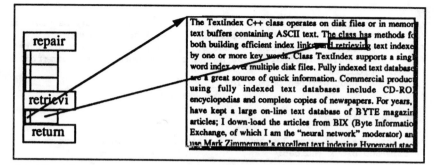

Figure 11.2 Compact data structures used to index text in multiple files.

How can the data structure in Fig. 11.1 be improved? It captures the concept to use for building indices, but you can reduce the storage requirement significantly. Figure 11.1 shows a pointer from each name in name storage space to a 16-bit file pointer. Unfortunately, for the simple design shown in this figure, this pointer from the name space element to the first file pointer must be greater than 16 bits (a limit of 65,536 file pointers is too restrictive). To eliminate this extra pointer storage, place a list of file pointers in memory directly after the word key to combine name space storage and file pointer storage. Figure 11.2 shows how to do this.

Figure 11.2 is almost complete. You may be asking, though, how do I tell which five byte blocks of memory are word keys (first eight characters only) and which two byte blocks are file pointers? With the data structures shown in Fig. 11.2, the only way to answer this question is to start at the beginning of the combined name and pointer space, since you know that the first byte is the first byte of a five-byte name key. After a five-byte name key, you can determine how many two-byte blocks are file pointers, since the last file pointer for a name key does not have bit 0 set.

It would be very slow to start searching the combined name and pointer space from the beginning. However, adding one more small pointer table that points to the first name key for each letter of the alphabet enables a search for a given word to at least start near the desired word key. These pointers are made 32 bits each, so the combined name and pointer space can be large.

11.3 Implementation of the TextIndex Class

The following listing shows the include file defining the TextIndex class:

```
// File: TextInd.h
//
// Description: Header file for the text indexing class
//
// Copyright 1992 by Mark Watson Associates
```

```
//
//          No binary rights reserved: this software library may be used in
//          compiled form without restrictions.  All source rights
//          reserved: Source code to the GUI library can not be distributed
//          (on bulletin boards, or as part of shareware or commercial
//          products)
//          without written permission.
//

#include "char_v.h"

// Change the following 3 constant definitions to allow fewer or more
// file and block indices:

const int MAX_FILE_NAMES       = 8;
const int BITS_FOR_FILE_INDEX  = 3;
const int BITS_FOR_BLOCK_INDEX = 12;  // Constraint: 12 = 8 + 3 + 1

const int BLOCK_SIZE = 512;

void free_strings(char **s);

class filePointer {
public:
    unsigned block_index   : BITS_FOR_BLOCK_INDEX;
    unsigned file_index    : BITS_FOR_FILE_INDEX;
    unsigned end_of_list   : 1;
};

class char_5_block {  // 5 bit character, 'A' = 0, .. 'Z' = 25, end-of-
                      // line = 26.
public:
    unsigned n0 : 5;
    unsigned n1 : 5;
    unsigned n2 : 5;
    unsigned n3 : 5;
    unsigned n4 : 5;
    unsigned n5 : 5;
    unsigned n6 : 5;
    unsigned n7 : 5;
    unsigned n8 : 5;
    int equal(char_5_block *b);
};

// When we build the index data structures, we will build the index in
// place in the namePointerSpace data area. This will involve shifting
// large blocks of memory around, but will make the code much simpler.
// In virtual memory systems, this may cause excessive page faulting.

class TextIndex {
public:
    char_vect namePointerSpace;  // this will grow dynamically
    long topNamePointerSpace;       // size of data in namePointerSpace
      long firstCharIndex[28]; // first character position in the
name/pointer
                                // space for each letter of the alphabet
    char *file_names[MAX_FILE_NAMES];
    int number_of_files;

    // various utility methods:
    Long firstHitIndex(char *name); // index in name/pointer space of
```

```
                                    // the first file/file block pointer
      void decodeFilePointer(filePointer *filePtr,
                    int &last_pointer_flag,    // equals 0 for last
                                               // entry
                  int &file_index,         // file index for
                                           // this entry
                    int &file_block_index);    // file blocks
                                               // size=4096
      void setFilePointer(filePointer *filePtr,
                    int last_pointer_flag,     // equals 0 for last
                                               // entry
                  int file_index,          // file index for this
                                           // entry
                    int file_block_index);  // file blocks size=4096

    // class utilities:
     TextIndex(char **fileList, int num_files);  // constructor for
                                                 // building index
     TextIndex(char *fileName);    // constructor for reloading an old
                                   // index
    ~TextIndex();
     void buildIndex_helper(char *file_name, int file_number);
     void buildIndex();
     void addWordToIndex(char *word, int file_count, int block_count);

    // File I/O methods:
    int save(char *indexFileName);
    int restore(char *indexFileName);

    // For retrieval:
    Char **regionTextBlocks(char *name); // returns 0 if name not indexed
    int regionIndex(int occurence, int &file, int &block); // returns 0
                                                //if name not indexed
    void get_text(char *buffer, int buffer_size, int file, int block);

    // Utilities for converting between 5 bit compact character codes and
    // 8 bit character codes:
    void c_5_to_8(char_5_block *compactChars, Char *bufferFor8BitChars);
    void c_8_to_5(Char*eightBitChars,char_5_block *bufferForCompactChars);

    int convert_5_to_8(int bit_5);
    int convert_8_to_5(int bit_8);

    // Utility to print out the index table for debugging:
    void print_out();
};
```

The class filePointer defines the file position pointer structure seen in Fig. 11.2. The class char_5_block implements a packed character set that uses five bits per character.

The TextIndex class has two constructors:

```
    TextIndex(char **fileList, int num_files);  // constructor for
                                                // building index
    TextIndex(char *fileName);    // constructor for reloading an old
                                  // index
```

The first constructor accepts a list of filenames and the number of file-names; an in-memory index structure is built for these files. The second constructor simply reloads an existing index structure from a disk file.

The following listing shows the implementation of the TextIndex class:

```
// File: TextInd.cp
//
// Description: Source file for the text indexing class
//
// Copyright 1992 by Mark Watson Associates
//
//         No binary rights reserved: this software library may be used in
//         compiled form without restrictions.  All source rights
//         reserved: Source code to this file can not be distributed
//         (on bulletin boards, or as part of shareware or commercial
//         products)
//         without written permission.
//
//         This software is provided "as is". The user accepts all
//         responsibility for its use.
//

#include "applib.h"
#include "TextInd.h"

extern "C" { void exit(int); int toupper(int); };

//
// String equality comparison. Ignore case.
//
static int STR_EQUAL(Char *s1, Char *s2, int num_to_compare)
{
    for (int i=0; i<num_to_compare; i++) {
        int c1 = s1[i];
        if (c1 >= 'a' && c1 <= 'z')  c1 += 'A' - 'a';
        int c2 = s2[i];
        if (c2 >= 'a' && c2 <= 'z')  c2 += 'A' - 'a';
        if (c1 != c2)  return 0;
    }
    return 1;
}

//
// Utility to free storage for a NULL terminated list of strings:
//
void free_strings(char **s)
{
    int count = 0;
    while (s[count] != (char *)0) {
        delete s[count];
        count++;
    }
    delete s;
}

//
// Compare to compact character blocks for equality:
```

```
//
int char_5_block::equal(char_5_block *b) {
    if (n0==b->n0 && n1==b->n1 && n2==b->n2 && n3==b->n3 &&
        n4==b->n4 && n5==b->n5 && n6==b->n6 && n7==b->n7 &&
        n8==b->n8)    return 1;
    return 0;
};
//
// For a given name, find the first file/block pointer in the current
// index:
//
Long TextIndex::firstHitIndex(char *name) // index in name/pointer space
                                          // of
{                                         // the first file/file block
                                          // pointer
    char_5_block compact_chars;
    c_8_to_5(name, &compact_chars);
    int compact_first_char = convert_8_to_5(name[0]);
    Long firstIndex = firstCharIndex[compact_first_char];
    Long endIndex = topNamePointerSpace;
    // look for next non-blank entry in table firstCharIndex:
    for (int bc=compact_first_char +1; bc < 26; bc++) {
        if (firstCharIndex[bc] != -1) {
            endIndex = firstCharIndex[bc];
            break; // out the for loop
        }
    }

    // Search the table until we find a new index entry with the first
    // compact
    // character code > bc, OR we reach the end of the namePointerSpace:
    int last_element, file_number, block_number;
    char name[10];
    while (firstIndex < endIndex) {
        if(compact_chars.equal((char_5_block*)&
           (namePointerSpace[firstIndex])))
               return firstIndex + sizeof(char_5_block);
        // No match, so skip past this compact name field:
        firstIndex += sizeof(char_5_block);
        // Then skip past file pointers:
        do {
            decodeFilePointer((filePointer
 *)&(namePointerSpace[firstIndex]), last_element,
                        file_number, block_number);
            firstIndex += sizeof(filePointer);
        } while (firstIndex < endIndex && last_element != 0);
    }
    return -1;
}

//
// Decode a compact file pointer:
//
void TextIndex::decodeFilePointer(filePointer *filePtr,
                        int &last_pointer_flag,   // equals 1 for
                                                  // last entry
                        int &file_index,          // file index for
                                                  // this entry
                        int &file_block_index)    // file blocks
```

```
size=BLOCK_SIZE
{
    filePointer * fp = (filePointer *)filePtr;
    last_pointer_flag = fp->end_of_list;
    file_index = fp->file_index;
    file_block_index = fp->block_index;
}
```

```
//
// Encode a compact file pointer:
//
void TextIndex::setFilePointer(filePointer *filePtr,
                          int last_pointer_flag,   // equals 0 for last
                                                   // entry
                          int file_index,          // file index for
                                                   // this entry
                          int file_block_index)    // file blocks
                                                   // size=BLOCK_SIZE
{
    filePtr->end_of_list = last_pointer_flag;
    filePtr->file_index  = file_index;
    filePtr->block_index = file_block_index;
}
```

```
//
// TextIndex constructor for building a new index:
//
TextIndex::TextIndex(char **fileList, int num_files)  // constructor for
building index
{
    for (int i=0; i<26; i++) firstCharIndex[i] = -1;
    for (i=0; i<num_files; i++) {
        file_names[i] = new char[strlen(fileList[i]) + 1];
        strcpy(file_names[i],fileList[i]);
    }
    number_of_files = num_files;
    topNamePointerSpace = 0;
    buildIndex();
}
```

```
//
// TextIndex constructor for restoring from an exsting index file:
//
    TextIndex::TextIndex(char *fileName)     // constructor for reloading
                                             // an old index
{
    restore(fileName);
}
```

```
//
// TextIndex destructor:
//
TextIndex::~TextIndex()
{
}
```

```
//
// Local helper function to extract individual words from a string:
//
```

```
static void parse_words(char *word_buf, char *words[], int &num_words)
{
    int count = 0;
    int charCount = 0;
    for (int k=0; k<8; k++)
        for (int l=0; l<256; l++)  words[k][l] = '\0';
    int len = strlen(word_buf);
    for (int i=0; i<len; i++) {
        if (word_buf[i] < 'A') {
            if (count < 7) count++; // only allow eight words (we should
                                    // never hit this limit)
            charCount = 0;
        }
        else
            words[count][charCount++] = word_buf[i];
    }
    num_words = count + 1;
}


//
// Add a new word to an existing index:
//
void TextIndex::addWordToIndex(char *word, int file_count, int
block_count)
{
    if (file_count > 7) {
        Warning("Warning from TextIndex::addWordToIndex: file_count is
stored as 3 bits. Skip word.");
        return;
    }

    // We start by finding where we need to insert the new index. Here
    // are the
    // cases we need to handle:
    //
    //  1)    No indices for any word starting with the first character
    //        of 'word'.
    //        We need to search backwards in the small table
    //        'firstCharIndex' in
    //        order to find the insertion point.
    //  2)    Indices exist for any word starting with the first
    //        character of 'word'
    //        but none for 'word' itself.
    //  3)    An index exists for the word 'word', add a
    //        pointer with the current
    //        file and block indices.
    //  4)    An index exists for the word 'word' with matching file and
    //        block indices; we don't have to do anything in this
    //        case.
    //
    // Note: in cases 1, 2, and 3: we need to adjust all pointers
    //       in the small table 'firstCharIndex' after the
    //       entry for the first letter of 'word'.

    char_5_block compact_chars;
    c_8_to_5(word, &compact_chars);
    int compact_first_char = convert_8_to_5(word[0]);
    if (firstCharIndex[compact_first_char] == -1) { // case # 1
        // search forewards in table firstCharIndex:
```

```
        Long lastIndex;
        for (int bc=compact_first_char + 1; bc < 26; bc++)
            if (firstCharIndex[bc] != -1) {
                lastIndex = firstCharIndex[bc];
                // We have found the insertion point. First update
                // firstCharIndex[]:
                for (int g=bc; g<26; g++)   // Note: we start at bc, not (bc
                                            // + 1) here!
                    if (firstCharIndex[g] != -1)
                        firstCharIndex[g] +=
                            sizeof(char_5_block) + sizeof(filePointer);
                firstCharIndex[compact_first_char] = lastIndex;
                // Now shift the data in namePointerSpace:
                for (Long t=topNamePointerSpace-1; t>=lastIndex; t--)
                    namePointerSpace[(long)(t+sizeof(char_5_block) +
                                    sizeof(filePointer))] =
                        namePointerSpace[t];
                topNamePointerSpace +=
                    sizeof(char_5_block) + sizeof(filePointer);
                c_8_to_5(word,(char_5_block
*)&(namePointerSpace[lastIndex]));
                setFilePointer((filePointer *)&(namePointerSpace[
                        (long)(lastIndex + sizeof(char_5_block))]),
                            0,file_count, block_count);
                return;
            }
        // We did not find a first char index in the table with an
            // index value > compact_first_char so we must have the case
            //  where  we  are  adding  something  to  the  end  of
            //  namePointerSPace:
        lastIndex = topNamePointerSpace;
        if (firstCharIndex[compact_first_char] < 0)
            firstCharIndex[compact_first_char] = lastIndex;
        topNamePointerSpace += sizeof(char_5_block) + sizeof(filePointer);
        c_8_to_5(word,(char_5_block *)&(namePointerSpace[lastIndex]));
        setFilePointer((filePointer *)&(namePointerSpace[lastIndex +
                                    sizeof(char_5_block)]),
                        0,file_count, block_count);
        return;
    }
    if (firstCharIndex[compact_first_char] != -1) { // case  3 (MUST be
                                                    // before case 2 code!!
        Long lastIndex = firstCharIndex[compact_first_char];
        // Search the table until we find a new index entry with the first
        // compact
        //  character code > bc, OR we reach the end of the
        //  namePointerSpace:
        do {
            if (compact_chars.equal((char_5_block
                *)&(namePointerSpace[lastIndex]))) {
                // See if the current file/block combination is already in
                // the
                // table for this keyword:
                Long fileIndex = lastIndex + sizeof(char_5_block);
                int last_p = 1; int file_num, block_num;
                while (last_p != 0) {
                    decodeFilePointer((filePointer *)
                                    &(namePointerSpace[fileIndex]),
                                last_p, file_num, block_num);
                    if (file_num == file_count && block_num == block_count)
```

```
{
                        return;
                    }
                    fileIndex += sizeof(filePointer);
                }
                if (firstCharIndex[compact_first_char] < 0)
                    firstCharIndex[compact_first_char] = lastIndex;
                // We have found the insertion point.
                // First update firstCharIndex[]:
                for (int g=compact_first_char+1; g<26; g++)
                    if (firstCharIndex[g] != -1)
                        firstCharIndex[g] += sizeof(filePointer);
                // Now shift the data in namePointerSpace:
                Long fpSize = sizeof(filePointer);
                for (Long t=topNamePointerSpace-1;
                    t>=lastIndex + sizeof(char_5_block);
                    t--)
                    namePointerSpace[t + fpSize] = namePointerSpace[t];
                topNamePointerSpace += sizeof(filePointer);
                setFilePointer((filePointer *) &(namePointerSpace[lastIndex
+
                        sizeof(char_5_block)]), 1, // 1 not 0!!
                            file_count, block_count);
                return;
            }
            // skip past the compact name field:
            lastIndex += sizeof(char_5_block);
            // skip past file pointers:
            while (lastIndex < topNamePointerSpace &&
                (namePointerSpace[lastIndex] & 256) != 0)
            lastIndex += sizeof(filePointer);
            lastIndex += sizeof(filePointer);
        } while (lastIndex < topNamePointerSpace);
    }
    if (firstCharIndex[compact_first_char] != -1) { // case # 2
        Long lastIndex = firstCharIndex[compact_first_char];
        // We have found the insertion point. First update
        //  firstCharIndex[]:
        for (int g=compact_first_char+1; g<26; g++)
            if (firstCharIndex[g] != -1)
                firstCharIndex[g]+=sizeof(char_5_block)+
                sizeof(filePointer);
        // Now shift the data in namePointerSpace:
        for (Long t=topNamePointerSpace-1;
            t>=lastIndex;
            t--)
            namePointerSpace[t+sizeof(char_5_block) + sizeof(filePointer)]
=
            namePointerSpace[t];
        topNamePointerSpace += sizeof(char_5_block) + sizeof(filePointer);
        c_8_to_5(word, (char_5_block *)&(namePointerSpace[lastIndex]));
        setFilePointer((filePointer *) &(namePointerSpace[lastIndex +
                sizeof(char_5_block)]),0,file_count, block_count);
        return;
    }
}

//
// Build a new index in memory from the current file list:
```

```
//
void TextIndex::buildIndex_helper(char *file_name, int file_number)
{
    char *words[8]; // up to 8 256 character words
    for (int i=0; i<8; i++) words[i] = new char[256];
    filebuf in_file;
    if (in_file.open(file_name, input)==0) {
        char buf5[256];
        sprintf(buf5,"Could not open input file %s",file_name);
        Warning(buf5);
        exit(1);
    }
    long charCount = 0;
    istream in_stream(&in_file);
    char word_buf[256];
    in_stream >> word_buf;
    while (!in_stream.eof()) {
        int len = strlen(word_buf);
        int blockCount = (int)(charCount / BLOCK_SIZE);
        charCount = in_stream.tellg();
        for (int j=0; j<len; j++) {
            word_buf[j] = toupper(word_buf[j]);
            if (word_buf[j] < 'A' || word_buf[j] > 'Z')  word_buf[j] = '
';
        }
        int num_words;
        parse_words(word_buf, words, num_words);
        for (int m=0; m<num_words; m++)
            if (strlen(words[m]) > 2)    // skip 1 and 2 letter words
                addWordToIndex(words[m], file_number, blockCount);
        in_stream >> word_buf;
    }
    in_file.close();
    for (i=0; i<8; i++) delete words[i];
}

void TextIndex::buildIndex() // returns 0 for OK, 1 for ERROR
{
    for (int f=0; f<number_of_files; f++) {
        buildIndex_helper(file_names[f], f);
    }
}

//
// Save the current index to a disk file:
//
int TextIndex::save(char *indexFileName)
{
    filebuf out_file;
    if (out_file.open(indexFileName, output)==0) {
        char buf5[256];
        sprintf(buf5,"Could not open output file %s",indexFileName);
        Warning(buf5);
        exit(1);
    }

    ostream out_stream(&out_file);
    out_stream.write((unsigned char *)&number_of_files, sizeof(int));
    out_stream.write((unsigned   char  *)&topNamePointerSpace,
```

```
sizeof(long));
    out_stream.write((unsigned char *)firstCharIndex, 28 * sizeof(long));
    out_stream.write((unsigned    char    *)&(namePointerSpace[0]),
topNamePointerSpace);       for (int i=0; i<number_of_files; i++)
        out_stream << file_names[i] << "\n";
    out_file.close();

    return 0;
}


//
// Restore an exisitng index from disk:
//
int TextIndex::restore(char *indexFileName)
{
    filebuf in_file;
    if (in_file.open(indexFileName, input)==0) {
        char buf5[256];
        sprintf(buf5,"Could not open input file %s",indexFileName);
        Warning(buf5);
        exit(1);
    }
    istream in_stream(&in_file);
    in_stream.read((unsigned char *)&number_of_files, sizeof(int));
    in_stream.read((unsigned char *)&topNamePointerSpace, sizeof(long));
    in_stream.read((unsigned char *)firstCharIndex, 28 * sizeof(long));
    in_stream.read((unsigned    char    *)&(namePointerSpace[0]),
topNamePointerSpace);
    for (int i=0; i<number_of_files; i++) {
        file_names[i] = new char[64];
        in_stream >> file_names[i];
    }
    in_file.close();

    return 0;
}


//
//  Collect text regions containing a specified word:
//

static int last_block[64], last_file[64];
static int numReturnedRegions = 0;

Char **TextIndex::regionTextBlocks(char *input_name) // returns 0 if name
not indexed
{
    int len = strlen(input_name);  if (len > 8)  len = 8;
    if (len < 2) {
        return (Char **)0;
    }

    char name[64];
    sprintf(name,"%s",input_name);
    for (int m=0; m<strlen(name); m++)
        if (name[m] >= 'a' && name[m] <= 'z')  name[m] += 'A' - 'a';

    Long firstIndex = firstHitIndex(name);
    if (firstIndex < 0) {
```

```
        char buf8[256];
        sprintf(buf8,"No occurrences of %s",input_name);
        Warning(buf8);
        return (Char **)0;
    }


    char **returnList = new char * [64]; // limit of 64 returned text
                                         // regions
    numReturnedRegions = 0;

    // Loop over all fileblock pointers for this index table entry for
    // 'name':
    int last_element, file_number, block_number;
    do {
        decodeFilePointer((filePointer *)&(namePointerSpace[firstIndex]),
                          last_element,
                          file_number, block_number);
        // Collect text from this file/block pointer to
        // return to calling function:

        filebuf in_file;
        if (in_file.open(file_names[file_number], input)==0) {
            Warning("Could not open input file ");
            exit(1);
        }
        long charCount = 0;

        istream in_stream(&in_file);
        char word_buf[BLOCK_SIZE+28];
        long init_file_pos = block_number * BLOCK_SIZE - 12;
        if (init_file_pos < 0)  init_file_pos = 0;
        in_stream.seekg(init_file_pos);
        in_stream.read(word_buf,BLOCK_SIZE+26);
        int num_chars_read = in_stream.gcount();

        for (int n=0; n<(num_chars_read - len); n++) {
            if (STR_EQUAL(name, &(word_buf[n]), len) == 1) {
                // For debug, just spill the surrounding characters of
                // the match to stderr:
                int first = n - 32;    if (first < 0)  first = 0;
                int last = first + 90;
                if (last > num_chars_read) last = num_chars_read;
                returnList[numReturnedRegions] = new char[2 + last -
first];
                for (int l=first; l<last; l++)
                    if (word_buf[l] > 20)
                        returnList[numReturnedRegions][l-first] =
                            word_buf[l];
                    else
                        returnList[numReturnedRegions][l-first] = ' ';
                returnList[numReturnedRegions][last-first] = '\0';
                  last_file[numReturnedRegions] = file_number;
                  last_block[numReturnedRegions] = block_number;
                if (numReturnedRegions < 63) numReturnedRegions++;
            }
        }

        in_file.close();
```

```
        // Bump the file pointer index:
        firstIndex += sizeof(filePointer);
    } while (last_element == 1);
    returnList[numReturnedRegions] = (char *)0;
    return returnList;
}


int TextIndex::regionIndex(int occurence, int &file, int &block)
// returns 0 if name not indexed
{
    if (numReturnedRegions < 1 || occurence > (numReturnedRegions-1)) {
        Warning("No occurences of selected word");
        return 0;
    }

    file = last_file[occurence];
    block = last_block[occurence];
    return 1;
}

void TextIndex::get_text(char *buffer, int buffer_size, int file, int
block)
{
    filebuf in_file;
    if (in_file.open(file_names[file], input)==0) {
//          cerr << "Could not open input file " << file_names[f] << "\n";
        exit(1);
    }
    istream in_stream(&in_file);
    char word_buf[BLOCK_SIZE+28];
    long init_file_pos = block * BLOCK_SIZE - 12;
    if (init_file_pos < 0)  init_file_pos = 0;
    in_stream.seekg(init_file_pos);
    in_stream.read(buffer,buffer_size-1);
    int num_chars_read = in_stream.gcount();
    buffer[num_chars_read] = '\0';
}


// Utilities for converting between 5 bit compact character codes and
// 8 bit character codes:
void   TextIndex::c_5_to_8(char_5_block   *compactChars,   Char
*bufferFor8BitChars)
{
    bufferFor8BitChars[0] = convert_5_to_8(compactChars->n0);
    bufferFor8BitChars[1] = convert_5_to_8(compactChars->n1);
    bufferFor8BitChars[2] = convert_5_to_8(compactChars->n2);
    bufferFor8BitChars[3] = convert_5_to_8(compactChars->n3);
    bufferFor8BitChars[4] = convert_5_to_8(compactChars->n4);
    bufferFor8BitChars[5] = convert_5_to_8(compactChars->n5);
    bufferFor8BitChars[6] = convert_5_to_8(compactChars->n6);
    bufferFor8BitChars[7] = convert_5_to_8(compactChars->n7);
    bufferFor8BitChars[8] = convert_5_to_8(compactChars->n8);
    bufferFor8BitChars[9] = '\0';
}
void TextIndex::c_8_to_5(Char *originalEightBitChars,
                        char_5_block *bufferForCompactChars)
```

```
{   char eightBitChars[256];
    sprintf(eightBitChars, "%s            ", originalEightBitChars);
    bufferForCompactChars->n0 = convert_8_to_5(eightBitChars[0]);
    bufferForCompactChars->n1 = convert_8_to_5(eightBitChars[1]);
    bufferForCompactChars->n2 = convert_8_to_5(eightBitChars[2]);
    bufferForCompactChars->n3 = convert_8_to_5(eightBitChars[3]);
    bufferForCompactChars->n4 = convert_8_to_5(eightBitChars[4]);
    bufferForCompactChars->n5 = convert_8_to_5(eightBitChars[5]);
    bufferForCompactChars->n6 = convert_8_to_5(eightBitChars[6]);
    bufferForCompactChars->n7 = convert_8_to_5(eightBitChars[7]);
    bufferForCompactChars->n8 = convert_8_to_5(eightBitChars[8]);
}

int TextIndex::convert_5_to_8(int bit_5)
{   int bit_8;
    if (bit_5 == 26)
        bit_8 = '\n';
    else if (bit_5 == 27) // space character
        bit_8 = ' ';
    else
        bit_8 = bit_5 + 'A';
    return bit_8;
}

int TextIndex::convert_8_to_5(int bit_8)
{   int bit_5;
    if (bit_8 >= 'a' && bit_8 <= 'z')  bit_8 += 'A' - 'a';
    if (bit_8 == '\n')
        bit_5 = 26;
    else if (bit_8 == ' ')
        bit_5 = 27;
    else if (bit_8 >= 'A' && bit_8 <= 'Z')
        bit_5 = bit_8 - 'A';
    else
        bit_5 = 27;
    return bit_5;
}

void TextIndex::print_out()
{
#if 0
    cerr << "\n\nDebug printout of the index table: topNamePointerSpace="
        << topNamePointerSpace << "\n\nfirstCharIndex table:\n\n";
    for (int i=0; i<26; i++)
        cerr << "      " << i << " : " << firstCharIndex[i] << "\n";
    cerr << "\nTable (address, name, filepointers.....)\n\n";

    Long lastIndex = 0;
    // Search the table until we find a new index entry with the first
compact
    // character code > bc, OR we reach the end of the namePointerSpace:
    int last_element, file_number, block_number;
    char name[10];
    while (lastIndex < (topNamePointerSpace-1)) {
        for (int m=0; m<10; m++) name[m] = '\0';
        c_5_to_8((char_5_block *)&(namePointerSpace[lastIndex]), (Char
*)name);
        cerr << "\n  Address: " << lastIndex << ", name: " << name << " ";
        // skip past the compact name field:
```

```
        lastIndex += sizeof(char_5_block);
        // skip past file pointers:
        do {
            decodeFilePointer((filePointer
*)&(namePointerSpace[lastIndex]),
                            last_element,
                            file_number, block_number);
            cerr << " block #: " << block_number;
            lastIndex += sizeof(filePointer);
        } while (lastIndex < (topNamePointerSpace-1) &&
                last_element != 0);
    }
    cerr << "\n";
#endif
}

// Test code:

#if 0

// define this flag to test restore-from-file option:
//#define RESTORE 1

char *testFileList[] = {"sample.txt"};

void Warning(char *message)
{
    cerr << message << "\n";
}

void main()
{

#ifndef RESTORE
    TextIndex ti(testFileList,1);
#endif

#ifdef RESTORE
    TextIndex ti("test.index");
#endif

    ti.print_out();

    cerr << "Calling regionTextBlocks: design\n";
    char **s = ti.regionTextBlocks("design");
    int count = 0;
    while (s[count] != (char *)0) {
        cerr << "match: " << s[count] << "\n";
        count++;
    }
    cerr << "Freeing string storage:\n";
    free_strings(s);

#ifndef RESTORE
    ti.save("test.index");
#endif
}

#endif
```

The function int STR_EQUAL (Char *s1, Char *s2, int num_to_compare) compares strings for equality while ignoring uppercase/lowercase differences. The function free_strings(char **s) frees all storage for a null-terminated list of character strings.

The method int char_5_block::equal (char_5_block *b) compares packed five-bit character names for equality. The method Long TextIndex:: firstHitIndex(char *name) finds the first file/block pointer in an index for a given name.

The utility method that unpacks the file/block pointer variable shown in Fig. 11.2 is:

```
void TextIndex::decodeFilePointer(filePointer *filePtr,
                        int &last_pointer_flag,
                        int &file_index,
                        int &file_block_index)
```

The method that sets the internal fields of a compact file/block pointer variable is:

```
void TextIndex::setFilePointer(filePointer *filePtr,
                        int last_pointer_flag,
                        int file_index,
                        int file_block_index)
```

The constructor TextIndex::TextIndex(char **fileList, int num_files) creates an in-memory index for the list of files passed in its argument list. The constructor TextIndex::TextIndex(char *fileName) creates an in-memory index by reloading an existing index from a disk file.

The utility function that extracts space-delimited words from a character buffer is:

```
void parse_words(char *word_buf, char *words[], int &num_words)
```

The method that adds a single word to the in-memory index is:

```
void   TextIndex::addWordToIndex(char *word, int file_count, int
block_count)
```

The method void TextIndex::buildIndex( ) is a utility method that loops over all input files for building an in-memory index.

The method int TextIndex::save(char *indexFileName) saves the in-memory index to a named disk file. The method int TextIndex::restore(char *indexFileName) reads an existing index file into memory.

The utility function Char **TextIndex::regionTextBlocks(char *input_name) returns a list of strings showing the regions surrounding a given word in the text files that are currently indexed. The function free_ strings(char **s) is useful for freeing the storage for this list of strings. The method for opening the indexed disk files and reading back a large block of text is the utility:

```
int TextIndex::get_text(char *buffer, int buffer_size,
int file, int block)
```

The method that converts eight-bits-per-character names to packed five-bits-per-character names is:

```
void  TextIndex::c_5_to_8(char_5_block *compactChars, Char
*bufferFor8BitChars)
```

The method that converts packed five-bits-per-character names to eight-bits-per-character names is:

```
void  TextIndex::c_5_to_8(char_5_block *compactChars, Char
*bufferFor8BitChars)
```

The method int TextIndex::convert_5_to_8(int bit_5) converts a single five-bit character to an eight-bit character. The method int TextIndex::convert_8_to_5(int bit_8) converts an eight-bit character to a packed five-bit character. The method TextIndex::print_out( ) can print out the index table to file *stderr* for systems-supporting text output.

11.4 Using the TextIndex Class

There are two steps to using the TextIndex class: creating an index file from one or more text files, and using an index file to browse the original text files. Usually, both steps are implemented in one application program. This section lists two very short test programs, one to build index files, and one to retrieve text. Chapter 14 shows how to use the TextIndex class to build a complete text-retrieval application program.

11.4.1 Using the TextIndex Class to build index files

The following listing shows how to build an index file:

```
#include "TextInd.h"

char *testFileList[] = {"sample.txt"}; // List up to 8 files here

void Warning(char *message) // Need to define a warning message callback
{
    cerr << message << "\n";
}

void main()
```

```
{
    TextIndex ti(testFileList,1); // Build the index file in memory
    ti.save("test.index"); // Save the index file to disk
}
```

The function Warning needs to be defined because the TextIndex class uses the GUI Library Warning function to notify the user of execution errors. The GUI Library is not used for the following short example program, however, so the function Warning must be defined to prevent an undefined function link error when you compile and link this sample program.

The list of source text files is defined in the variable testFileList. The constructor used for the TextIndex class uses a list of filenames and the number of items in this filename list to build an index in memory. The method *save* writes an index to a disk file.

11.4.2 Using the TextIndex Class to read Index files

The following listing shows how to use an existing index file:

```
#include "TextInd.h"

void Warning(char *message) // Need to define a warning message callback
{
    cerr << message << "\n";
}
void main()
{
    TextIndex ti("test.index");  // Read an existing index file

    ti.print_out();  // Use the debug method 'print_out' to list index

    cerr << "Calling regionTextBlocks: design\n";
    char **s = ti.regionTextBlocks("design");  // Do a search of index
    int count = 0;
    // Loop and print out all text regions with "design"
    while (s[count] != (char *)0) {
        cerr << "match: " << s[count] << "\n";
        count++;
    }
    cerr << "Freeing string storage:\n";
    free_strings(s);
}
```

The constructor for the TextIndex class has a single argument: a text string containing the path and filename for an existing index file. In this example, the class constructor is using an index created with the short example program in the previous section.

The method regionTextBlocks retrieves text blocks surrounding the keyword "design." The method regionTextBlocks returns a list of strings containing the desired text. Note that you must free the storage allocated by regionTextBlocks after you are done using the returned text strings. The utility function free_strings is used to free a list of strings.

Example Applications

12

Hierarchical Information Browser

It is useful to organize information as objects in hierarchies in which low-level objects can inherit information from objects higher in the hierarchies. For the Hierarchical Information Browser (HIB) developed in this chapter, the data objects are simply character strings. However, arbitrary data can be contained in the strings and labeled with arbitrary attribute names.

12.1 Example HIB Data

A short example will help you get an idea of how you might use hierarchical information. The following listing shows one data object per line; each object is simply stored as character strings:

```
name: man parent: human beard: yes tall: yes works: yes
name: woman parent: human tall: no works: yes
name: John parent: man
name: human number_eyes: 2
name: Jill parent: woman
```

Each attribute name ends with a colon. The attribute *parent:* has a special meaning to the HIB system—objects inherit attribute values from parent objects. In this simple example, *man* is a parent object to *John* and *human* is a parent object to *man*. Therefore, if you ask whether John has two eyes, you get the information that John does indeed have two eyes, because object *John* indirectly inherits from object *human*. Figure 12.1

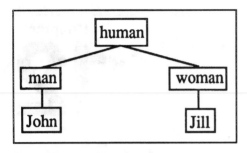

Figure 12.1 Sample information hierarchy.

shows the relationship between these five data objects.
The following listing shows a larger data set:

```
name: human
name: man parent: human beard: yes job: yes
name: woman parent: human job: yes
name: Mark parent: man height: 6'4" weight: 202
name: Carol parent: woman height: 5'11" weight: 141

name: computer
name: main-frame parent: computer
name: personal computer parent: computer
name: Macintosh parent: personal computer processor: 68XXX
name: PC-clone parent: personal computer processor: 386

name: Mac Plus parent: Macintosh memory: 1Meg price: $950 processor:
68000
name: Mac Classic parent: Macintosh memory: 2Meg price: $1150 processor:
68000
name: Mac Classic II parent: Macintosh memory: 4Meg price: $1350
processor: 68030

name: LeadingTECHNOLOGY parent: PC-clone
name: Northgate parent: PC-clone
name: Dell parent: PC-clone

name: plant
name: food plant parent: plant
name: garden plant parent: plant
name: rose parent: garden plant
name: grass parent: garden plant
name: juniper parent: garden plant
name: tree parent: garden plant
name: orange tree parent: citrus tree
name: lemon tree parent: citrus tree
name: apple tree parent: tree
name: peach tree parent: tree
name: citrus tree parent: tree

name: workstation parent: computer operating-system: UNIX
name: Sun parent: workstation
```

```
name: DEC parent: workstation
name: HP parent: workstation

name: IPC parent: Sun
name: SPARC 1+ parent: Sun

name: DEC 3100 parent: DEC
name: DEC 5000 parent: DEC

name: 710 parent: HP
name: 720 parent: HP
```

Figure 12.2 illustrates a Macintosh-based HIB browser window showing these objects.

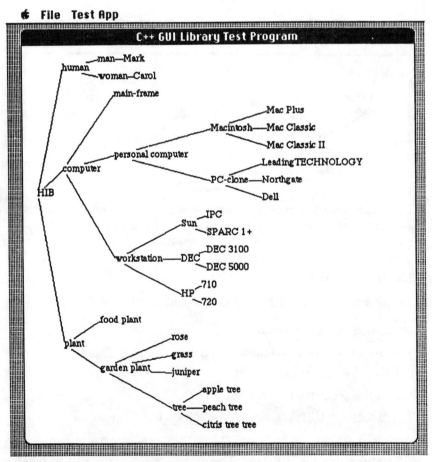

Figure 12.2 Sample HIB database on a Macintosh.

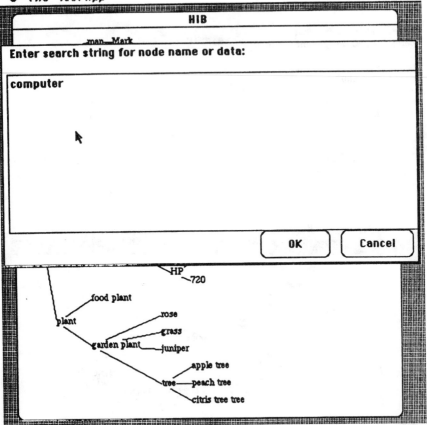

Figure 12.3 The HIB search mode is used to locate all nodes containing the word *computer*.

12.2 HIB Functionality

The HIB system has the following functionality:

- ASCII text files can be read into an in-memory database.
- The hierarchical relationship between data objects is displayed.
- Existing HIB objects can be edited.
- New HIB objects can be created.
- The in-memory HIB database can be written to a single ASCII output file.

Initially, input files for the HIB can be created from database files, a text editor, and within the HIB itself. The user interface to the HIB system has the following functionality:

- Any visible node can be selected with the mouse.
- The current display tree can be zoomed to the region containing the se-lected node.
- Selected nodes can be edited.
- Selected nodes can be deleted.
- A search mode selects all nodes containing a keyword and displays them for selection.

Figures 12.3 through 12.9 demonstrate the user interaction with the HIB program. There are two ways to select nodes in a HIB display. The first method is to simply click on a node with the mouse pointer. The second

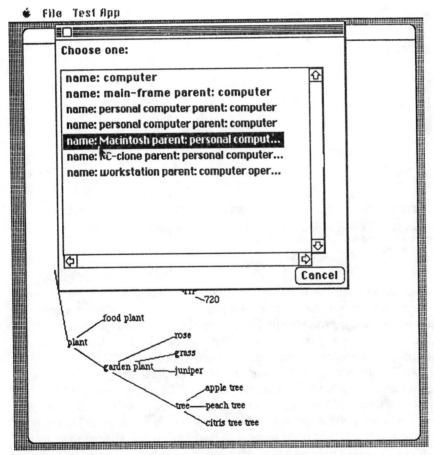

Figure 12.4 The HIB search for all nodes containing the word *computer* yields a list containing one entry for every occurrence of the word.

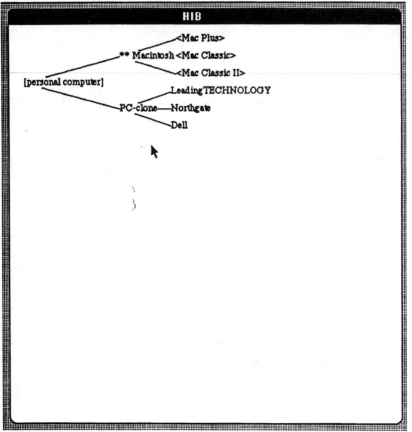

Figure 12.5 The user selected the node for *Macintosh* in Fig. 12.4. The selected node is marked with asterisks (**) while parent nodes are enclosed in square brackets ([ ]) and child nodes are enclosed in angle brackets (< >).

method is to use the text search mode: as seen in Fig. 12.3, the user can specify a keyword. All nodes containing the keyword in their data are displayed in a list, as seen in Fig. 12.4. When the user selects an item from this list, the corresponding node is selected and the HIB tree display is zoomed to the region containing this node, as seen in Fig. 12.5.

All data for a node is stored as an ASCII character string containing attributes and attribute values. Figure 12.6 shows the use of the node edit menu option. Figures 12.7 and 12.8 show the creation of a new data node. A do_edit method dialog box shows a new data template; the user must fill in the node name and the parent node name, followed by optional attribute names and values. Figure 12.9 shows a newly created node added to the HIB tree display.

File   Test   App

HIB

<Mac Ding>

Node edit:

name: Macintosh parent: personal computer processor: 68XXX

OK   Cancel

Figure 12.6 The user selected the node for *Macintosh* in Fig. 12.4. By choosing the *edit* menu option, the data associated with node *Macintosh* can be edited.

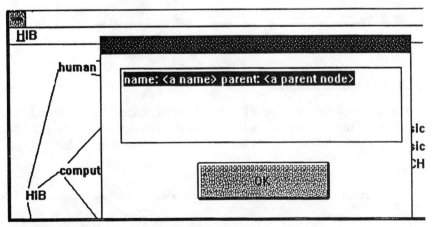

HIB

human

name: <a name> parent: <a parent node>

comput

HIB

OK

Figure 12.7 The user selects the *add node* menu option and is shown a template for editing a new object.

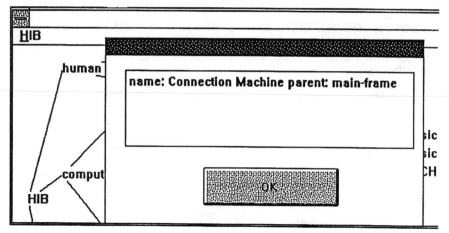

Figure 12.8 The user has filled in values for the node name and parent node name from the template shown in Fig. 12.7.

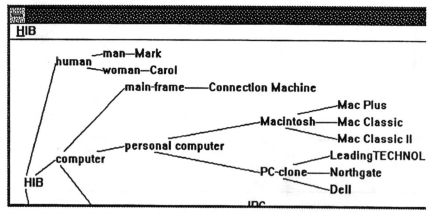

Figure 12.9 The node *Connection Machine* is added as a child of node *main-frame*.

12.3 HIB Implementation

The main application for the HIB is fairly simple, since it builds on both the GUI class library and the TGraph class library developed in Chapter 6. The entire implementation for the HIB program is contained in the file HIB.cp:

```
// FIle HIB.cp
//
// Description: This file contains the data manipulation classes for the
// HIB system.
//
//
// Copyright 1992 by Mark Watson Associates
```

```
//
//        No binary rights reserved: this software library may be used in
//        compiled form without restrictions.  All source rights
//        reserved: Source code to the GUI library can not be distributed
//          (on bulletin boards, or as part of shareware or commercial
//          products)
//        without written permission.
//
//        This software is provided "as is". The user accepts all
//        responsibility for its use.
//

#include "applib.h"
#include "Grapher.h"
#include "char_v.h"

// Define character manipulation primatives for getting attribute
// names and and attribute values:

//
// String equality comparison. Ignore case.
//
static int STR_EQUAL(char *s1, char *s2, int num_to_compare)
{
    for (int i=0; i<num_to_compare; i++) {
        int c1 = s1[i];
        if (c1 >= 'a' && c1 <= 'z')  c1 += 'A' - 'a';
        int c2 = s2[i];
        if (c2 >= 'a' && c2 <= 'z')  c2 += 'A' - 'a';
        if (c1 != c2)  return 0;
    }
    return 1;
}

int get_attribute_value(char *buf, char *attribute,
                                      char *returned_value, int
len_returned_value)
{
    int alen = strlen(attribute);
    int blen = strlen(buf);
    for (int i=0; i< (blen - alen); i++) {
        if (STR_EQUAL(&(buf[i]), attribute, alen)) {

            // found the attribute name:
            if (buf[i+alen] != ':')  break;  // attribute name in another
                                             // string

            // find the starting position of the next attribute:
            for (int index = i + alen + 2; index < blen; index++) {
                if (buf[index] ==':') {
                    int end = index -1;
                    for (int j=index-1; j>i+alen+1; j--) {
                        end = j - 1;
                        if (buf[j] == ' ')  break; // out of the for loop
                    }
                    int len2 = end - (i+alen+2)  + 1;
                    // make sure we don't write past the end
                    // of the returned_value buffer:
                    if   (len2  >   len_returned_value)     len2  =
```

```
len_returned_value;
                for (int k=0; k<len2; k++)
                    returned_value[k] = buf[k+i+alen+2];
                returned_value[len2] = '\0';
                return 1;
            }
        }

        // no following attribute, simply copy the rest of buf to the
        // returned_value buffer:
        int len2 = blen - (i+alen+2) + 2;

        // make sure we don't write past the end of the
        // returned_value buffer:
        if (len2 > len_returned_value)  len2 = len_returned_value;
        for  (int  k=0;  k<len2;  k++)      returned_value[k]   =
buf[k+i+alen+2];
        returned_value[len2] = '\0';
        return 1;
        }
    }
    return 0;
}

static TGraph *my_graph = (TGraph *)NULL;

static char my_text[100];

void TAppWindow::update_display()
{
    if (my_graph != (TGraph *)NULL)
        my_graph->Draw();
    plot_string(30, 30, my_text);
}

static int selected_node = -1;

void TAppWindow::mouse_down(int x, int y)

{
    int node_id = my_graph->closestNode(x, y);
    my_graph->setSelection(node_id); // if node_id = -1, then deselect
all nodes
    selected_node = node_id;
    clear_display();
    update_display();
}

void TAppWindow::mouse_up(int, int)
{
}

void TAppWindow::mouse_move(int, int)
{
}

void TAppWindow::idle_proc()
{
}
```

```
void TAppWindow::do_menu_action(int item_number)
{
    if (item_number == 1) {
        // load an ASCII file:
        if (my_graph == (TGraph *)NULL)
            my_graph = new TGraph(this, "HIB");
        else { // zap old tree:
            my_graph->t.num = 1; // leave the root node
        }
        char file_name[256];
        if (choose_file_to_read("Load ASCII file", "hib", file_name))
            Warning("Error opening file");
        else {
            filebuf in_file;
            if (in_file.open(file_name, input)==0) {
                char buf5[256];
                sprintf(buf5,"Could not open input file %s",file_name);
                Warning(buf5);
                exit(1);
            }
            // read the file:
            istream in_stream(&in_file);
            char buffer[256];
            char name[50], parent[50];
            in_stream.getline(buffer,255);
            while (!in_stream.eof()) {
                int len = strlen(buffer);
                if (get_attribute_value(buffer, "name", name, 50)) {
                    if (get_attribute_value(buffer, "parent", parent, 50))
                    {
                        my_graph->add_child(name, parent);
                    } else {
                        my_graph->add_child(name, "HIB");
                    }
                    int my_id = my_graph->name_to_id(name);
                    if (my_id>-1) {
                        my_graph->t.nodes[my_id].private_data =
                            new char[strlen(buffer)+1];
                        sprintf(my_graph->t.nodes[my_id].private_data,
                            "%s",buffer);
                    }
                }
                in_stream.getline(buffer,255);
            }
            in_file.close();
        }
        my_graph->do_layout();
        clear_display();
        update_display();
    }
    if (item_number == 2) {  // Save to file
        char file_name[256];
        if (choose_file_to_write("Save ASCII file",  file_name))
            Warning("Error opening file");
        else {
            filebuf out_file;
            if (out_file.open(file_name, output)==0) {
                char buf5[256];
                sprintf(buf5,"Could not open input file %s",file_name);
```

```
                Warning(buf5);
                exit(1);
            }
            // write the file:
            ostream out_stream(&out_file);
            for (int i=0; i<my_graph->t.num; i++)
                out_stream << (char *)my_graph->t.nodes[i].private_data <<
"\n";
            out_file.close();
        }
    }
    if (item_number == 3) {  // Clear database in memory
        my_graph->t.num = 1;
        clear_display();
        update_display();
    }
    if (item_number == 4) {  // Redraw from selected node
        int sel = my_graph->getSelectedNode();
        if (sel > -1) {
            my_graph->do_layout(sel);
            clear_display();
            update_display();
        }
    }
    if (item_number == 5) {  // Reset display from root of tree
        my_graph->do_layout();
        clear_display();
        update_display();
    }
    if (item_number == 6) {  // Search mode
        char buf[256];
        do_edit("Enter search string for node name or data:", buf);
        int len = strlen(buf);
        if (len > 1) {
            // count the number of occurences of this string in the
            // database:
            int count = 0;
            int *indices = new int[my_graph->t.num + 1];
            for (int k=0; k<my_graph->t.num; k++) {
                int len2 = strlen(my_graph->t.nodes[k].private_data);
                for (int i=0; i<len2 - len + 1; i++)
                    if (STR_EQUAL(&(my_graph->t.nodes[k].private_data[i]),
                                                    buf, len))
                        indices[count++] = k;
            }
            if (count > 0) {
                char **cp = new char *[count + 1];
                for (int i = 0; i<count; i++)
                cp[i] = my_graph->t.nodes[indices[i]] .private_data;
                int sel2 = choose_one_from_list("Choose one:", cp, count);
                if (sel2 > -1) {
                    int selected_node_index = indices[sel2];

                    // choose the top node of the display to be the
                    // parent node of this selected
                    // node, IF the parent exists:
                    int top = my_graph-
>t.nodes[selected_node_index].parent_id;
                    if (top == -1)  top = selected_node_index;
```

```
                    my_graph->do_layout(top);
                    my_graph->setSelection(selected_node_index);
                    selected_node = selected_node_index;
                    clear_display();
                    update_display();
                }
                delete indices;
                delete cp;
            }
        }
    }
    if (item_number == 7) {  //  Edit selected node
        if (selected_node > -1) {
            char buf[256];
            sprintf(buf,"%s",my_graph-
>t.nodes[selected_node].private_data);
            delete my_graph->t.nodes[selected_node].private_data;
            do_edit("Node edit:", buf);
            my_graph->t.nodes[selected_node].private_data =
                new char[strlen(buf)+1];
            sprintf(my_graph-
>t.nodes[selected_node].private_data,"%s",buf);
        }
    }
    if (item_number == 8) {  //  Delete selected node
        if (selected_node > -1) {
            // update all parent pointers:
            for (int i=0; i<my_graph->t.num; i++) {
                if (my_graph->t.nodes[i].parent_id == selected_node)
                    my_graph->t.nodes[i].parent_id = 0; // point to root of
                                                        // tree
                if (my_graph->t.nodes[i].parent_id > selected_node)
                    my_graph->t.nodes[i].parent_id--;
            }
            // remove the selected node:
            for (i=selected_node; i<my_graph->t.num-1; i++) {
                for (int k=0; k<TEXT_SIZE; k++)
                    my_graph->t.nodes[i].name[k] =
                        my_graph->t.nodes[i+1].name[k];
                my_graph->t.nodes[i].parent_id =
                    my_graph->t.nodes[i+1].parent_id;
                my_graph->t.nodes[i].plot_node=
                    my_graph->t.nodes[i+1].plot_node;
                my_graph->t.nodes[i].private_data =
                    my_graph->t.nodes[i+1].private_data;
                my_graph->t.nodes[i].selectionFlag =
                    my_graph->t.nodes[i+1].selectionFlag;
            }
            my_graph->t.num--;
            my_graph->do_layout();
            my_graph->setSelection(-1);
            selected_node = -1;
            clear_display();
            update_display();
        }
    }
    if (item_number == 9) {  //  Create a new node
        char buf[256];
        sprintf(buf,"name: <a name> parent: <a parent node>");
```

```
        do_edit("Make a new node:", buf);
        char name[50], parent[50];
        if (get_attribute_value(buf, "name", name, 50)) {
            if (get_attribute_value(buf, "parent", parent, 50)) {
                my_graph->add_child(name, parent);
                int my_id = my_graph->name_to_id(name);
                my_graph->t.nodes[my_id].private_data =
                    new char[strlen(buf)+1];
                sprintf(my_graph->t.nodes[my_id].private_data,"%s",buf);
                my_graph->do_layout();
                my_graph->setSelection(-1);
                selected_node = -1;
                clear_display();
                update_display();
            } else show_info("No parent node specified");
        } else show_info("No node name specified");
    }
    if (item_number == 10) {  // Quit
        exit(0);
    }
}
}


INIT_PROGRAM

    // anything can go here
    my_text[0] = '\0';

    RUN_PROGRAM;
}
```

The TGraph class contains most of the functionality needed to implement the HIB program. The function STR_EQUAL compares two character strings for equality, ignoring case. The function get_attribute_value returns the value of a named attribute in a character string.

Most of the functionality of the HIB application is defined in the callback method do_menu_action. The following menu actions are supported:

- Load an ASCII file containing HIB data.
- Save the current HIB database to an ASCII file.
- Clear the in-memory database.
- Redraw the tree display, zooming in on the selected node.
- Redraw the entire tree display.
- Search for and list all nodes that contain a target string.
- Edit the data associated with the currently selected node.
- Delete the selected node and make all children of this deleted node children of the top tree node.
- Create a new node.

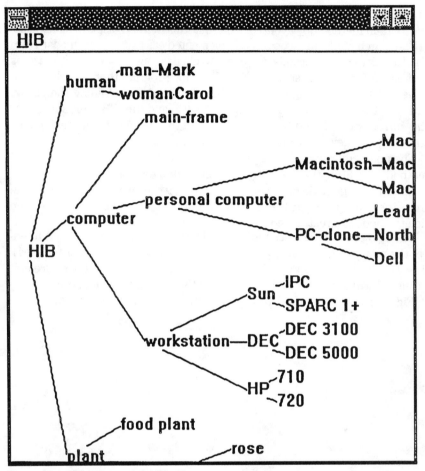

Figure 12.10 HIB browser under Windows.

The HIB program loads data files by reading each line of the file and using the get_attribute_value function to retrieve the node name and the parent node's name; the entire line of data is stored with the node in the attribute private_data. The TGraph method add_child is used to create new nodes.

The HIB program saves data to ASCII files by writing the private_data text string for each node to a file. The in-memory database is cleared by setting the number of tree nodes to one (saving the root HIB node) and redrawing the tree display.

The tree display is zoomed to the region surrounding the currently selected node by using the TGraph method do_layout(int selected_node) to lay out the tree with a new root node. Note that in the TGraph implementation, this method flags all nodes that are not children of the new tree root as undrawable. The tree display is recalculated from the HIB root node by using the TGraph method do_layout( ). Note that this method displays all nodes.

The search mode menu option is implemented easily using two modal TApp Window dialog box methods: do_edit and choose_one_from_list. The user is first asked for a target search string. The HIB program then searches each node for the data string, creating a list of all nodes containing the string. The user then selects on element from this list, and the HIB program selects the current node for editing and zooms the tree display to the region surrounding this newly selected node.

The node edit option is implemented by using the TAppWindow do_edit method for editing the currently selected node's data string.

The HIB program deletes a node by removing the currently selected node from the node array in the current TGraph object. The children of the deleted node are reattached to the root HIB node.

The HIB program creates new nodes by using the do_edit method to enter the new node name and parent name (with optional named attributes). The TGraph method add_child creates a new tree node, and the entire edit string returned from do_edit is copied to the new node's data string.

Figure 12.10 shows the HIB browser implemented under Windows.

13

Handwriting Classifier

The neural network class designed and implemented in Chapter 10 is used in this chapter to write an application that recognizes handwritten characters. This is a very simple application because of the reuse of the neural network and GUI class libraries. This program serves as a good example of capturing mouse motion in an application window.

13.1 User Interface

There are four functions that must be controlled by the user interface:

- Record training data.
- Train neural network and then save the weights to a file.
- Reload weights from a file.
- Test for recognition.

When recording training data, the program prompts the user to draw a sequence of characters in the application window. When testing recognition, the user draws a character in the application window and the program identifies it. Figure 13.1 shows the application window containing the hand-drawn character *2*.

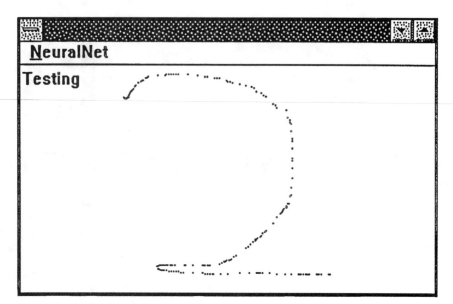

Figure 13.1 Application window containing the character *2*.

13.2 Implementation of the Handwriting Classifier

As the following listing shows, this is a simple application because it builds on existing C++ class libraries:

```
// File: hand.cp
//
// Description: Handwriting recognition system.
//              This demo uses the TNeuralNet Class
//
// Copyright 1992 by Mark Watson Associates
//
//        No binary rights reserved: this software library may be used in
//        compiled form without restrictions.  All source rights
//        reserved: Source code to the GUI library can not be distributed
//        (on bulletin boards, or as part of shareware or commercial
//        products)
//        without written permission.
//
//        This software is provided "as is". The user accepts all
//        responsibility for its use.
//

#include "applib.h"
#include "TNeural.h"
#include "int_vect.h"    // Use smart vector to store points
#include "double_v.h"    // Use smart vector to store points

int nump = 0;    // count the number of points stored
int_vect xp(500), yp(500);
//   USER DEFINED CALLBACK(S):
```

```
// Keep track of current mode of operation:
//   0:  do nothing
//   1:  recording training data
//   2:  currently training network
//   3:  testing recognition

static int current_mode = 0;

// Data for neural network: 7x9 input, 10 output neurons

TNeuralNet nnet(63,6,10); // 63 inputs, 6 hidden, 10 output neurons

double_vect input_examples(1000), output_examples(200);
static int num_training_examples = 0;
static int training_input_counter = 0;
static int training_output_counter = 0;

double in_vect[63];

char *symbols[] = {"0","1","2","3","4","5","6","7","8","9"};

// Utility to convert captured points that were drawn with the
// mouse into a small 63 element vector (63 = 9x7):

void convert_to_2D(TAppWindow *tw)
{
    int min_x = 9999; int max_x = -1; int min_y = 9999; int max_y = -1;
    for (int i=0; i<nump; i++) {
            if (min_x > xp[i]) min_x = xp[i];
            if (max_x < xp[i]) max_x = xp[i];
            if (min_y > yp[i]) min_y = yp[i];
            if (max_y < yp[i]) max_y = yp[i];
    }
    if (min_x >= max_x) min_x = max_x - 1;
    if (min_y >= max_y) min_y = max_y - 1;
    for (i=0; i<63; i++) in_vect[i] = 0.1;
    for (i=0; i<nump; i++) {
            int x = (int)(((float)(xp[i] - min_x)/(float)(max_x -
min_x))*7.0);
            int y = (int)(((float)(yp[i] - min_y)/(float)(max_y -
min_y))*9.0);
            if (x < 0) x = 0;  if (x > 6) x = 6;
            if (y < 0) y = 0;  if (y > 8) y = 8;
            in_vect[x*9+y] = 0.9;
            tw->plot_line(10+x,70+y,10+x,70+y);
    }
}

static int training_step = 0;

static void save_training_data(TAppWindow *tw)
{
    convert_to_2D(tw);
    for (int i=0; i<63; i++)
        input_examples[training_input_counter++] = in_vect[i];
    for (i=0; i<10; i++)
        if (i != training_step)
            output_examples[training_output_counter++] = 0.1;
        else
```

```
                output_examples[training_output_counter++] = 0.9;
     num_training_examples++;
}

static int recall_value = 0;

void recall_pattern(TAppWindow *tw)
{
    convert_to_2D(tw);
    nnet.forward_pass(in_vect);
    // Find the largest output activation:
    double max_act = -9999.0;
    int max_index = 0;
    for (int i=1; i<10; i++)
    if(net,output_activations[i] >
       nnet.output_activations[max_index])
           max_index = i;
    recall_value = max_index;
}

void TAppWindow::update_display()
{
    if (current_mode == 1) {
        plot_string(2,15,"Recording");
    }
    if (current_mode == 2) {
        plot_string(2,15,"Training");
    }
    if (current_mode == 3) {
        plot_string(2,15,"Testing");
    }
}

static int down_flag = 0;

void TAppWindow::mouse_down(int x, int y)
{
    down_flag = 1;
    if (current_mode == 1 || current_mode == 3) {
            if (x < 20 && y < 20) {
                if (current_mode == 1) {
                    save_training_data(this);
                    nump = 0;
                    for (long delay=0; delay<456000; delay++) ;
                    clear_display();
                    training_step += 1;
                    if (training_step < 10) {
                        nump = 0;
                        clear_display();
                        plot_string(30,50,symbols[training_step]);
                }
                    else current_mode = 0;
                    return;
            }
                if (current_mode == 3) {
                    recall_pattern(this);
                    nump = 0;
                    current_mode = 0;
                    clear_display();
```

```
                plot_string(50,50,symbols[recall_value]);
                return;
            }
        }
            xp[nump] = x;
            yp[nump] = y;
            nump++;
            plot_line(x,y,x+1,y+1);
    }
}

void TAppWindow::mouse_up(int, int)
{
    down_flag = 0;
}

void TAppWindow::mouse_move(int x, int y)
{
    if (down_flag)  mouse_down(x, y);
}

void TAppWindow::do_menu_action(int item_number)
{
    if (item_number == 1) { // Record training data
            current_mode = 1;
            training_step = 0;
            nump = 0;
            clear_display();
            plot_string(30,50,symbols[0]);
    }
    if (item_number == 2) { // Train network and save weights
            for (int j=0; j<4; j++) {
                double error = nnet.auto_train(30,num_training_examples,
                    &(input_examples[0]), &(output_examples[0]));
                char buf[80];
                sprintf(buf,"Error=%f",error);
                clear_display();
                plot_string(10,80,buf);
            }
            char output_filename[255];
            if (choose_file_to_write("Output file name:", output_filename)
!= 0) {
                Warning("Could not open/write to file name");
            } else {
                    nnet.save(output_filename);
            }
            current_mode = 2;
    }
    if (item_number == 3) { // Reload saved weights
            char input_filename[255];
            if (choose_file_to_read("Weight file:", "dat", input_filename)
!= 0) {
                Warning("Could not open/read to file name");
            } else {
                nnet.restore(input_filename);
            }
    }
    if (item_number == 4) { // test recognition
            current_mode = 3;
```

```
       }
   }


INIT_PROGRAM

   // anything can go here

   RUN_PROGRAM;
}
```

This application uses two int_vect smart vectors to hold the x-y coordinates of points drawn in the TAppWindow. Two double_vect smart vectors
are used to hold input and output neuron values for neural network training
data. An instance of the TNeuralNet class is allocated statically:

```
// Data for neural network: 7× 9 input, 10 output neurons
TNeuralNet nnet(63,6,10); // 63 inputs, 6 hidden, 10 output neurons
```

This program is set up for learning the numbers zero through nine. A list
of character strings is used to prompt the user during training:

```
char *symbols[] = {"0","1","2","3","4","5","6","7","8","9"};
```

The utility function convert_to_2D(TAppWindow *tw) converts the
points captured while the program user is drawing in a TAppWindow into a
two-dimensional down-sampled input array, which will be the input for the
neural network. This utility function is called from function save_train-
ing_data(TAppWindow *tw), which accumulates training data sets.
    The function recall_pattern(TAppWindow *tw) calls convert_to_2D( ) to
convert the current drawing in the TAppWindow to a two-dimensional input vector, calls the method TNeuralNet::forward_pass( ) to propagate
these input values through the neural net, and identifies the hand-drawn
character by examining the neural network's output neurons to find the
output neuron with the largest activation energy.
    The method TAppWindow::mouse_down( ) uses a global variable, cur-
rent_mode, to determine what to do in response to a mouse-down event. If
the current mode equals 1, the method terminates data collection for the
current drawing, saves this training data set for the current character, in-
crements the character type count (variable training_step), and clears the
screen. If the current mode equals 3, the program is in recall mode and the
current drawing is identified. If the current mode is equal to 2, the method
saves the current x-y mouse coordinates in the int_vect smart vectors xp[ ]
and yp[ ].
    The method TAppWindow::do_menu_action( ) supports the options that
record training data, train the neural network and save the weights to a disk
file for later use, reload an existing set of neural network weights, and test
for recognition.

14

Intelligent Text Browser

The text-indexing C++ class developed in Chapter 11 is used to build a general-purpose text browsing program in this chapter. The use of existing class libraries makes it very easy to develop this application.

14.1 User Interface

Four functions must be controlled by the text browser's user interface:

- Load an existing index file into memory.
- Index one or more text files.
- Save the current index data structures to a data file.
- Perform a search of indexed text databases.

These four functions are controlled by the application's menu.

Figure 14.1 shows the text browser application running on a Sun workstation; a new text file is indexed and added to an index file. Most of the time spent running this application involves the use of the search mode. Figure 14.2 shows a generic do_edit dialog box used for entering a search word.

In Fig. 14.3, a choose_one_from_list dialog box provides a list of text regions surrounding the key word searched for. Figure 14.4 shows a selection of a text region from the dialog box. Figure 14.5 shows text retrieved from an indexed text file shown in the application's main window. The text is displayed using the application window's scrolling_text methods.

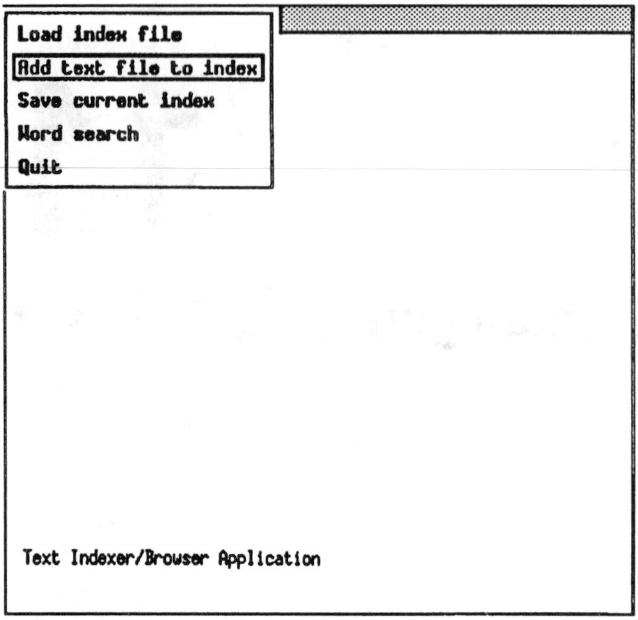

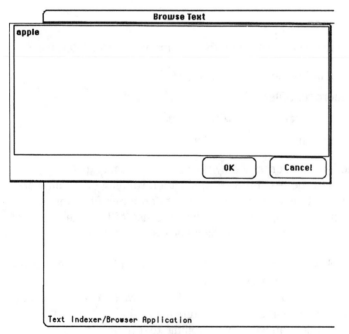

Figure 14.1 Text browser application menu options shown on a Sun workstation.

Figure 14.2 Search mode: find all occurrences of apple in text database.

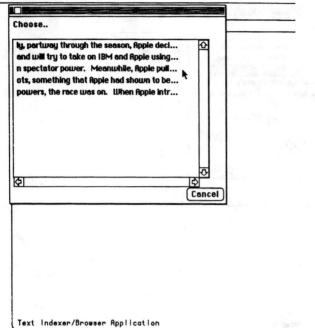

Figure 14.3 A dialog box with a list of text regions containing the key word.

14.2   Implementation of the Text Browser Application

This application is very simple to implement because it uses the TextInd class from Chapter 11 for indexing and searching large text databases. The only complexity in the application is a 30-line block of code in method TAppWindow::do_menu_action() that performs a word search. The following steps are taken for word-searching a text database (implemented in about 30 lines of code):

- Use a TAppWIndow::do_edit() call to ask the user for a search word.
- Use the method TextInd::regionTextBlocks() to retrieve a one-line region surrounding every occurrence of the search word in the text database.
- Count the number of strings returned by TextInd::regionTextBlocks().
- Use a TAppWindow::choose_one_from_list() call to select one occurrence of the target word in its original context.
- Use the method TextInd::get_text() to retrieve a block of text surrounding the user's selection from the original text file.
- Use TAppWindow::put_scrolling_text to display the selected text.

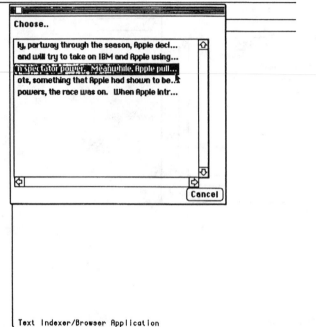

Figure 14.4 Selection of a text region containing the keyword.

The implementation of the text browser is as follows:

```
// File: textbr.cp
//
// Description: Free Text Browser Application.
//              This application uses the TextInd Class
//
// Copyright 1992 by Mark Watson Associates
//
//       No binary rights reserved: this software library may be used in
//       compiled form without restrictions.  All source rights
//       reserved: Source code to the GUI library can not be distributed
//       (on bulletin boards, or as part of shareware or commercial
//       products)
//       without written permission.
//
//       This software is provided "as is". The user accepts all
//       responsibility for its use.
//

#include "applib.h"
#include "TextInd.h"
#include "char_v.h"

TextIndex *ti = 0;

void TAppWindow::update_display()
```

```
{
}
void TAppWindow::idle_proc()    // no background processing in this
                                // application
{
}
void TAppWindow::mouse_down(int x, int y)
{
}

void TAppWindow::mouse_up(int, int)
{
}

void TAppWindow::mouse_move(int x, int y)
{
}

void TAppWindow::do_menu_action(int item_number)
{
    if (item_number == 1) { // Load existng index
        char file_name[256];
        if (choose_file_to_read("Load existing index:", "idx", file_name))
            Warning("Error opening file");
         else
            ti = new TextIndex(file_name);
    }
    if (item_number == 2) { // Create an index file
        if (ti == (TextIndex *)0) {  // We need to create a new index
            char *fileList[8];
            for (int m=0; m<8; m++) fileList[m] = new char[128];
            int get_next_file = 1;
            int count_files = 0;
            while (get_next_file && (count_files < 8)) {
                if (choose_file_to_read("Choose another text file to add:",
                                    "txt", fileList[count_files])) {
                    get_next_file = 0;
                } else count_files++;
            }
            if (count_files > 0)
                ti = new TextIndex(fileList,count_files);
        }
        else
            Warning("Current index in memory");
    }

    if (item_number == 3) { // Save the current index
        char output_file[256];
        if (choose_file_to_write("Enter output file ending in .idx:",
                            output_file))
            Warning("Could not open output file");
         else {
            ti->save(output_file);
        }
    }
    if (item_number == 4) { // Word Search
        if (ti != 0) {
            char target_word[256], buf[256];
            do_edit("Enter the search word:", target_word);
```

```
                char **s = ti->regionTextBlocks(target_word);
                if (s != (char **)0) {
                    int count = 0;
                    while (s[count] != (char *)0) {
                        count++;
                    }
        int user_selection =
        choose_one_from_list("Choose..",s,count);
                    free_strings(s);
                    int file, block;
                    if (ti->regionIndex(user_selection, file, block)) {
                        sprintf(buf,"file=%d, block=%d",file,block);
                        put_scrolling_text(buf);
                        char *buf2 = new char[BLOCK_SIZE + 2];
                        ti->get_text(buf2,BLOCK_SIZE,file,block);
                        int text_len = strlen(buf2);
                        for (int j=0; j<(text_len - 20); j++) {
                            int eol_flag = 0;
                            for (int l=0; l<255; l++) buf[l] = '\0';
                            for (int i=j; i<text_len; i++) {
                                if ((i-j) < 254) {
                                    buf[i-j] = buf2[i];
                                    if (buf2[i] < 30) {
                                        buf[i-j] = '\0';
                                        j = i;
                                        eol_flag = 1;
                                        break;
                                    }
                                }
                            }
                            if (eol_flag == 0) {
                                delete buf2;
                                return;
                            }
                            if (strlen((char *)buf) < 255) {
                                put_scrolling_text(buf);
                            }
                        }
                        delete buf2;
                    }
                }
        } else
            Warning("No active index");
    }
}


INIT_PROGRAM

    // anything can go here
    current_window->init_scrolling_text();
        current_window->put_scrolling_text("Text  Indexer/Browser
Application");
    RUN_PROGRAM;
}
```

 ⚫ **File   Test App**

```
▓▓▓▓▓▓▓▓▓▓▓▓▓▓▓▓▓▓▓▓▓▓▓▓▓▓▓▓▓▓▓▓▓▓▓▓▓▓▓▓▓▓▓▓▓▓▓▓▓▓▓▓▓▓▓▓▓▓▓▓▓▓▓▓▓
                         Browse Text
─────────────────────────────────────────────────────────────────
single disk drive, no expansion slots, and more appearances of
the system Bomb than was appreciated, the Mac's icon-based
aerodynamics and Motorola power pushed the competition up a
file=0, block=6


                              ▸

A Design Hiccup?

  IBM's new Micro Channel Architecture (MCA) induction system
was supposed to bring the next leap in performance. But racing
teams and fans seemed a bit disenchanted. A new fuel (OS/2) was
very expensive (memory) and difficult to obtain in a complete
blend (the missing add-on Managers). Some performance was to be
gained in an endurance race, but a large season-pass investment
was required of the spectators.
  This new design, similar but not quite equal in magnitude to
file=0, block=7
, has not become the darling of the racing set.
In fact, some mutual competitors, after test-driving the MCA
machines, decided to form their own racing consortium. They are
using the proven AT-bus design and will try to take on IBM and
Apple using the large numbers inherent in spectator power.
  Meanwhile, Apple pulled the tarp off a boxy entry called the
Macintosh II, complete with expansion slots. And while it
retains the spirit behind the technology of the original Mac,
```

Figure 14.5 Retrieved text.

15

3D Chess

If you've ever seen Captain Kirk and Commander Spock playing 3D chess in the original StarTrek television series, you've probably wanted to try playing 3D chess yourself. This chapter gives you that chance. It starts by stating a set of rules for 3D chess. (If you don't like these rules, make up your own rules and change the program!) Next, the user interface is designed. Then, a set of C⁺⁺ classes that play chess is designed. This chapter ends with a complete implementation, including GUI, of a 3D chess program.

15.1 Rules for 3D Chess

I assume that you know how to play chess. 3D chess uses three chessboards stacked on top of each other. In 3D chess, every piece can move on its current board level, in the same way that it moves in chess. Additionally, each piece in 3D chess can move up or down one level. To make this clear, I use the following 3D chess notation:

```
chess_piece_location = <level index> <rank index> <row index>
```

In setting up the chess pieces at the beginning of a game, the human player's pieces are placed on level 1. For example, if you are playing the white pieces, the white king is placed on 1E1 (level 1, rank E, row 1). The computer's pieces are placed on level 3. For example, the black queen is on 3D8 (level 3, rank D, row 8).

All pieces either move up or down a level, or move normally. There is one exception to this rule for moving pieces: the first time that a pawn moves, the player may optionally move the pawn both forward and up or down one level.

All pieces, including pawns, can capture when moving up or down one level. Pawns are much stronger pieces than in normal 2D chess. A pawn on its initial square can capture pieces on five squares: by the normal two diagonal captures on the current level, by changing levels, by changing levels and moving forward one square, and by changing levels and moving forward two squares. During test play, I found that it was difficult to prevent pawns from promoting (i.e., reaching the eighth rank and becoming a queen or other piece of choice). As a result of this test play, I decided to prohibit pawn promotion in my version of 3D chess.

I have found that a useful strategy, when possible, is to leave most of my pawns on their original squares to control my half of the middle board level. I try to move most of my pieces to the middle level before starting any attack on the computer's king.

The game is over when one of the kings is checkmated, or when both players agree to a draw.

15.2   User Interface Design for a 3D Chess Program

Figure 15.1 shows the window layout for the 3D chess program. I find it difficult to play against chess programs that use a 3D perspective to show the board and pieces. For 3D chess, I find it easiest to view the three levels in a flat perspective.

The move list area of the playing window shows a historic record of the moves played in the current game. The current move evaluations area of the playing window shows the best 3D chess moves currently under consideration by the program.

15.3   C++ Classes to Play 3D Chess

The first step in designing the C++ classes to play 3D chess is to decide how to encode the data necessary to keep track of the current state of the chessboard, the lookahead tree, and move generation data. In order to make move generation (for one playing level) more efficient, the 8-by-8 square chessboard is surrounded on three sides with four rows and two columns of additional empty squares, as shown in Fig. 15.2.

The *board* class maintains state information for a 3D chessboard and methods for generating piece moves on the board. The following listing shows the class definition:

```
class board {
public:
```

```
int brd[360];
int bcontrol[360];
int wcontrol[360];
int current_side;    // toggles between -1 and 1 for lookahead
int move_from[MAX_MOVES]; // "from squares" for legal moves
int move_to[MAX_MOVES];    // "to squares" for legal moves
int move_value[MAX_MOVES];  // static evaluation of this move
int num_possible_moves;

void set_pieces();   // beginning of game setup
void generate_moves(int protect);
int generate_moves_from_square(int index, int protect);
board();
board & operator = (board &b);
};
```

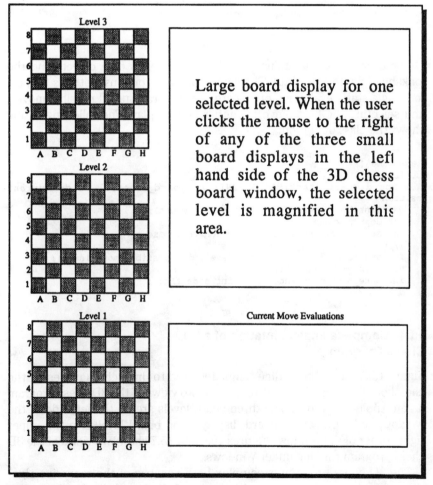

Figure 15.1 Window layout for 3D chessboard display.

110	111	112	113	114	115	116	117	118	119
100	101	102	103	104	105	106	107	108	109
90	91	92	93	94	95	96	97	98	99
80	81	82	83	84	85	86	87	88	89
70	71	72	73	74	75	67	77	78	79
60	61	62	63	64	65	66	67	68	69
50	51	52	53	54	55	56	57	58	59
40	41	42	43	44	45	46	47	48	49
30	31	32	33	34	35	36	37	38	39
20	21	22	23	24	25	26	27	28	29
10	11	12	13	14	15	16	17	18	19
0	1	2	3	4	5	6	7	8	9

Figure 15.2 Square indices for level 1. The shaded squares are legal squares and the unshaded squares are off of the chessboard.

The *game* class maintains a stack of board class data objects and the lookahead depth and width. The game class also contains methods for performing a static evaluation of a board position, ranking all possible moves, and selecting the best move for either side to play. The following listing shows the class definition:

```
class game {
public:
        board board_stack[MAX_DEPTH]; // board_stack[0] holds current
position
      game(int look_ahead_depth, int search_width);
      int depth, width;
      // use a static evaluation function to impose a
      // partial ordering on the moves:
      int static_evaluation(int brd_level, int possible_move_index);
      void rank_moves(int level);
      int make_best_move(int level, int side_flag);
};
```

15.4 Complete Implementation of a 3D Chess Program

Figure 15.3 shows the outline templates used to draw chess pieces on the chessboard. Figures 15.4 and 15.5 show two views of the 3D chess program on an Apple Macintosh. The three board levels are on the left side of the window, and an enlarged board display of on board level is in the upper right corner of the window. Figures 15.6 and 15.7 show two views of the 3D chess program running under Windows.

The 3D chess program is complex both because of the recursive algorithm for playing 3D chess and because of the board display. In under-

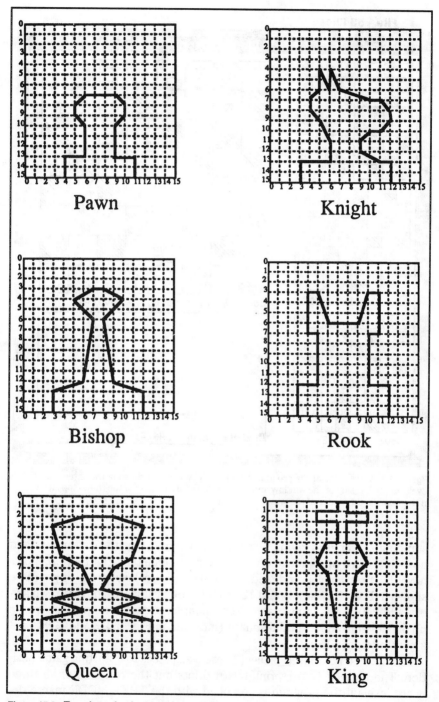

Pawn

Knight

Bishop

Rook

Queen

King

Figure 15.3 Templates for drawing chess pieces.

Figure 15.4 View of 3D chess program on an Apple Macintosh showing the three board levels on the left side of the window and an enlarged board display of the third (top) level in the upper right corner of the window.

standing the chess-playing algorithm, it is important to first understand how the board and piece control arrays are indexed. Figure 15.2 shows how the first level is indexed. To move up one level from any square shown in Fig. 15.2, simply add 120 to the index value. To move up two levels, add 240 to the index value. For example, to move the player's queen up one level from her initial square (index 25 in Fig. 15.2), add 120 to get a new index of 145.

The method board::set_pieces( ) resets all pieces to a starting game position. The method board::print_board prints out the contents of all three board levels if the program is compiled with the TEXT_MODE macro defined. The method board::print_possible_moves( ) prints out the possible moves from the current board position if the program is compiled with the TEXT_MODE macro defined.

The utility method board::generate_moves_from_square( ) generates possible moves for the piece on a given square. This method may look complex (since it is about 200 lines of code), but it is really simple: the array index_table maps a piece type into a starting array index in the array piece_table. Array piece_table contains a series of offsets that are added to a pieces-current board index. For example, a bishop is of piece type 3, and index_table[3] equals 10. The entries in array piece_table starting at index 10 (until you reach a zero value) are –9, –11, 9, 11, and 0. To move a bishop, you start by repetitively adding –9 to its index until it either runs off of the

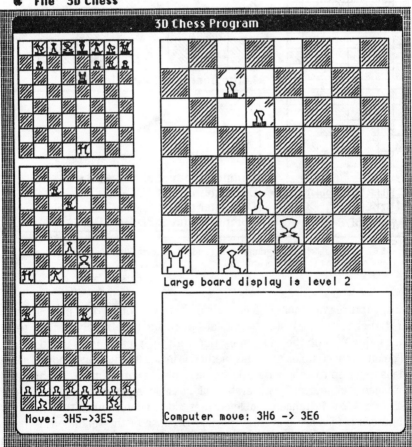

Figure 15.5 View of 3D chess program similar to Fig. 15.4, showing an enlarged board display of the second (middle) board level.

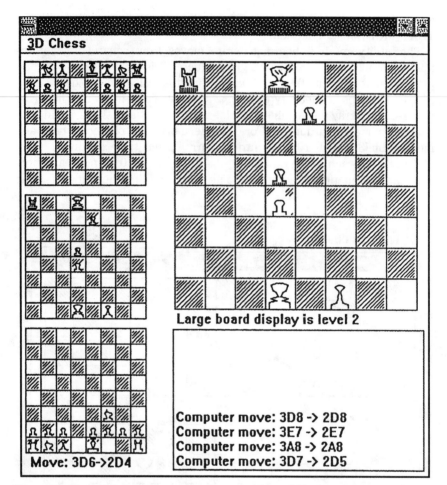

Figure 15.6 View of 3D chess program running under Microsoft Windows showing an enlarged view of the first (bottom) board level.

board, captures an enemy piece, or runs into one of its own pieces. Then you start again on the bishop's original square and repetitively add −11 to its board index. You do the same operation with the piece offsets 9 and 11.

The only real complexity in this method is in calculating pawn moves, since code is required to handle the special cases of pawn movement. The method board::generate_moves() generates all possible moves for a side. These methods use the instance variable current_side to determine if the human or computer's pieces are currently moving. Because of the recursion used for move generation and evaluation, these methods calculate moves for both sides.

The constructor game::game(int look_ahead_depth, int search_width) sets up a game by copying the search limit parameters and using the method board::set_pieces( ) to initialize the board. The *game* class has an array of boards (board_stack[ ]) as an instance variable. The board at index zero is the current board position, and high indexed boards in the array are used for the recursive lookahead.

The method game::static_evaluation(int brd_level, int possible_move_index) evaluates a move using static evaluation from squares defined by the following code:

```
int to_square =
    board_stack[brd_level].move_to[possible_move_index];
int from_square =
    board_stack[brd_level].move_from[possible_move_index];
```

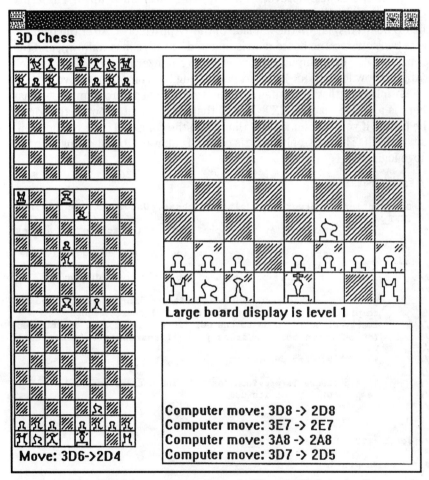

Figure 15.7 View of 3D chess program running under Microsoft Windows showing an enlarged view of the second (middle) board level.

The method game::rank_moves(int level) ranks all possible moves. The argument *level* defines an index into the array board_stack[ ]. This method uses the static evaluation function to rank moves.

The method game::make_best_move(int level, int side_flag) uses recursion to rank moves based on possible future moves by the opponent and itself.

When drawing the board displays, pieces are drawn using shape template arrays. These templates hold x-y coordinates to draw the coordinates of a square from the origin. The enlarged board display uses the same templates with a scaling factor to increase the plot size.

Event handling is easy to implement in the 3D chess program. As usual, menu events are handled by the program. The user is also allowed to interact with the program by clicking in the TAppWindow; the program processes the mouse-up events in TAppWindow::mouse_up(). The array hilight_square_list[2] holds the square indices of up to two mouse clicks in the 3D board display on the left side of the TAppWindow. After the user selects two squares, the board data is updated, the screen is redrawn, and the global variable do_computer_move is set to a nonzero value as a flag to tell TAppWindow:idle_ proc( ) to start calculating the computer's move.

The following listing contains the entire 3D chess program. Note that there is a define macro TEXT_MODE that is commented out at the top of the listing; if you uncomment this line, then the compiled code will not contain the GUI. This text-only mode is useful if you want to test changes to the move logic.

```
// File: chess3d.cp
//
// Description: A program to play 3D chess. Uncomment the '#define
// TEXT_MODE'
//              statement at the top of the listing to produce a "text
//              only"
//              version of the program (useful for debugging). See
//              chapter 15
//              for details on lookahead logic and board display.
//
//      No binary rights reserved: this software library may be used in
//      compiled form without restrictions.  All source rights
//      reserved: Source code to the GUI library can not be distributed
//      (on bulletin boards, or as part of shareware or commercial
//      products)
//      without written permission.
//
//      This software is provided "as is". The user accepts all
//      responsibility for its use.
//


// #define TEXT_MODE

#include "applib.h"

const int MAX_DEPTH = 5;
```

```
const int MAX_MOVES = 120;

const int WHITE = 1;
const int BLACK =-1;

const int PAWN = 1;
const int KNIGHT = 2;
const int BISHOP = 3;
const int ROOK = 4;
const int QUEEN = 5;
const int KING = 6;

// conversion from [row, column, level] indices to linear index:
int get_index(int row, int col, int level)
{
    return 22+col+row*10+level*120;
}
void index_to_coords(int index, int &row, int &col, int &level)
{
    level = index / 120;
    int coord_in_level = index - 120 * level;
    row = (coord_in_level/10) - 2;
    col = coord_in_level - (row+2)*10 - 2;
}

class board {
public:
    int brd[360];
    int bcontrol[360];
    int wcontrol[360];

    int current_side;  // toggles between -1 and 1 for lookahead

    int move_from[MAX_MOVES]; // "from squares" for legal moves
    int move_to[MAX_MOVES];   // "to squares" for legal moves
    int move_value[MAX_MOVES];  // static evaluation of this move
    int num_possible_moves;
    void set_pieces();  // beginning of game setup
#ifdef TEXT_MODE
    void print_board();
    void print_possible_moves();
#endif
    // defines move_to and move_from:
    void generate_moves(int protect);
    int generate_moves_from_square(int index, int protect);

    board();

    board & operator = (board &b);
};

static int player_side = 1;  // 1->human plays white, -1->human plays
black

class game {
public:
    board board_stack[MAX_DEPTH]; // board_stack[0] holds current
position
    game(int look_ahead_depth, int search_width);
```

```
    int depth, width;
    // use a static evaluation function to impose a
    // partial ordering on the moves:
    int static_evaluation(int brd_level, int possible_move_index);
    void rank_moves(int level);
    int make_best_move(int level, int side_flag);
};


board::board()
{
    num_possible_moves = 0;
    for (int i=0; i<360; i++)
        brd[i] = bcontrol[i] = wcontrol[i] = 0;
}


// Define the = operator for board:
board & board::operator = (board &b)
{
    for (int i=0; i<360; i++) {
        brd[i] = b.brd[i];
        bcontrol[i] = b.bcontrol[i];
        wcontrol[i] = b.wcontrol[i];
    }
    current_side = b.current_side;
    num_possible_moves = b.num_possible_moves;
    for (i=0; i<num_possible_moves; i++) {
        move_from[i] = b.move_from[i];
        move_to[i] = b.move_to[i];
        move_value[i] = b.move_value[i];
    }
    return (*this);
}



// Set up the initial board position:
void board::set_pieces()
{
    for (int i=0; i<360; i++) { // zero out board squares
        brd[i] = 0;
    }
    for (i=0; i<12; i++) { // off brd squares (see Figure 15.2)
        brd[10*i] = brd[10*i+120] = brd[10*i+240] = 7;
        brd[10*i+1] = brd[10*i+121] = brd[10*i+241] = 7;
    }
    for (i=2; i< 10; i++) { // off brd squares (see Figure 15.2)
        brd[i] = brd[i+120] = brd[i+240] = 7;
        brd[i+10] = brd[i+130] = brd[i+250] = 7;
        brd[i+100] = brd[i+220] = brd[i+320] = 7;
        brd[i+110] = brd[i+230] = brd[i+350] = 7;
    }

    for (i=32; i<40; i++) brd[i] = WHITE * PAWN;
    brd[22] = WHITE * ROOK;        brd[23] = WHITE * KNIGHT;
    brd[24] = WHITE * BISHOP;        brd[25] = WHITE * QUEEN;
    brd[26] = WHITE * KING;        brd[27] = WHITE * BISHOP;
    brd[28] = WHITE * KNIGHT;        brd[29] = WHITE * ROOK;

    for (i=82+240; i<90+240; i++) brd[i] = BLACK * PAWN;
    brd[92+240] = BLACK * ROOK; brd[93+240] = BLACK * KNIGHT;
    brd[94+240] = BLACK * BISHOP;    brd[95+240] = BLACK * QUEEN;
    brd[96+240] = BLACK * KING; brd[97+240] = BLACK * BISHOP;
```

```
        brd[98+240] = BLACK * KNIGHT;    brd[99+240] = BLACK * ROOK;
}

#ifdef TEXT_MODE
// Print out the board to stderr:
void board::print_board()
{
    // Loop over squares on all three levels:
    for (int i=99+2*120; i>=0; i-=10) {
        if (i==99+2*120) cerr << "\n\nLevel 3:\n";
        if (i==99+120) cerr <<    "\nLevel 2:\n";
        if (i== 99) cerr <<    "\nLevel 1:\n";
    for (int j=0; j<8; j++) {
        int ind = i - 7 + j;
        if (brd[ind] != 7) { // not off of the board:
            if (brd[ind] == 0) {
                int index = ind % 120;
                int row = (index / 10) % 2;
                int col = (index - ((index / 10) * 10)) % 2;
                if (row == 0) {
                    if (col == 0) cerr << " X ";
                      else        cerr << " . ";
                } else {
                        if (col == 1) cerr << ".X.";
                          else        cerr << " . ";
                    }
            } else {
                if (brd[ind] < 0) cerr << " B";
                 else             cerr << " W";
                int ptype = brd[ind]; if (ptype < 0) ptype = -ptype;
                if (ptype == PAWN) cerr << "P";
                if (ptype == KNIGHT) cerr << "N";
                if (ptype == BISHOP) cerr << "B";
                if (ptype == ROOK) cerr << "R";
                if (ptype == QUEEN) cerr << "Q";
                if (ptype == KING) cerr << "K";
            }
        }
    }
        if (brd[i] != 7)   cerr << "\n";
    }
    cerr << "\n";
}

void board::print_possible_moves()
{   int row1, col1, level1, row2, col2, level2;
    for (int i=0; i<num_possible_moves; i++) {
        index_to_coords(move_from[i], row1, col1, level1);
        index_to_coords(move_to[i], row2, col2, level2);
        cerr << "From level " << level1 <<", row " << row1 << ", col " <<
                col1 << " to: level " << level2 <<", row " << row2 <<
                ", col " << col2 << "  value: " << move_value[i] << "\n";
    }
}
#endif

// Defines move_to and move_from generating possible moves:
void board::generate_moves(int protect)
{
    num_possible_moves = 0;
    for (int i=0; i<360; i++)
```

```
        if (brd[i] != 7 && brd[i] != 0) {
            if (current_side == -1 && brd[i] < 0)
                generate_moves_from_square(i, protect);
            if (current_side == 1  && brd[i] > 0)
                generate_moves_from_square(i, protect);
        }
    return;
}


static int index_table[] = {0, 12, 15, 10, 1, 6, 6};
static int piece_table[] = {0, 1, -1, 10, -10, 0, 1, -1, 10, -10, -9,
                    -11, 9, 11, 0, 8, -8, 12, -12, 19, -19, 21,
                    -21, 0, 10, 20, 0, 0, 0, 0, 0};
static int control[] = {0, 12, 10, 10, 9, 8, 8};
int board::generate_moves_from_square(int index, int protect)
{
    int level = index / 120;
    int ind = index - 120*level;  // index inside a level
    int num_moves = 0;
    int ptype = brd[index]; if (ptype < 0) ptype = -ptype;

    // Regardless of piece type, allow movement up or down a level to
    // either a blank square or for a capture:
    if (level < 2) { // check for moving up a level:
        if (brd[index] > 0) { // white piece
            if (brd[index+120] <= 0) {
                move_from[num_possible_moves] = index;
                move_to[num_possible_moves++] = index + 120;
                            if (current_side==1) wcontrol[index +
120]+=control[ptype];
                            else                bcontrol[index +
120]+=control[ptype];
            }
        }
        if (brd[index] < 0) { // black piece
            if (brd[index+120] >= 0) {
                move_from[num_possible_moves] = index;
                move_to[num_possible_moves++] = index + 120;
                            if (current_side==1) wcontrol[index +
120]+=control[ptype];
                            else                bcontrol[index +
120]+=control[ptype];
            }
        }
    }

    if (level > 0) { // check for moving down a level:
        if (brd[index] > 0) { // white piece
            if (brd[index-120] <= 0) {
                move_from[num_possible_moves] = index;
                move_to[num_possible_moves++] = index - 120;
                            if (current_side==1) wcontrol[index -
120]+=control[ptype];
                            else                bcontrol[index -
120]+=control[ptype];
            }
        }
        if (brd[index] < 0) { // black piece
            if (brd[index-120] >= 0) {
```

```
                    move_from[num_possible_moves] = index;
                    move_to[num_possible_moves++] = index - 120;
                              if (current_side==1)  wcontrol[index -
120]+=control[ptype];
                         else                        bcontrol[index -
120]+=control[ptype];
                }
        }
    }

    switch (ptype) {
        case PAWN:  // There are MANY special cases for pawns:
            int row = (ind / 10) - 2; // index rows starting with 0
            if (current_side == BLACK) {
                if (row == 6 && level == 2) { // pawn has not moved yet:
                    if (brd[index-20]==0) {
                        move_from[num_possible_moves] = index;
                        move_to[num_possible_moves++] = index-20;
                        if (brd[index-20-120] <= 0) { // empty or capture
                                                     // OK
                            move_from[num_possible_moves] = index;
                            move_to[num_possible_moves++] = index-20-120;
                        }
                    }

                }
                if (brd[index-10]==0) { // not blocked:
                    move_from[num_possible_moves] = index;
                    move_to[num_possible_moves++] = index-10;
                    if (row==6 && level == 2) {
                        if (brd[index-10-120] <= 0) { // empty or capture
                                                     // OK
                            move_from[num_possible_moves] = index;
                            move_to[num_possible_moves++] = index-10-120;
                        }
                    }
                }
                if (brd[index-9] != 7 && brd[index-9]!=0) {
                    if (brd[index-9] < 0) {
                        move_from[num_possible_moves] = index;
                        move_to[num_possible_moves++] = index-9;
                    }
                }
                if (brd[index-11] != 7 && brd[index-11]!=0) {
                    if (brd[index-11] < 0) {
                        move_from[num_possible_moves] = index;
                        move_to[num_possible_moves++] = index-11;
                    }
                }
            } else { // WHITE
                if (row == 1) { // pawn has not moved yet:
                    if (brd[index+20]==0) {
                        move_from[num_possible_moves] = index;
                        move_to[num_possible_moves++] = index+20;
                        if (brd[index+20+120] <= 0) { // empty or capture
                                                     // OK
                            move_from[num_possible_moves] = index;
                            move_to[num_possible_moves++] = index+20+120;
                        }
                    }
                }
```

```
        }
        if (brd[index+10]==0) { // not blocked:
            move_from[num_possible_moves] = index;
            move_to[num_possible_moves++] = index+10;
            if (row==1) {
                if (brd[index+10+120] <= 0) { // empty or capture
                    move_from[num_possible_moves] = index;
                    move_to[num_possible_moves++] = index+10+120;
                }
            }
        }
        if (brd[index+9] != 7 && brd[index+9]!=0) {
            if (brd[index+9] < 0) {
                move_from[num_possible_moves] = index;
                move_to[num_possible_moves++] = index+9;
            }
        }
        if (brd[index+11] != 7 && brd[index+11]!=0) {
            if (brd[index+11] < 0) {
                move_from[num_possible_moves] = index;
                move_to[num_possible_moves++] = index+11;
            }
        }
    }
    // Fill in control arrays for all possible pawn captures:
    for (int k=22; k<360; k++) {
        if (brd[k] == BLACK*PAWN) {
            bcontrol[k-9] += 12;
            bcontrol[k-11] += 12;
        }
        if (brd[k] == WHITE*PAWN) {
            wcontrol[k+9] += 12;
            wcontrol[k+11] += 12;
        }
    }
    break;

case KNIGHT: // after pawn moves, the other piece moves are
             // simple:
case BISHOP:
case ROOK:
case QUEEN:
case KING:
    int move_index = index_table[ptype];
    for (int table_loop=move_index; piece_table[table_loop]!=0;
        table_loop++) {
        if (ptype == KNIGHT || ptype == KING) {
            if (brd[index + piece_table[table_loop]] != 7) {
                if (brd[index + piece_table[table_loop]] *
                  current_side <= 0) {
                    move_from[num_possible_moves] = index;
                    move_to[num_possible_moves++] =
                     index + piece_table[table_loop];
                    if (current_side==1)
                      wcontrol[index + piece_table[table_loop]]+=
                        control[ptype];
                      else
```

```
                        bcontrol[index + piece_table[table_loop]]+=
                            control[ptype];
                } else {
                    if (brd[index + piece_table[table_loop]] *
                    current_side > 0 && protect==1) {
                            if (current_side==1)
                            wcontrol[index+
                    piece_table[table_loop]]+=
                                control[ptype];
                    else
                            bcontrol[index+
                    piece_table[table_loop]]+=
                                control[ptype];
                    }
                }
        }
    } else {   // BISHOP, ROOK, or QUEEN:
        for (int sq=index+piece_table[table_loop]; ;
            sq+=piece_table[table_loop]) {
            if (brd[sq] == 7)  break;  // off of board
            if (brd[sq] == 0) {
                move_from[num_possible_moves] = index;
                move_to[num_possible_moves++] = sq;
                if (current_side==1)
                  wcontrol[s q] = wcontrol[s q]+
                                control[ptype];
                  else
                  bcontrol[s q] = bcontrol[s q]+
                                control[ptype];
            }
            if (brd[sq] != 0) {
                int capture_sign = 1;
              if (brd[sq] < 0) capture_sign = -1;
                if (protect == 1) {
                    if (capture_sign == current_side) {
                        if (current_side==1)
                        wcontrol[sq]+=control[ptype];
                          else
                        bcontrol[sq]+=control[ptype];
                        break; // protect friendly piece
                    }
                }
                if (capture_sign != current_side) {
                    move_from[num_possible_moves] = index;
                    move_to[num_possible_moves++] = sq;
                    if (current_side==1)
                    wcontrol[sq]+=control[ptype];

                    else
                  bcontrol[sq]+=control[ptype];
                  break; // capture
            } else {
                break;
            }
        }
    }
}
if (num_possible_moves > 0)
```

```
                    if (move_to[num_possible_moves-1] < 22  ||
                        move_to[num_possible_moves-1] > 340)
                        num_possible_moves--;
            }
            break;
    }

    return num_possible_moves;
}

game::game(int look_ahead_depth, int search_width)
{
    depth = look_ahead_depth; width = search_width;
    board_stack[0].set_pieces();
}

// Static evaluation function:

static int p_value[] = {0, 1, 3, 3, 5, 9, 1000};

const int LEVEL_MOVE_BONUS = 3;

int game::static_evaluation(int brd_level, int possible_move_index)
{
    int value = 0;

    if (brd_level > (MAX_DEPTH - 2)) {
#ifdef TEXT_MODE
        cerr << "Error in static evaluation\n";
#endif
        return 0;
    }
    // Copy board to next board stack level:
    board_stack[brd_level+1] = board_stack[brd_level];
    int *b = (int *)&(board_stack[brd_level+1].brd);

int to_square = board_stack[brd_level].move_to[possible_move_index];
int from_square = board_stack[brd_level].move_from [possible_move
_index];

    b[to_square] = b[from_square];
    b[from_square] = 0;
for (int i=0; i<360; i++) {
    board_stack[brd_level+1].wcontrol[i] = 0;
    board_stack[brd_level+1].bcontrol[i] = 0;
}

int side_moving = board_stack[brd_level+1].current_side;

if (side_moving == BLACK) {
    if ((to_square / 120) < (from_square / 120))
        value += LEVEL_MOVE_BONUS;
    if (b[to_square-9] == WHITE*PAWN ||
        b[to_square-11] == WHITE*PAWN)
          value -= 50 * (p_value[-b[to_square]] - p_value[PAWN]);
} else {  // side_moving == WHITE
    if ((to_square / 120) > (from_square / 120))
        value += LEVEL_MOVE_BONUS;
```

```
        if (b[to_square+9] == BLACK*PAWN ||
           b[to_square+11] == BLACK*PAWN)
             value -= 50 * (p_value[b[to_square]] - p_value[PAWN]);
}

if (b[to_square] == BLACK*QUEEN || b[to_square] == WHITE*QUEEN)
    value -= 2;
if (b[to_square] == BLACK*KING || b[to_square] == WHITE*KING)
    value -= 3;

board_stack[brd_level+1].current_side = 1;
for (i=22; i<360; i++)
    if (board_stack[brd_level+1].brd[i] != 7 &&
        board_stack[brd_level+1].brd[i] > 0)
          board_stack[brd_level+1].generate_moves_from_square(i, 1);

board_stack[brd_level+1].current_side = -1;
for (i=22; i<360; i++)
    if (board_stack[brd_level+1].brd[i] != 7 &&
        board_stack[brd_level+1].brd[i] < 0)
          board_stack[brd_level+1].generate_moves_from_square(i, 1);

// Static evaluation based on control and material:
for (i=22; i<360; i++) {
    if (b[i] != 7) {
        int ptype = b[i]; if (ptype < 0)  ptype = - ptype;
        int pside = 1; if (b[i] < 0) pside = -1;
        int relative_control =
          board_stack[brd_level+1].wcontrol[i] -
          board_stack[brd_level+1].bcontrol[i];
        value += side_moving * relative_control / 10;
        value += side_moving * 100 * p_value[ptype] * pside;
        if (b[i] != 0) {
            if (b[i] > 0 && relative_control < 0)
                value -= side_moving * 15 * p_value[ptype];
            if (b[i] < 0 && relative_control > 0)
                value += side_moving * 15 * p_value[ptype];
        }
        if (b[i] == WHITE * KING) {
            if (side_moving == WHITE)
                if (board_stack[brd_level+1].bcontrol[i]>0)
                  value-=1000;
            if (side_moving == BLACK)
                if (board_stack[brd_level+1].bcontrol[i]>0)
                  value+=10; // bonus for checking
        }
        if (b[i] == BLACK * KING) {
            if (side_moving == BLACK)
                if (board_stack[brd_level+1].wcontrol[i]>0)
                  value-=1000;
            if (side_moving == WHITE)
                if (board_stack[brd_level+1].wcontrol[i]>0)
                  value+=10; // bonus for checking
        }
    }
}
int relative_control = board_stack[brd_level+1].wcontrol[to_square] -
                       board_stack[brd_level+1].bcontrol[to_square];
if (side_moving == 1 && relative_control < 0)
```

```
        value -= 75*p_value[b[to_square]];
    if (side_moving ==-1 && relative_control > 0)
        value -= 75*p_value[-b[to_square]]; // sign of b[] < negative

    return value;
}
```

```
// Use a static evaluation function to impose a
// partial ordering on the moves:

static char *column_name[] = {"A","B","C","D","E","F","G","H","Z"};

void game::rank_moves(int level)
{
    for (int i=0; i<board_stack[level].num_possible_moves; i++) {
        board_stack[level].move_value[i] = static_evaluation(level, i);
    }
    // Bubble sort the top 'width' moves to the top of the move
    // list. (NOTE: a bubble sort is very efficient only if the
    // number of items being moved is less than 16).
    for (i=0; i<width; i++) {
        int max = -9999;
        int max_index = 0;
        for (int j=i+1; j<board_stack[level].num_possible_moves; j++) {
            if (board_stack[level].move_value[j] > max) {
                max = board_stack[level].move_value[j];
                max_index = j;
            }
        }

        int temp = board_stack[level].move_value[max_index];
        board_stack[level].move_value[max_index] =
            board_stack[level].move_value[i];
        board_stack[level].move_value[i] = temp;
        temp = board_stack[level].move_from[max_index];
        board_stack[level].move_from[max_index] =
            board_stack[level].move_from[i];
        board_stack[level].move_from[i] = temp;
        temp = board_stack[level].move_to[max_index];
        board_stack[level].move_to[max_index] =
            board_stack[level].move_to[i];
        board_stack[level].move_to[i] = temp;
    }
#ifdef TEXT_MODE
    int num_loop = width;
    if (num_loop > board_stack[level].num_possible_moves)
        num_loop = board_stack[level].num_possible_moves;

    for (i=0; i<num_loop; i++) {
        cerr << "LEVEL=" << level << " ";
        cerr << "From: " << board_stack[level].move_from[i] <<
                ", to: " << board_stack[level].move_to[i];
        int levelX, row, col;

            index_to_coords(board_stack[level].move_from[i], row, col,
levelX);
            cerr << "  (" << (levelX+1) << column_name[col] <<
                (row + 1) << " -> ";
```

```
                index_to_coords(board_stack[level].move_to[i], row, col, levelX);
                cerr << (levelX+1) << column_name[col] << (row + 1) << ")"
                    << ", value= " << board_stack[level].move_value[i]
                    << "\n";
        }
#endif
    return;
}


int game::make_best_move(int level, int side_flag)
{
#ifdef TEXT_MODE
    cerr << "MAKE_BEST_MOVE: level=" << level << ", side_flag=" <<
            side_flag << "\n";
#endif
    if (level >= depth) {
        board_stack[level].current_side = side_flag;
        board_stack[level].generate_moves(0);
        rank_moves(level);
        if (board_stack[level].num_possible_moves > 0) {
            int to_square    = board_stack[level].move_to[0];
            int from_square = board_stack[level].move_from[0];
            board_stack[level].brd[to_square] =
                board_stack[level].brd[from_square];

            board_stack[level].brd[from_square] = 0;
        }
        return board_stack[level].num_possible_moves;
    } else {   // do a limited lookahead:
        board_stack[level].current_side = side_flag;
        board_stack[level].generate_moves(0);
        rank_moves(level);
        for (int w=0; w<width; w++) {
            int to = board_stack[level].move_to[w];
            int from = board_stack[level].move_from[w];
            int save = board_stack[level].brd[from];
#ifdef TEXT_MODE
            cerr << "looking ahead: from=" << from << ", to: " <<
                    to << "\n";
#endif
            board_stack[level+1] = board_stack[level];
                                board_stack[level+1].brd[to]    =
board_stack[level+1].brd[from];
            board_stack[level+1].brd[from] = 0;
            board_stack[level+1].current_side = -side_flag;
            make_best_move(level+1, -side_flag);
            board_stack[level].move_value[w] -=
                board_stack[level + 1].move_value[0];
        }
        // sort the moves:
        for (int i=0; i<width; i++) {
            int max = board_stack[level].move_value[i];
            int max_index = i;
            int width2 = width;
            if (width2>board_stack[level].num_possible_moves)
                width2=board_stack[level].num_possible_moves;
            for (int j=i+1; j<width2; j++) {
                if (board_stack[level].move_value[j] > max) {
                    max = board_stack[level].move_value[j];
                    max_index = j;
```

```
                }
            }
            int temp = board_stack[level].move_value[max_index];
            board_stack[level].move_value[max_index] =
                board_stack[level].move_value[i];
            board_stack[level].move_value[i] = temp;
            temp = board_stack[level].move_from[max_index];
            board_stack[level].move_from[max_index] =
                board_stack[level].move_from[i];
            board_stack[level].move_from[i] = temp;
            temp = board_stack[level].move_to[max_index];
            board_stack[level].move_to[max_index] =
                board_stack[level].move_to[i];
            board_stack[level].move_to[i] = temp;
        }
        if (level == 0) {
            int to = board_stack[level].move_to[0];
            int from = board_stack[level].move_from[0];
            board_stack[level].brd[to] = board_stack[level].brd[from];
            board_stack[level].brd[from] = 0;
#ifndef TEXT_MODE
            int levelX1, row1, col1, levelX2, row2, col2;
            index_to_coords(board_stack[0].move_from[0], row1, col1,
                levelX1);
            index_to_coords(board_stack[0].move_to[0], row2, col2,
                levelX2);
            char buf2[128];
            sprintf(buf2,"Computer move: %d%s%d -> %d%s%d",
                    levelX1+1,column_name[col1],
                        row1+1, levelX2+1, column_name[col2], row2+1);
            current_window->put_scrolling_text(buf2);
#endif
#ifdef TEXT_MODE
            int levelX, row, col;
                index_to_coords(board_stack[0].move_from[0], row, col,
levelX);
            cerr << "\nMOVE:   (" << (levelX+1) << column_name[col] <<
                (row + 1) << " -> ";
            index_to_coords(board_stack[0].move_to[0], row, col, levelX);
            cerr << (levelX+1) << column_name[col] << (row + 1) << ")"
                << ", value= " << board_stack[level].move_value[i]
                << "\n";
#endif
        }
    }
}


#ifdef TEXT_MODE
void main()
{
    game b(1,4);

    // For a test, let the computer generate moves for both sides:
    for (int loop=0; loop<70; loop++) {
        if (b.make_best_move(0, 1) == 0)  break;
        b.board_stack[0].print_board();
        if (b.make_best_move(0,-1) == 0)  break;
        b.board_stack[0].print_board();
```

```
        }
}
                                    ////////////////
                                    //            //
#else                                        // GUI mode: //
                                    //            //
                                    ////////////////

static char my_text[100];
static char blowup_level_name[50];
static game g(1,3);
static int *b; // utility pointer directly to lookahead level 0 game
board

const int row_spacing = 16;
const int col_spacing = 16;
const int level_spacing = 138;

// See Figure 15.3:

static int x_pawn_template[] = { 4,  4,  6,  6, 5, 5, 6, 9, 10, 10,
                                 9,  9, 11, 11};
static int y_pawn_template[] = {15, 13, 13, 10, 9, 8, 7, 7,  8,  9,
                                10, 13, 13, 15};

static int x_knight_template[] = { 3,  3,  6,  6, 5, 4, 4, 5, 5, 6, 6, 7,
                                   10, 11, 12, 12, 11, 10,  9,  9, 11, 12,
                                   12};
static int y_knight_template[] = {15, 13, 13, 11, 9, 8, 7, 6, 6, 6, 4, 6,
                                    7,  7,  8, 9, 10, 10, 11, 12, 13, 13,
                                   15};

static int x_bishop_template[] = { 3,  3,  6, 7, 5, 7, 8, 10, 8,  9,
                                   12, 12};
static int y_bishop_template[] = {15, 13, 12, 6, 4, 3, 3,  4, 6, 12,
                                   13, 15};

static int x_rook_template[] = { 3,  3,  5, 5, 4, 4, 5, 6, 9, 10, 11,
                                 11, 10, 10, 12, 12};
static int y_rook_template[] = {15, 12, 12, 7, 7, 3, 3, 6, 6,  3,  3,
                                 7,  7, 12, 12, 15};

static int x_queen_template[] = { 2,  2,  6,  3, 7, 6, 4, 3, 6, 9, 12,
                                  11,  9,  8, 12,  9, 13, 13};
static int y_queen_template[] = {15, 12, 11, 10, 9, 7, 6, 3, 2, 2,  3,
                                  6,  7,  9, 10, 11, 12, 15};

static int x_king_template[] = { 2,  2,  7,  6, 5, 6, 7, 7, 5, 5, 7, 7,
                                 8,  8, 10, 10, 8, 8, 9, 10, 9,  8, 13, 13};
static int y_king_template[] = {15, 12, 12, 7, 6, 4, 4, 2, 2, 1, 1, 0,
                                 0,  1,  1, 2, 2, 4, 4,  6, 7, 12, 12, 15};

static int *x_templates[] = {x_pawn_template, x_knight_template,
                             x_bishop_template, x_rook_template,
                             x_queen_template, x_king_template};

static int *y_templates[] = {y_pawn_template, y_knight_template,
                             y_bishop_template, y_rook_template,
```

```
                              y_queen_template, y_king_template};

static int num_templates[] = {14, 23, 12, 16, 18, 24};

static int blowup_level = 0;
static int hilight_square_list[2];
static int num_hilight_squares = 0;

static int redraw_small_boards = 1;
static int redraw_large_board = 1;
void TAppWindow::update_display()
{
    // Plot the 3 "mini-board" displays in the left third of the window:
    if (redraw_small_boards != 0)
        for (int level=2; level>=0;  level--) {
            for (int col=7; col>=0; col--) {
                for (int row=7; row>=0; row--) {
                    int index = get_index(row, col, level);
                    int x = 5 + col_spacing * col;
                    int y = 8 + level_spacing * (2 - level) +
                      row_spacing * (7 - row);
                    plot_line(x, y, x + col_spacing, y);
                    plot_line(x + col_spacing, y, x + col_spacing,
                            y + row_spacing);
                    plot_line(x + col_spacing, y + row_spacing,
                            x, y + row_spacing);
                    plot_line(x, y + row_spacing, x, y);
                    // Check for hilighted squares:
                    for (int k=0; k<num_hilight_squares; k++)
                        if (hilight_square_list[k] == index) {
                            plot_line(x+1, y+1, x + col_spacing-1, y+1);
                            plot_line(x + col_spacing-1, y+1,
                                    x + col_spacing-1, y + row_spacing-1);
                            plot_line(x + col_spacing-1,
                                    y + row_spacing-1, x+1,
                                    y + row_spacing-1);
                            plot_line(x+1, y + row_spacing-1, x+1, y+1);
                        }
                    // Shade the dark squares:
                    int rr = row % 2;
                    int cc = col % 2;
                    if ((rr == 0 && cc == 0) || (rr == 1 && cc == 1)) {
                        plot_line(x+2, y+4, x+4, y+2);
                        plot_line(x+(row_spacing - 4), y+col_spacing-2,
                                x+row_spacing-2, y+(col_spacing-4));
                        if (b[index] == 0) {
                            plot_line(x + 2, y+col_spacing-2,
                                    x + row_spacing-2, y+2);
                            plot_line(x + 2, y+7, x+7, y+2);
                            plot_line(x+(row_spacing - 7), y+col_spacing-
                                2,
                                    x+row_spacing-2, y+(col_spacing-7));
                            plot_line(x + 2, y+10, x+10, y+2);
                            plot_line(x + (row_spacing - 10),
                                    y + col_spacing-2, x+row_spacing-2,
                                    y + (col_spacing-10));
                        } else {
                            if (b[index] >= -4 && b[index] <= 4) {
                                plot_line(x + row_spacing-6, y+2+4,
                                    x + row_spacing-2, y+2);
```

```
                    plot_line(x+2, y+7, x+7, y+2);
                    if (b[index]==-1 || b[index]==1) {
                        plot_line(x+2, y+10, x+10, y+2);
                    }
            } else {
                plot_line(x+row_spacing-4, y+2+2,
                        x+row_spacing-2, y+2);
            }
        }
    }
    if (b[index] != 0 && b[index] != 7) {
        int ptype = b[index];
      if (ptype < 0)   ptype = -ptype;
        ptype -= 1;
        if (ptype >= 0 && ptype < 7) {
            int num = num_templates[ptype];
            for (int i=0; i< (num-1); i++)
                plot_line(x + x_templates[ptype][i],
                    y + y_templates[ptype][i],
                        x + x_templates[ptype][i+1],
                    y + y_templates[ptype][i+1]);
        }
        if (b[index] == -1 * player_side) {
            plot_line(x+9, y+13, x+6, y+7);
            for (int m=5; m<11; m++)
                plot_line(x+m, y+row_spacing,
                        x+m, y+row_spacing-2);
        }
        if (b[index] == -2 * player_side) {
            plot_line(x+9, y+12, x+6, y+6);
            for (int m=4; m<12; m++)
                plot_line(x+m, y+row_spacing,
                        x+m, y+row_spacing-2);
        }
        if (b[index] == -3 * player_side) {
            plot_line(x+9, y+12, x+7, y+6);
            plot_line(x+8, y+6, x+7, y+3);
            for (int m=4; m<12; m++)
                plot_line(x+m, y+row_spacing, x+m,
                        y+row_spacing-2);
        }
        if (b[index] == BLACK*ROOK * player_side ||
         b[index] == BLACK*QUEEN * player_side ||
         b[index] == BLACK*KING * player_side)   {
            int m;
            if (b[index] == BLACK*ROOK * player_side)
                for (m=4; m<12; m++)
                    plot_line(x+m, y+row_spacing, x+m,
                        y+row_spacing-3);
              else
                for (m=3; m<13; m++)
                plot_line(x+m, y+row_spacing, x+m,
                    y+row_spacing-3);
        if (b[index] == BLACK*ROOK * player_side) {
            plot_line(x+7,y+12,x+6, y+7);
            plot_line(x+9,y+12,x+8, y+7);
            plot_line(x+5, y+6, x+10, y+6);
        }
        if (b[index] == BLACK*QUEEN * player_side) {
```

```
                            plot_line(x+7, y+6, x+5, y+4);
                            plot_line(x+9, y+6, x+7, y+4);
                    }
                    if (b[index] == BLACK*KING * player_side) {
                            plot_line(x+8, y+12, x+6, y+4);
                            plot_line(x+9, y+7, x+8, y+4);
                    }
                }
            }
        }
    }
}

// Plot the large board display:
if (redraw_large_board!= 0)
    for (int col=7; col>=0; col--) {
        for (int row=7; row>=0; row--) {
            int index = get_index(row, col, blowup_level);
            int x = 20 + col_spacing*2 *col + 9 * col_spacing;
            int y = 8 + row_spacing*2 * (7 - row);
            plot_line(x, y, x + col_spacing*2, y);
            plot_line(x + col_spacing*2, y, x + col_spacing*2,
                    y + row_spacing*2);
            plot_line(x + col_spacing*2, y + row_spacing*2,
                    x, y + row_spacing*2);
            plot_line(x, y + row_spacing*2, x, y);
            // Shade the dark squares:
            int rr = row % 2;
            int cc = col % 2;
            if ((rr == 0 && cc == 0) || (rr == 1 && cc == 1)) {
                plot_line(x+2, y+4, x+4, y+2);
                plot_line(x+(row_spacing*2 - 4), y+col_spacing*2-2,
                        x+row_spacing*2-2, y+(col_spacing*2-4));
                if (b[index] == 0) {
                    plot_line(x+2, y+col_spacing*2-2,
                            x+row_spacing*2-2, y+2);
                    plot_line(x+2, y+7, x+7, y+2);
                    plot_line(x+(row_spacing*2 - 7),
                            y+col_spacing*2-2, x+row_spacing*2-2,
                            y+(col_spacing*2-7));
                    plot_line(x+2, y+10, x+10, y+2);
                    plot_line(x+(row_spacing*2 - 10),
                            y+col_spacing*2-2, x+row_spacing*2-2,
                            y+(col_spacing*2-10));
                    plot_line(x+2, y+13, x+13, y+2);
                    plot_line(x+(row_spacing*2 - 13),
                            y+col_spacing*2-2, x+row_spacing*2-2,
                            y+(col_spacing*2-13));
                    plot_line(x+2, y+17, x+17, y+2);
                    plot_line(x+(row_spacing*2 - 17),
                            y+col_spacing*2-2, x+row_spacing*2-2,
                            y+(col_spacing*2-17));
                    plot_line(x+2, y+21, x+21, y+2);
                    plot_line(x+(row_spacing*2 - 21),
                            y+col_spacing*2-2, x+row_spacing*2-2,
                            y+(col_spacing*2-21));
                    plot_line(x+2, y+25, x+25, y+2);
                    plot_line(x+(row_spacing*2 - 25),
                            y+col_spacing*2-2, x+row_spacing*2-2,
```

```
                            y+(col_spacing*2-25)));
            } else {
                plot_line(x+(row_spacing*2 - 2)-8, y+2+4,
                        x+(row_spacing*2 - 2)-4, y+2);
                plot_line(x+(row_spacing*2 - 2) -4,  y+2+8,
                        x+(row_spacing*2 - 2), y+2+4);
              if (b[index] >= -4 && b[index] <= 4) {
                  plot_line(x+row_spacing*2-2-8, y+2+8,
                          x+row_spacing*2-2, y+2);
                  plot_line(x+2, y+7, x+7, y+2);
                  plot_line(x+2, y+10, x+10, y+2);
              } else {
                  plot_line(x+row_spacing*2-2-6, y+2+6,
                          x+row_spacing*2-2, y+2);
              }
            }
        }
        if (b[index] != 0 && b[index] != 7) {
            int ptype = b[index];
          if (ptype < 0)  ptype = -ptype;
            ptype -= 1;
            if (ptype >= 0 && ptype < 7) {
                int num = num_templates[ptype];
                for (int i=0; i< (num-1); i++)
                    plot_line(x+x_templates[ptype][i]*2,
                            y+y_templates[ptype][i]*2+1,
                                x+x_templates[ptype][i+1]*2,
                                y+y_templates[ptype][i+1]*2+1);
            }
            if (b[index] == -1 * player_side) {
                plot_line(x+18, y+26, x+12, y+14);
                for (int m=5; m<11; m++)
                    plot_line(x+m*2, y+row_spacing*2-1,
                            x+m*2, y+row_spacing*2-4);
            }
            if (b[index] == -2 * player_side) {
                plot_line(x+18, y+24, x+12, y+12);
                for (int m=4; m<12; m++)
                    plot_line(x+m*2, y+row_spacing*2-1,
                            x+m*2, y+row_spacing*2-4);
            }
            if (b[index] == -3 * player_side) {
                plot_line(x+18, y+24, x+14, y+12);
                plot_line(x+16, y+12, x+14, y+6);
                for (int m=4; m<12; m++)
                    plot_line(x+m*2, y+row_spacing*2-1,
                            x+m*2, y+row_spacing*2-4);
            }
            if (b[index] == BLACK*ROOK * player_side ||
              b[index] == BLACK*QUEEN * player_side ||
              b[index] == BLACK*KING  * player_side)     {
                int m;
                if (b[index] == BLACK*ROOK * player_side)
                    for (m=4; m<12; m++)
                        plot_line(x+m*2, y+row_spacing*2-1,
                                x+m*2, y+row_spacing*2-6);
                else
                    for (m=3; m<13; m++)
                        plot_line(x+m*2, y+row_spacing*2-1,
```

```
                                      x+m*2, y+row_spacing*2-6);
                    if (b[index] == BLACK*ROOK * player_side) {
                        plot_line(x+14,y+24,x+12, y+14);
                        plot_line(x+18,y+24,x+16, y+14);
                        plot_line(x+10, y+12, x+20, y+12);
                    }
                    if (b[index] == BLACK*QUEEN * player_side) {
                        plot_line(x+14, y+12, x+10, y+8);
                        plot_line(x+18, y+12, x+14, y+8);
                    }
                    if (b[index] == BLACK*KING * player_side) {
                        plot_line(x+16, y+24, x+12, y+8);
                        plot_line(x+18, y+14, x+16, y+8);
                    }
                }
            }
        }
    }

    sprintf(blowup_level_name,"Large board display is level %d",
            blowup_level+1);
    plot_string(10 * row_spacing + 6, 2* level_spacing +2,
                blowup_level_name);
    plot_string(10, 3 * level_spacing + 12, my_text);
}

static int do_computer_move = 0;

void TAppWindow::mouse_up(int x, int y)
{
    int level = 2 - (y - 8)/level_spacing;
    int row = 7 - ((y - ((2 - level) * level_spacing) - 8) /
row_spacing);
int col = (x - 5) / col_spacing;
if (level>=0 && level<3 && row>=0 && row<8 && col>=0 && col < 8) {
    // Legal square selected on one of the three "mini-boards":
    int index = get_index(row, col, level);
    if (num_hilight_squares<2) {
        hilight_square_list[num_hilight_squares++] = index;
        if (num_hilight_squares == 1) {
            redraw_large_board = 0;
            update_display();
            redraw_large_board = 1;
        }
        if (num_hilight_squares == 2) {
            // Human selected a move. First check for a castle:
            if (hilight_square_list[0] == 26 &&
                hilight_square_list[1] == 28) {
                if (b[26] == WHITE*KING &&
                    b[29] == WHITE*ROOK &&
                    b[27] == 0 &&
                    b[28] == 0) {
                        // castle king side:
                        b[26] = b[29] = 0;
                        b[27] = WHITE*ROOK;
                        b[28] = WHITE*KING;
                } else {
                    Warning("Illegal King side castle attempted");
                    num_hilight_squares = 0;
```

```
                            return;
                        }
                } else if (hilight_square_list[0] == 26 &&
                        hilight_square_list[1] == 24) {
                        if (b[26] == WHITE*KING &&
                            b[22] == WHITE*ROOK &&
                            b[23] == 0 &&
                            b[24] == 0 &&
                            b[25] == 0) {
                                // castle queen side:
                                b[26] = b[22] = 0;
                                b[24] = WHITE*ROOK;
                                b[25] = WHITE*KING;
                        } else {
                            Warning("Illegal Queen side castle attempted");
                            num_hilight_squares = 0;
                            return;
                        }
                } else {
                    b[hilight_square_list[1]] = b[hilight_square_list[0]];
                    b[hilight_square_list[0]] = 0;
                }
                num_hilight_squares = 0;
                sprintf(my_text,"CALCULATING...");
                erase_rect(1, 9*col_spacing, 600, 1);
                erase_rect(1, 600, 2* level_spacing +6, 10*col_spacing);
                sprintf(my_text,"CALCULATING...");
                erase_rect(1, 9*col_spacing, 600, 1);
                erase_rect(1, 2* level_spacing -2, 30*col_spacing,
                            2* level_spacing -2);
            clear_display();
            update_display();
            // Set flag so method idle_proc() will calculate
            // the computer's move:
                do_computer_move = 1;
            }
        }
    } else { // click outside mini-boards:
        if (level>=0 && level<3) {
            // switch board levels for large display:
            blowup_level = level;
            // erase_rect(1, 9*col_spacing, 600, 1);
            erase_rect(1, 600, 2* level_spacing +6, 10*col_spacing);
            redraw_small_boards = 0;
            update_display();
            redraw_small_boards = 1;
        }
    }
}

void TAppWindow::mouse_down(int, int)
{
}

void TAppWindow::mouse_move(int, int)
{
}

void TAppWindow::idle_proc()
```

```
{
    if (do_computer_move != 0) {
        do_computer_move = 0;
        g.make_best_move(0,-1);
        sprintf(my_text,"Player's turn");
        clear_display();
        update_display();
    }
}

void TAppWindow::do_menu_action(int item_number)
{
    if (item_number == 1) {
        player_side = 1;
        g.board_stack[0].set_pieces();
        for (int m=0; m<14; m++)  put_scrolling_text("  ");
        sprintf(my_text,"  ");
        clear_display();
        update_display();
    }
    if (item_number == 2) {
        // swap sides and let the computer play white:
        player_side = -1;
        sprintf(my_text,"CALCULATING...");
        g.board_stack[0].set_pieces();
        for (int m=0; m<14; m++)  put_scrolling_text("  ");
        do_computer_move = 1;
        clear_display();
        update_display();
    }
    if (item_number == 3) {
        char buf[128];
        choose_file_to_write("Choose an output game file:", buf);
        filebuf out_file;
        if (out_file.open(buf, output)!=0) {
            ostream out_stream(&out_file);
            out_stream << player_side << "\n";
            for (int m=0; m<360; m++) out_stream << b[m] << "\n";
            out_file.close();
        } else show_info("Could not open file for writing!");
    }
    if (item_number == 4) {
        char buf[128];
        choose_file_to_read("Choose a game file:", "ch", buf);
        filebuf in_file;
        if (in_file.open(buf, input)!=0) {
            istream in_stream(&in_file);
            in_stream >> player_side;
            for (int m=0; m<360; m++) in_stream >> b[m];
            in_file.close();
            clear_display();
            update_display();
        } else show_info("Could not open file for reading!");

    }
    if (item_number == 5)  {
        exit(0);
    }
}
```

```
INIT_PROGRAM

    // anything can go here:
    my_text[0] = '\0';
    blowup_level_name[0] = '\0';
    b = (int *)&(g.board_stack[0].brd);
    current_window->init_scrolling_text(2* level_spacing +11,
                                        27 * row_spacing - 10,
                                        2* level_spacing +150,
                                 10 * row_spacing + 4);

    RUN_PROGRAM;
}
#endif
```

A

Generic GUI Class Reference

The application class is not "visible" to the application programmer using the C++ GUI library. The constructor for the application class is hidden inside a C macro (INIT_PROGRAM) which is defined in the file applib.h.

The following table shows the TAppWindow class methods that are used in application programs:

Method	Use
void update_display()	Draws in the document window
void mouse_down(int x, int y)	Called with mouse-down coordinates
void mouse_up(int x, int y)	Called with mouse-up coordinates
void mouse_move(int x, int y)	Called with mouse-move coordinates
void do_menu_action(int menu_item_number)	Executes menu actions
void plot_line(int x1, int y1, int x2, int y2)	Plots a line
void plot_string(int x, int y, char *str)	Plots a string
void plot_rect(int top, int right, int bottom, int left)	Plots a rectangle

void init_scrolling_text(int top,
        int right,
        int bottom,
        int left)
	Initializes a scrolling text field of a specified size

void init_scrolling_text()	Initializes a scrolling text field that fills the default document window

Method	Use
void put_scrolling_text(char *buf)	Inserts a line of text into a scrolling text field
int string_height(char *str)	Returns an int value in pixels of a string height
int string_width(char *str)	Returns an int value in pixels of a string width
void do_edit(char *prompt, char *buf)	Modal dialog box utility for editing the character string buf
void show_info(char *info_buf)	Modal dialog box utility to display a character string
int choose_one(char *prompt1, char *prompt2)	Modal dialog box utility to display two choices; returns int value 1 or 2
int choose_one_from_list(char *prompt, char **list_items, int num_items)	Modal dialog box utility to display a selection list; returns index of item selected (or -1 for Cancel)
void idle_proc()	Called for background processing

Microsoft Windows Class Implementation

B.1 Windows Resource Files

Chess resource file: chess.rc

```
#include "..\include\windows.h"

whello ICON test.ico

MyMenu MENU PRELOAD
    BEGIN
        POPUP "&3D Chess"
            BEGIN
                MENUITEM "&New game (play white)", 1
                MENUITEM "&New game (play black)", 2
                MENUITEM "&Save current game position", 3
                MENUITEM "&Reload old game position", 4
                MENUITEM "&Exit...", 5
            END
    END

AboutBox DIALOG 55, 51, 178, 92
STYLE WS_POPUP | WS_DLGFRAME
CAPTION " "
BEGIN
  CONTROL "Default About message goes here..." 101, "STATIC", WS_CHILD |
WS_VISIBLE | WS_BORDER | WS_TABSTOP | 0x1L, 11, 8, 162, 42
    CONTROL "OK" 1002, "BUTTON", WS_CHILD | WS_VISIBLE | WS_TABSTOP, 55,
61, 76, 21
END

EditBox DIALOG 55, 51, 178, 92
STYLE WS_POPUP | WS_DLGFRAME
CAPTION " "
BEGIN
```

```
   EDITTEXT  102,    11, 8, 162, 42,  ES_AUTOVSCROLL
   CONTROL "OK" 1002, "BUTTON", WS_CHILD | WS_VISIBLE | WS_TABSTOP, 55,
61, 76, 21
END

ListBox DIALOG 18, 39, 186, 115
STYLE WS_POPUP | WS_DLGFRAME
CAPTION " "
BEGIN
   CTEXT "The Title" 100,    5, 3, 173, 12
   CONTROL "LISTBOX" 102, "LISTBOX", WS_CHILD | WS_VISIBLE | WS_BORDER |
WS_VSCROLL | 0x3L, 5, 17, 173, 80
   CONTROL "Cancel" 103, "BUTTON", WS_CHILD | WS_VISIBLE | WS_TABSTOP,
124, 100, 54, 12
END
FileInBox DIALOG 55, 51, 178, 220
STYLE WS_POPUP | WS_DLGFRAME
CAPTION " "
BEGIN
   EDITTEXT  102,    11, 8, 102, 12, ES_MULTILINE
   EDITTEXT  103,    11, 24, 102, 12, ES_MULTILINE
    LISTBOX     104,    11, 58, 140, 125, (LBS_NOTIFY | WS_VSCROLL |
WS_BORDER)
   LTEXT "lll",105,    11, 40, 100, 12
   CONTROL "OK" 1002, "BUTTON", WS_CHILD | WS_VISIBLE | WS_TABSTOP, 55,
190, 76, 21
END

FileOutBox DIALOG 55, 51, 178, 220
STYLE WS_POPUP | WS_DLGFRAME
CAPTION " "
BEGIN
   EDITTEXT  102,    11, 8, 102, 12, ES_MULTILINE
   EDITTEXT  103,    11, 24, 102, 12, ES_MULTILINE
    LISTBOX     104,    11, 58, 140, 125, (LBS_NOTIFY | WS_VSCROLL |
WS_BORDER)
   LTEXT "lll",105,    11, 40, 100, 12
   CONTROL "OK" 1002, "BUTTON", WS_CHILD | WS_VISIBLE | WS_TABSTOP, 55,
190, 76, 21
END
```

Drawing program resource file: draw.rc

```
#include "windows.h"

whello ICON test.ico

MyMenu MENU PRELOAD
    BEGIN
        POPUP "&Draw"
            BEGIN
                MENUITEM "&Clear screen", 1
                MENUITEM "&Save drawing", 2
                MENUITEM "&Reload drawing", 3
            END
    END

AboutBox DIALOG 55, 51, 178, 92
STYLE WS_POPUP | WS_DLGFRAME
```

```
CAPTION " "
BEGIN
  CONTROL "Default About message goes here..." 101, "STATIC", WS_CHILD |
WS_VISIBLE | WS_BORDER | WS_TABSTOP | 0x1L, 11, 8, 162, 42
  CONTROL "OK" 1002, "BUTTON", WS_CHILD | WS_VISIBLE | WS_TABSTOP, 55,
61, 76, 21
END

EditBox DIALOG 55, 51, 178, 92
STYLE WS_POPUP | WS_DLGFRAME
CAPTION " "
BEGIN
  EDITTEXT 102,    11, 8, 162, 42,  ES_AUTOVSCROLL
  CONTROL "OK" 1002, "BUTTON", WS_CHILD | WS_VISIBLE | WS_TABSTOP, 55,
61, 76, 21
END

ListBox DIALOG 18, 39, 186, 115
STYLE WS_POPUP | WS_DLGFRAME
CAPTION " "
BEGIN
  CTEXT "The Title" 100,    5, 3, 173, 12
  CONTROL "LISTBOX" 102, "LISTBOX", WS_CHILD | WS_VISIBLE | WS_BORDER |
WS_VSCROLL | 0x3L, 5, 17, 173, 80
  CONTROL "Cancel" 103, "BUTTON", WS_CHILD | WS_VISIBLE | WS_TABSTOP,
124, 100, 54, 12
END

FileInBox DIALOG 55, 51, 178, 220
STYLE WS_POPUP | WS_DLGFRAME
CAPTION " "
BEGIN
  EDITTEXT  102,    11, 8, 102, 12, ES_MULTILINE
  EDITTEXT  103,    11, 24, 102, 12, ES_MULTILINE
  LISTBOX       104,    11, 58, 140, 125, (LBS_NOTIFY | WS_VSCROLL |
WS_BORDER)
  LTEXT  "111",105,    11, 40, 100, 12
  CONTROL "OK" 1002, "BUTTON", WS_CHILD | WS_VISIBLE | WS_TABSTOP, 55,
190, 76, 21
END

FileOutBox DIALOG 55, 51, 178, 220
STYLE WS_POPUP | WS_DLGFRAME
CAPTION " "
BEGIN
  EDITTEXT  102,    11, 8, 102, 12, ES_MULTILINE
  EDITTEXT  103,    11, 24, 102, 12, ES_MULTILINE
  LISTBOX       104,    11, 58, 140, 125, (LBS_NOTIFY | WS_VSCROLL |
WS_BORDER)
  LTEXT  "111",105,    11, 40, 100, 12
  CONTROL "OK" 1002, "BUTTON", WS_CHILD | WS_VISIBLE | WS_TABSTOP, 55,
190, 76, 21
END
```

Handwriting recognition program resource file: hand.rc

```
#include "windows.h"

whello ICON test.ico
```

```
MyMenu MENU PRELOAD
    BEGIN
        POPUP "&NeuralNet"
            BEGIN
                MENUITEM "&Collect training cases", 1
                MENUITEM "&Train and write weights to disk", 2
                MENUITEM "&Reload weights from disk", 3
                MENUITEM "&Test", 4
            END
    END

AboutBox DIALOG 55, 51, 178, 92
STYLE WS_POPUP | WS_DLGFRAME
CAPTION " "
BEGIN
  CONTROL "Default About message goes here..." 101, "STATIC", WS_CHILD |
WS_VISIBLE | WS_BORDER | WS_TABSTOP | 0x1L, 11, 8, 162, 42
  CONTROL "OK" 1002, "BUTTON", WS_CHILD | WS_VISIBLE | WS_TABSTOP, 55,
61, 76, 21
END

EditBox DIALOG 55, 51, 178, 92
STYLE WS_POPUP | WS_DLGFRAME
CAPTION " "
BEGIN
  EDITTEXT 102,   11, 8, 162, 42, ES_AUTOVSCROLL
  CONTROL "OK" 1002, "BUTTON", WS_CHILD | WS_VISIBLE | WS_TABSTOP, 55,
61, 76, 21
END

ListBox DIALOG 18, 39, 186, 115
STYLE WS_POPUP | WS_DLGFRAME
CAPTION " "
BEGIN
  CTEXT "The Title" 100,   5, 3, 173, 12
  CONTROL "LISTBOX" 102, "LISTBOX", WS_CHILD | WS_VISIBLE | WS_BORDER |
WS_VSCROLL | 0x3L, 5, 17, 173, 80
  CONTROL "Cancel" 103, "BUTTON", WS_CHILD | WS_VISIBLE | WS_TABSTOP,
124, 100, 54, 12
END

FileInBox DIALOG 55, 51, 178, 220
STYLE WS_POPUP | WS_DLGFRAME
CAPTION " "
BEGIN
  EDITTEXT 102,   11, 8, 102, 12, ES_MULTILINE
  EDITTEXT 103,   11, 24, 102, 12, ES_MULTILINE
  LISTBOX    104,   11, 58, 140, 125, (LBS_NOTIFY | WS_VSCROLL |
WS_BORDER)
  LTEXT "111",105,   11, 40, 100, 12
  CONTROL "OK" 1002, "BUTTON", WS_CHILD | WS_VISIBLE | WS_TABSTOP, 55,
190, 76, 21
END

FileOutBox DIALOG 55, 51, 178, 220
STYLE WS_POPUP | WS_DLGFRAME
CAPTION " "
BEGIN
  EDITTEXT 102,   11, 8, 102, 12, ES_MULTILINE
```

```
    EDITTEXT  103,   11, 24, 102, 12, ES_MULTILINE
    LISTBOX      104,     11, 58, 140, 125, (LBS_NOTIFY | WS_VSCROLL |
WS_BORDER)
    LTEXT  "lll",105,   11, 40, 100, 12
    CONTROL "OK" 1002, "BUTTON", WS_CHILD | WS_VISIBLE | WS_TABSTOP, 55,
190, 76, 21
END
```

GUI test program resource file: test.rc

```
#include "..\include\windows.h"

whello ICON test.ico

MyMenu MENU PRELOAD
    BEGIN
        POPUP "&TestMenu"
            BEGIN
                MENUITEM "&Test Grapher Class", 1
                MENUITEM "&Get a text string", 2
                MENUITEM "&About this program", 3
                MENUITEM "&Single list box test", 4
                  MENUITEM "&Choose one of 2 choices", 5
                MENUITEM "&Test scrolling text", 6
                  MENUITEM "&Test plot utilities", 7
            END
    END

AboutBox DIALOG 55, 51, 178, 92
STYLE WS_POPUP | WS_DLGFRAME
CAPTION " "
BEGIN
  CONTROL "Default About message goes here..." 101, "STATIC", WS_CHILD |
WS_VISIBLE | WS_BORDER | WS_TABSTOP | 0x1L, 11, 8, 162, 42
  CONTROL "OK" 1002, "BUTTON", WS_CHILD | WS_VISIBLE | WS_TABSTOP, 55,
61, 76, 21
END

EditBox DIALOG 55, 51, 178, 92
STYLE WS_POPUP | WS_DLGFRAME
CAPTION " "
BEGIN
  EDITTEXT  102,   11, 8, 162, 42, ES_MULTILINE
  CONTROL "OK" 1002, "BUTTON", WS_CHILD | WS_VISIBLE | WS_TABSTOP, 55,
61, 76, 21
END

FileInBox DIALOG 55, 51, 178, 220
STYLE WS_POPUP | WS_DLGFRAME
CAPTION " "
BEGIN
  EDITTEXT  102,   11, 8, 102, 12, ES_MULTILINE
  EDITTEXT  103,   11, 24, 102, 12, ES_MULTILINE
  LISTBOX      104,     11, 58, 140, 125, (LBS_NOTIFY | WS_VSCROLL |
WS_BORDER)
  LTEXT  "lll",105,   11, 40, 100, 12
  CONTROL "OK" 1002, "BUTTON", WS_CHILD | WS_VISIBLE | WS_TABSTOP, 55,
190, 76, 21
END
```

```
FileOutBox DIALOG 55, 51, 178, 220
STYLE WS_POPUP | WS_DLGFRAME
CAPTION " "
BEGIN
   EDITTEXT   102,    11, 8, 102, 12, ES_MULTILINE
   EDITTEXT   103,    11, 24, 102, 12, ES_MULTILINE
   LISTBOX      104,      11, 58, 140, 125, (LBS_NOTIFY | WS_VSCROLL |
WS_BORDER)
   LTEXT  "111",105,    11, 40, 100, 12
   CONTROL "OK" 1002, "BUTTON", WS_CHILD | WS_VISIBLE | WS_TABSTOP, 55,
190, 76, 21
END


ListBox DIALOG 18, 39, 186, 165
STYLE WS_POPUP | WS_DLGFRAME
CAPTION " "
BEGIN
   LTEXT "The Title" 100,    5, 3, 173, 12
   LISTBOX      104,      11, 20, 140, 125, (LBS_NOTIFY | WS_VSCROLL |
WS_BORDER)
   CONTROL "Cancel" 103, "BUTTON", WS_CHILD | WS_VISIBLE | WS_TABSTOP,
124, 150, 54, 12
END


MListBox DIALOG 10, 35, 259, 151
STYLE WS_POPUP | WS_DLGFRAME
CAPTION " "
BEGIN
   CTEXT "A Title" 100,    2, 3, 255, 14
   CONTROL "LISTBOX" 102, "LISTBOX", WS_CHILD | WS_VISIBLE | WS_BORDER |
WS_VSCROLL | 0x3L, 2, 19, 131, 112
   CONTROL "LISTBOX" 103, "LISTBOX", WS_CHILD | WS_VISIBLE | WS_BORDER |
WS_VSCROLL | 0x3L, 135, 19, 122, 116
   CONTROL "Done" 104, "BUTTON", WS_CHILD | WS_VISIBLE | WS_TABSTOP, 188,
135, 63, 13
END
```

Text browser program resource file: textbr.rc

```
#include "..\include\windows.h"

whello ICON test.ico

MyMenu MENU PRELOAD
    BEGIN
        POPUP "&FreeTextBrowser"
            BEGIN
                MENUITEM "&Load index", 1
                MENUITEM "&Add text file to current index", 2
                MENUITEM "&Save current index", 3
                MENUITEM "&Word search...", 4
            END
    END


AboutBox DIALOG 55, 51, 178, 92
STYLE WS_POPUP | WS_DLGFRAME
CAPTION " "
BEGIN
   CONTROL "Default About message goes here..." 101, "STATIC", WS_CHILD |
```

```
    WS_VISIBLE | WS_BORDER | WS_TABSTOP | 0x1L, 11, 8, 162, 42
      CONTROL "OK" 1002, "BUTTON", WS_CHILD | WS_VISIBLE | WS_TABSTOP, 55,
    61, 76, 21
    END


    EditBox DIALOG 55, 51, 178, 92
    STYLE WS_POPUP | WS_DLGFRAME
    CAPTION " "
    BEGIN
      EDITTEXT 102,  11, 8, 162, 42, ES_MULTILINE
      CONTROL "OK" 1002, "BUTTON", WS_CHILD | WS_VISIBLE | WS_TABSTOP, 55,
    61, 76, 21
    END

    FileInBox DIALOG 55, 51, 178, 220
    STYLE WS_POPUP | WS_DLGFRAME
    CAPTION " "
    BEGIN
      EDITTEXT 102,   11, 8, 102, 12, ES_MULTILINE
      EDITTEXT 103,   11, 24, 102, 12, ES_MULTILINE
      LISTBOX     104,    11, 58, 140, 125, (LBS_NOTIFY | WS_VSCROLL |
    WS_BORDER)
      LTEXT "lll",105,   11, 40, 100, 12
      CONTROL "OK" 1002, "BUTTON", WS_CHILD | WS_VISIBLE | WS_TABSTOP, 55,
    190, 76, 21
    END

    FileOutBox DIALOG 55, 51, 178, 220
    STYLE WS_POPUP | WS_DLGFRAME
    CAPTION " "
    BEGIN
      EDITTEXT 102,   11, 8, 102, 12, ES_MULTILINE
      EDITTEXT 103,   11, 24, 102, 12, ES_MULTILINE
      LISTBOX     104,    11, 58, 140, 125, (LBS_NOTIFY | WS_VSCROLL |
    WS_BORDER)
      LTEXT "lll",105,   11, 40, 100, 12
      CONTROL "OK" 1002, "BUTTON", WS_CHILD | WS_VISIBLE | WS_TABSTOP, 55,
    190, 76, 21
    END


    ListBox DIALOG 18, 39, 186, 165
    STYLE WS_POPUP | WS_DLGFRAME
    CAPTION " "
    BEGIN
      LTEXT "The Title" 100,   5, 3, 173, 12
      LISTBOX     104,    11, 20, 140, 125, (LBS_NOTIFY | WS_VSCROLL |
    WS_BORDER)
      CONTROL "Cancel" 103, "BUTTON", WS_CHILD | WS_VISIBLE | WS_TABSTOP,
    124, 150, 54, 12
    END
```

B.2 Windows-Specific GUI Include Files

File applib.h

```
// File: applib.h
//
// Description: Header file for the Microsoft Windows class library.
//              Derived from the Borland C++ example programs.  Library
```

```
//                    setup to use small or medium memory models.
//
// Copyright 1992 by Mark Watson Associates
//
//          No binary rights reserved: this software library may be used in
//          compiled form without restrictions.  All source rights
//          reserved: Source code to the GUI library can not be distributed
//          (on bulletin boards, or as part of shareware or commercial
//          products)
//          without written permission.
//
//          This software is provided "as is". The user accepts all
//          responsibility for its use.
//

#ifndef __applib
#define __applib

#include <windows.h>

#include <stdlib.h>
#include <string.h>
#include <fstream.h>
#include <iostream.h>

#include "apptypes.h"

extern "C" { void sprintf(...); void exit(int); };

#define output (ios::out)
#define input (ios::in)

long FAR PASCAL _export WndProc( HWND hWnd, WORD iMessage,
                WORD wParam, LONG lParam );

class Application
{
public:
    // For Windows interface:
    static HANDLE instanceHandle;
    static HANDLE applicationRegisteredFlag;
    static int showWindowFlag;
    static int processEventMessages( void );
};

const int MAX_TEXT_LINES = 24;
const int MAX_TEXT_LINE_SIZE = 80;

class TAppWindow
{
protected:
    HWND hWnd;
private:
    static char windowName[20];
public:
    HBRUSH backgroundBrush;
    HBRUSH blackBrush;
    // Data for supporting scrolling text:
    short  top_text_clip,  right_text_clip,  bottom_text_clip,
left_text_clip;
```

```
    char *saved_text[MAX_TEXT_LINES]; // ring buffer for saved text
    int number_of_saved_lines;
    int current_ring_buffer_start;
    int in_scrolling_text_mode; // =1 for in text mode
    int redraw_both_text_and_graphics;

    static void registerWindow( void );
    TAppWindow( void );
    void plot_line(int x1, int y1, int x2, int y2);
    void plot_string(int x, int y, char *cp);
    void plot_rect(int top, int right, int bottom, int left);
    void erase_rect(int top, int right, int bottom, int left);
    int string_height(char *)
      {//  TEXTMETRIC text_info;
       //  GetTextMetrics(current_hDC, &text_info);
       //  return text_info.tmHeight * 96;   // FIX: 96 is for VGA only!!
          return 13;
      }
    int string_width(char *str)
      {//  TEXTMETRIC text_info;
       //   GetTextMetrics(current_hDC, &text_info);
       //   return text_info.tmAveCharWidth * 96;    // FIX: 96 is for
                                                    // VGA only!!
          return 9 * strlen(str);
      }

    void clear_display();
    HWND GetHandle( void ) { return hWnd; };
    BOOL Show( int showWindowFlag ) { return ShowWindow( hWnd,
showWindowFlag ); };
    void Update( void ) { UpdateWindow( hWnd ); };

    long WndProc( WORD iMessage, WORD wParam, LONG lParam );
    void Paint( void );
    // Maintain a valid HDC only during paint operations:
    HDC current_hDC;

    // user defined callback(s):
    void update_display();
    void mouse_down(int, int );
    void mouse_up(int, int );
    void mouse_move(int, int );
    void do_menu_action(int);

    // for the About box:
    void do_about();
    void do_edit(char *prompt, char *str);
    void show_info(char *str) { do_edit(" ", str); }
    int choose_one_from_list(char *prompt,
               char **list_items, int number_of_items);
    int choose_one(char *prompt1, char *prompt2);
    int choose_file_to_write(char *prompt, char *returned_filename);
    int choose_file_to_read(char *prompt, char *extension, char
*returned_filename);

    void init_scrolling_text(int top, int right, int bottom, int left);
    void init_scrolling_text();
    void put_scrolling_text(char *str);
    void reset_scrolling_text();
```

```
    void idle_proc();
};

extern TAppWindow *current_window;
void Warning(char *);

// Use the test shown in Borland C++ examples for getting and setting
// TAppWindow pointers for various memory models:

// For small and medium memory models:
inline TAppWindow *GetPointer( HWND hWnd )
{
    return (TAppWindow *) GetWindowWord( hWnd, 0 );
}
inline void SetPointer( HWND hWnd, TAppWindow *pWindow )
{
    SetWindowWord( hWnd, 0, (WORD) pWindow );
}

// #pragma argsused
// #pragma option -w-aus
#define INIT_PROGRAM \
int PASCAL WinMain( HANDLE instanceHandle, HANDLE appRegisteredFlag,
LPSTR lpszCmdLine,\
            int showWindowFlag )\
{\
    Application::instanceHandle = instanceHandle;\
    Application::applicationRegisteredFlag = appRegisteredFlag;\
    Application::showWindowFlag = showWindowFlag;\
    if (Application::applicationRegisteredFlag == 0) {\
        TAppWindow::registerWindow();\
    }\
    TAppWindow MainWnd;\
    current_window = &MainWnd;

#define RUN_PROGRAM \
    return Application::processEventMessages();

#endif __applib
```

File apptypes.h

```
// File: apptypes.h
//
// Description: Define macros for intrinsic data types. This is useful
//              for portability to machines with a segmented memory
//              architecture.
//
// Copyright 1992 by Mark Watson Associates
//
//       No binary rights reserved: this software library may be used in
//       compiled form without restrictions.  All source rights
//       reserved: Source code to the GUI library can not be distributed
//       (on bulletin boards, or as part of shareware or commercial
//       products)
//       without written permission.
//
//       This software is provided "as is". The user accepts all
//       responsibility for its use.
//
```

```
#define Char char  FAR
#define Int int   // this can be either 16 or 32 bits
#define Long long // this needs to be 32 bits
#define Short short // this needs to be 16 bits
#define Double double FAR
#define Float float FAR
```

B.3   Windows-Specific GUI C++ Source Files

File applib.cpp

```
// File: applib.cpp
//
// Description: Source code for the Microsoft Windows Class library.
//              This library was written using Borland C++.
//
// Copyright 1992 by Mark Watson Associates
//
//        No binary rights reserved: this software library may be used in
//        compiled form without restrictions.  All source rights
//        reserved: Source code to the GUI library can not be distributed
//        (on bulletin boards, or as part of shareware or commercial
//        products)
//        without written permission.
//
//        This software is provided "as is". The user accepts all
//        responsibility for its use.
//

#include "applib.h"
TAppWindow *current_window;

char TAppWindow::windowName[] = "  ";  // Specify a window title name
here

HANDLE Application::applicationRegisteredFlag = 0;
int Application::showWindowFlag = 0;


int Application::processEventMessages(void)
{
    MSG eventMessage;
    // Keep running until the user kills the program:
    while (GetMessage(&eventMessage, NULL, 0, 0 )) {
    TranslateMessage(&eventMessage);
    DispatchMessage(&eventMessage);
    }
    return eventMessage.wParam;
}

HANDLE Application::instanceHandle = 0;

void TAppWindow::registerWindow( void )
{
    WNDCLASS wndclass;    // Structure used to register Windows class.
    wndclass.style = CS_HREDRAW | CS_VREDRAW;
    wndclass.lpfnWndProc = ::WndProc; // PASCAL type window callback proc
    wndclass.cbClsExtra = 0;  // don't allocate extra bytes
    wndclass.cbWndExtra = sizeof(TAppWindow *);
    wndclass.hInstance  = Application::instanceHandle;
```

```
      wndclass.hIcon  = LoadIcon( Application::instanceHandle, "GUIlib" );
      wndclass.hCursor= LoadCursor( NULL, IDC_ARROW );
      wndclass.hbrBackground = GetStockObject( WHITE_BRUSH );
      wndclass.lpszMenuName = "MyMenu";
      wndclass.lpszClassName = windowName;

      if (RegisterClass(&wndclass) == 0) exit( FALSE ); // register failed
   }

static int i_timer = 0;
int PASCAL DefaultTimer(HWND /* hWnd */ , WORD /* iMessage */ ,
                     WORD /* wParam */ , LONG /* lParam */)
{
    // MessageBeep(1);
    current_window->idle_proc();
    return 0;
}

// Do not create unless previously registered.
TAppWindow::TAppWindow( void )
  {
    hWnd = CreateWindow(windowName, windowName, WS_OVERLAPPEDWINDOW,
                     CW_USEDEFAULT, 0, CW_USEDEFAULT, 0, NULL,
                     NULL, Application::instanceHandle,
                     (LPSTR) this ); // This pointer stored as data

    if (hWnd == 0)     exit( FALSE );    // Failed to create a window!!

    FARPROC lpfnDefaultTimer = MakeProcInstance((FARPROC)DefaultTimer,
                     Application::instanceHandle);

    // Set up a 300 millisecond timer:
    if (!(i_timer=SetTimer(NULL, 0, 300, lpfnDefaultTimer))) {
        MessageBox(hWnd,"No available timer.","applib",
                     MB_ICONEXCLAMATION | MB_OK);
        exit(0);
    }

    Show( Application::showWindowFlag );
    Update();
    in_scrolling_text_mode = 0;
    redraw_both_text_and_graphics = 0;
    bottom_text_clip = 0;
    backgroundBrush = GetStockObject( WHITE_BRUSH );
    blackBrush = GetStockObject( BLACK_BRUSH );
}

// User application utility functions (external to Windows):
void TAppWindow::plot_line(int x1, int y1, int x2, int y2)
{
    if (current_hDC != (HDC)NULL) {
        MoveTo(current_hDC, x1, y1);
        LineTo(current_hDC, x2, y2);
    }
}
void TAppWindow::plot_string(int x, int y, char *cp)
{
    if (current_hDC != (HDC)NULL) {
        TextOut(current_hDC, x, y - 12, cp, strlen(cp));
    }
```

```
}
void TAppWindow::plot_rect(int top, int right, int bottom, int left)
{
    plot_line(left, top, right, top);
    plot_line(right, top, right, bottom);
    plot_line(right, bottom, left, bottom);
    plot_line(left, bottom, left, top);
}
void TAppWindow::erase_rect(int top, int right, int bottom, int left)
{
    if (current_hDC != (HDC)NULL) {
        SelectObject(current_hDC, backgroundBrush);
        SelectObject(current_hDC, GetStockObject(NULL_PEN));
        Rectangle(current_hDC, left, top, right, bottom);
        SelectObject(current_hDC, GetStockObject(BLACK_PEN));
    }
}


void TAppWindow::clear_display()
{
    InvalidateRect(hWnd,NULL,TRUE); // force a redraw via user's update
                                    // method
}

void TAppWindow::Paint( void )
{
    PAINTSTRUCT ps;
    RECT rect;
    HDC hDC;
//  RECT invalRect;
//  (void)GetUpdateRect(hWnd, invalRect, FALSE);   // call before
//  BeginPaint!
    hDC = BeginPaint( hWnd, &ps );
    // Save this hDC for other member functions:
    current_hDC = hDC;
    if (in_scrolling_text_mode == 0 || redraw_both_text_and_graphics ==
1)
        update_display(); // User defined callback
    if (bottom_text_clip > 0 &&
        (in_scrolling_text_mode == 0 || redraw_both_text_and_graphics ==
1)) {
        RECT r;
        SetRect(&r, left_text_clip+1, top_text_clip+1,
                right_text_clip-1,bottom_text_clip-1);
        FillRect(current_hDC, &r, backgroundBrush);
        // Refresh any user scrolling text:
        int next = current_ring_buffer_start;
        for (int i=0; i<(number_of_saved_lines - 1); i++) {
          next++;
          if (next > (number_of_saved_lines - 1))  next = 0;
          put_scrolling_text(saved_text[next]);
        }
    }
    EndPaint( hWnd, &ps );
    current_hDC = (HDC)NULL;
}


// Default Dialog About box:
int PASCAL DefaultAboutBox(HWND hWnd, WORD iMessage, WORD wParam,
```

```
                    LONG /* lParam */)
{
    switch (iMessage) {
        case WM_INITDIALOG:
            return TRUE;
        case WM_COMMAND:
            if (wParam == 1002) {   // OK button hit
                EndDialog(hWnd, 0);
                return TRUE;
            } else {
                return FALSE;
            }
        default:
            return FALSE;
    }
}

// Default Dialog Edit box:

static char FAR cpEdit[256];
static char FAR cpPrompt[128];
static char FAR cpExtension[14];

int PASCAL DefaultEditBox(HWND hWnd, WORD iMessage, WORD wParam,
                LONG /* lParam */)
{
    switch (iMessage) {
        case WM_INITDIALOG:
            SetDlgItemText(hWnd, 102, cpEdit);
            return TRUE;
        case WM_COMMAND:
            if (wParam == 1002) {   // OK button hit
                for (int i=0; i<256; i++)
                    cpEdit[i] = '\0';
                GetDlgItemText(hWnd, 102, &(cpEdit[0]), 80);
                EndDialog(hWnd, 0);
                return TRUE;
            } else {
                return FALSE;
            }
        default:
            return FALSE;
    }
}


static char FAR szFileSpec[32];
static char FAR szFileName[100];
static WORD FAR wFileAttribute, wFileStatus;

int PASCAL DefaultFileInBox(HWND hWnd, WORD iMessage, WORD wParam,
                        LONG lParam)
{   char buf[256];
    switch (iMessage) {
        case WM_INITDIALOG:
            SetDlgItemText(hWnd, 102, cpPrompt);  // set up prompt
            szFileSpec[0] = '*'; szFileSpec[1] = '.';
            if (cpExtension[0] == '\0')  szFileSpec[2] = '*';
             else {
```

```
                    for (int i=0; cpExtension[i] != '\0'; i++) {
                        szFileSpec[i+2] = cpExtension[i];
                        szFileSpec[i+3] = '\0';
                    }
                }
            wFileAttribute = 0x4010;
            SendDlgItemMessage(hWnd, 103, EM_LIMITTEXT, 80, 0L);
            DlgDirList(hWnd, szFileSpec, 104, 105, wFileAttribute);
            SetDlgItemText(hWnd, 103, szFileName);
            return TRUE;
        case WM_COMMAND:
            if (wParam == 1002) {  // OK button hit
                for (int i=0; i<256; i++)
                    cpEdit[i] = '\0';
                GetDlgItemText(hWnd, 103, &(cpEdit[0]), 80);
                EndDialog(hWnd, 0);
                return TRUE;
            } else
            if (wParam == 104) {  // List box
                WORD option = HIWORD( lParam);
                if (option == LBN_DBLCLK) {
                    if (DlgDirSelect(hWnd, szFileName, 104)) {
                        _fstrcat(szFileName, szFileSpec);
                        DlgDirList(hWnd, szFileName, 104, 105,
wFileAttribute);
                        SetDlgItemText(hWnd, 103, szFileSpec);
                    } else {
                        SetDlgItemText(hWnd, 103, szFileName);
                        SendMessage(hWnd, WM_COMMAND, 1002, 0L);
                    }
                    return TRUE;
                }
                if (option == LBN_SELCHANGE) {
                    if (DlgDirSelect(hWnd, szFileName, 104)) {
                        _fstrcat(szFileName, szFileSpec);
                    }
                    SetDlgItemText(hWnd, 103, szFileName);
                    return TRUE;
                }
                return TRUE;
            }
            else {
                return FALSE;
            }
        default:
            return FALSE;
    }
}

int PASCAL DefaultFileOutBox(HWND hWnd, WORD iMessage, WORD wParam,
                        LONG lParam)
{   char buf[256];
    switch (iMessage) {
        case WM_INITDIALOG:
            SetDlgItemText(hWnd, 102, cpPrompt);  // set up prompt
            szFileSpec[0] = '*';  szFileSpec[1] = '.'; szFileSpec[2] =
'*';
            szFileSpec[3] = '\0';
            szFileName[0] = '\0';
```

```
                wFileAttribute = 0x4010;
                SendDlgItemMessage(hWnd, 103, EM_LIMITTEXT, 80, OL);
                DlgDirList(hWnd, szFileSpec, 104, 105, wFileAttribute);
                SetDlgItemText(hWnd, 103, szFileName);
                return TRUE;
        case WM_COMMAND:
            if (wParam == 1002) {   // OK button hit
                for (int i=0; i<256; i++)
                    cpEdit[i] = '\0';
                GetDlgItemText(hWnd, 103, &(cpEdit[0]), 80);
                EndDialog(hWnd, 0);
                return TRUE;
            } else
            if (wParam == 104) { //  List box
                WORD option = HIWORD( lParam);
                if (option == LBN_DBLCLK) {
                    if (DlgDirSelect(hWnd, szFileName, 104)) {
                        _fstrcat(szFileName, szFileSpec);
                        DlgDirList(hWnd, szFileName, 104, 105,
wFileAttribute);
                        SetDlgItemText(hWnd, 103, szFileSpec);
                    } else {
                        SetDlgItemText(hWnd, 103, szFileName);
                        SendMessage(hWnd, WM_COMMAND, 1002, OL);
                    }
                    return TRUE;
                }
                if (option == LBN_SELCHANGE) {
                    if (DlgDirSelect(hWnd, szFileName, 104)) {
                        _fstrcat(szFileName, szFileSpec);
                    }
                    SetDlgItemText(hWnd, 103, szFileName);
                    return TRUE;
                }
                return TRUE;
            }
            else {
                return FALSE;
            }
        default:
            return FALSE;
    }
}

// Single List Dialog box:

// For selection from MODAL dialog boxes:
static int FAR theItem;        // NOTE: make this FAR!!
static LPSTR FAR the_list_items[64];
static int FAR the_number_of_list_items;


int PASCAL DefaultListBox(HWND hWnd, WORD iMessage, WORD wParam,
            LONG lParam)
{
    switch (iMessage) {
        case WM_INITDIALOG:
            for (int i=0; i<the_number_of_list_items; i++) {
                LPSTR lpStr = &(the_list_items[i][0]);
```

```
                SendDlgItemMessage(hWnd,104,LB_ADDSTRING,0,  (LONG)lpStr);
            }
            SetDlgItemText(hWnd, 100, cpPrompt);
            return TRUE;

    case WM_COMMAND:
        if (wParam == 103) {  // Cancel button hit
            EndDialog(hWnd, FALSE);
            return TRUE;
        } else
        if (wParam == 104) {  //  List box
            WORD option = HIWORD(lParam);
            if (option == LBN_DBLCLK || option == LBN_SELCHANGE)  {
                theItem =
                  (WORD)SendDlgItemMessage(hWnd,104,LB_GETCURSEL,0,0L);
                EndDialog(hWnd, TRUE);
                return TRUE;
            }
        }
    default:
        return FALSE;
    }
}

static FARPROC lpfnDefaultAboutBox;
static FARPROC lpfnDefaultEditBox;
static FARPROC lpfnDefaultListBox;
static FARPROC lpfnDefaultFileInBox;
static FARPROC lpfnDefaultFileOutBox;

long TAppWindow::WndProc( WORD iMessage, WORD wParam, LONG lParam)
{
    static int mouse_down_flag = 0;
    switch (iMessage)
    {
    // Menu item:
    case WM_COMMAND:
        do_menu_action(wParam);
        InvalidateRect(hWnd, NULL, TRUE);
        break;
    case WM_CREATE:
        lpfnDefaultAboutBox = MakeProcInstance((FARPROC)DefaultAboutBox,
                    Application::instanceHandle);
        lpfnDefaultEditBox = MakeProcInstance((FARPROC)DefaultEditBox,
                    Application::instanceHandle);
        lpfnDefaultListBox = MakeProcInstance((FARPROC)DefaultListBox,
                    Application::instanceHandle);
        lpfnDefaultFileInBox = MakeProcInstance((FARPROC)DefaultFileInBox,
                    Application::instanceHandle);
        l p f n D e f a u l t F i l e O u t B o x                =
MakeProcInstance((FARPROC)DefaultFileOutBox,
                    Application::instanceHandle);
        break;
    case WM_PAINT:
        Paint();
        break;
    case WM_LBUTTONDOWN:  // left button is down
        mouse_down_flag = 1;
        mouse_down(LOWORD(lParam), HIWORD(lParam));
```

```
//         InvalidateRect(hWnd, NULL, TRUE);
           break;
     case WM_MOUSEMOVE:   // left button is down
           if (mouse_down_flag)
              mouse_move(LOWORD(lParam), HIWORD(lParam));
//         InvalidateRect(hWnd, NULL, FALSE);      // FALSE->experiment
           break;
     case WM_LBUTTONUP:   // left button is down
           mouse_up(LOWORD(lParam), HIWORD(lParam));
           mouse_down_flag = 0;
           InvalidateRect(hWnd, NULL, TRUE);
           break;
     case WM_DESTROY:
             if (i_timer!=0)  KillTimer(NULL, i_timer);
             PostQuitMessage( 0 );
             break;
     default:
             return DefWindowProc( hWnd, iMessage, wParam, lParam );
     }
     return 0;
}

void TAppWindow::do_about()
{
    DialogBox(Application::instanceHandle,"AboutBox",
hWnd,lpfnDefaultAboutBox);
}

void TAppWindow::do_edit(char * /* prompt */ , char *buf)
{
    int len = strlen(buf); if (len > 255) len = 255;
    for (int i=0; i<len; i++) cpEdit[i] = buf[i]; cpEdit[len] = '\0';
    DialogBox(Application::instanceHandle,    "EditBox",
hWnd,lpfnDefaultEditBox);
    for (i=0; cpEdit[i] != '\0'; i++) buf[i] = cpEdit[i];
    buf[i] = '\0';
    return;
}

int TAppWindow::choose_one_from_list(char *prompt,
                     char **list_items, int number_of_items)
{   theItem = -12;
    the_number_of_list_items = number_of_items;
    int len = strlen(prompt); if (len > 127) len = 127;
    for (int i=0; i<len; i++) cpPrompt[i] = prompt[i]; cpPrompt[len] =
'\0';
    for (i=0; i<number_of_items && i < (64 - 1); i++)
          the_list_items[i] = list_items[i];
    DialogBox(Application::instanceHandle,"ListBox",
hWnd,lpfnDefaultListBox);

    return theItem;
}

int TAppWindow::choose_one(char *prompt1, char *prompt2)
{
    static char *list[2];
    list[0] = prompt1; list[1] = prompt2;
    return choose_one_from_list("Choose one:", list, 2);
}
```

```
long FAR PASCAL _export WndProc( HWND hWnd, WORD iMessage, WORD wParam,
                                 LONG lParam )
{
    // Pointer to the (C++ object that is the) window.
    TAppWindow *pWindow = GetPointer( hWnd );
    if ( pWindow == 0 )
    {
        if ( iMessage == WM_CREATE )
        {
            LPCREATESTRUCT lpcs;

            lpcs = (LPCREATESTRUCT) lParam;
            pWindow = (TAppWindow *) lpcs->lpCreateParams;

            // Store a pointer to this object in the window's extra
            // bytes;
            // this will enable to access this object (and its member
            // functions) in WndProc where we are
            // given only a handle to identify the window.
            SetPointer( hWnd, pWindow );

            // Now let the object perform whatever
            // initialization it needs for WM_CREATE in its own
            // WndProc.
            return pWindow->WndProc( iMessage, wParam, lParam );
        }
        else
            return DefWindowProc( hWnd, iMessage, wParam, lParam );
    }
    else
        return pWindow->WndProc( iMessage, wParam, lParam );
}

void TAppWindow::init_scrolling_text(int top, int right, int bottom, int
left)
{
    top_text_clip = top;
    right_text_clip = right;
    bottom_text_clip = bottom;
    left_text_clip = left;
    number_of_saved_lines = 1 + ((bottom_text_clip - top_text_clip) /
                                 string_height(" "));
    if (number_of_saved_lines < 4)
        number_of_saved_lines = 4;
    if (number_of_saved_lines > MAX_TEXT_LINES)
        number_of_saved_lines = MAX_TEXT_LINES;
    current_ring_buffer_start = 0;
    // Allocate storage for saved text lines:
    for (int i=0; i<number_of_saved_lines; i++)  {
      saved_text[i] = new char[MAX_TEXT_LINE_SIZE];
      saved_text[i][0] = '\0';
    }
    in_scrolling_text_mode = 1;
    redraw_both_text_and_graphics = 1;
}

void TAppWindow::init_scrolling_text()
{
    top_text_clip = 5;
```

```
      right_text_clip = 512;
      bottom_text_clip = 512;
      left_text_clip = 5;
      number_of_saved_lines = 1 + ((bottom_text_clip - top_text_clip) /
                                 string_height(" "));
      if (number_of_saved_lines > MAX_TEXT_LINES)
         number_of_saved_lines = MAX_TEXT_LINES;
      current_ring_buffer_start = 0;
      // Allocate storage for saved text lines:
      for (int i=0; i<number_of_saved_lines; i++)  {
        saved_text[i] = new char[MAX_TEXT_LINE_SIZE+1];
        saved_text[i][0] = '\0';
      }
      in_scrolling_text_mode = 1;
      redraw_both_text_and_graphics = 0;
}

void TAppWindow::put_scrolling_text(char *str)
{
  if (bottom_text_clip != 0) {
      HRGN hClipRgn = CreateRectRgn(left_text_clip-3, top_text_clip-3,
                                 right_text_clip+7, bottom_text_clip+5);
      SelectClipRgn(current_hDC, hClipRgn);
      RECT r, r2;
      SetRect(&r2, left_text_clip-2, top_text_clip, right_text_clip+6,
              bottom_text_clip+2);
      ScrollDC(current_hDC,0,-string_height(" ")-2,&r2,&r2,NULL,NULL);
      SetRect(&r, left_text_clip -1, bottom_text_clip - string_height(" "),
          right_text_clip + 5, bottom_text_clip + 6);
      FillRect(current_hDC, &r, backgroundBrush);
      plot_string(left_text_clip + 1, bottom_text_clip - 2, str);
      DeleteObject(hClipRgn);
      r2.bottom += 2;
      r2.top -= 2;
      FrameRect(current_hDC, &r2, blackBrush);
      if (strlen(str) < 256) {
         char buf[257];
         sprintf(buf,"%s", str);
         buf[MAX_TEXT_LINE_SIZE] = '\0';
         saved_text[current_ring_buffer_start][0]='\0';
         _fstrcat(saved_text[current_ring_buffer_start],(char far *)buf);
         current_ring_buffer_start++;
         if (current_ring_buffer_start > (number of saved lines - 1))
         current_ring_buffer_start = 0;
      }
  } else {
//    Warning("Need to call TAppWindow::init_scrolling_text.");
  }
}

void TAppWindow::reset_scrolling_text()
{
  // TBD
}

int TAppWindow::choose_file_to_read(char *prompt, char *extension,
                                 char *returned_filename)
{  cpEdit[0] = '\0';
   int len = strlen(prompt); if (len > 127) len = 127;
   for (int i=0; i<len; i++) cpPrompt[i] = prompt[i]; cpPrompt[len] =
```

```
'\0';
    len = strlen(extension); if (len > 12)  len = 12;
    for (i=0; i<len; i++) cpExtension[i] = extension[i];
    DialogBox(Application::instanceHandle, "FileInBox",
              hWnd,lpfnDefaultFileInBox);
    for (i=0; cpEdit[i] != '\0'; i++) returned_filename[i] = cpEdit[i];
    returned_filename[i] = '\0';
    return 0;          // TBD: return 1 on error, or User Cancel
}

int TAppWindow::choose_file_to_write(char *prompt,
                                     char *returned_filename)
{   cpEdit[0] = '\0';
    int len = strlen(prompt); if (len > 127) len = 127;
    for (int i=0; i<len; i++) cpPrompt[i] = prompt[i]; cpPrompt[len] =
'\0';
    DialogBox(Application::instanceHandle, "FileOutBox",
              hWnd,lpfnDefaultFileOutBox);
    for (i=0; cpEdit[i] != '\0'; i++) returned_filename[i] = cpEdit[i];
    returned_filename[i] = '\0';
    return 0;          // TBD: return 1 on error, or User Cancel
}

extern TAppWindow *current_window;

void Warning(char *buf)
{
    MessageBeep(0);
    current_window->do_edit(" ", buf);
}
```

B.4 Windows-Specific Smart Vector Include Files

File char_v.h

```
// File: char_v.h
//
// Description: Include file for the smart character vector class
//
// Copyright 1992 by Mark Watson Associates
//
//        No binary rights reserved: this software library may be used in
//        compiled form without restrictions.  All source rights
//        reserved: Source code to the GUI library can not be distributed
//        (on bulletin boards, or as part of shareware or commercial
//        products)
//        without written permission.
//
//        This software is provided "as is". The user accepts all
//        responsibility for its use.
//

#ifndef __char_vect
#define __char_vect

#ifndef __WINDOWS_H
#include "Windows.h"
#endif
```

```
#include <fstream.h>
#include "apptypes.h"

#define input (ios::in)
#define output (ios::out)

class char_vect {
    char FAR *p;  // For Microsoft Windows (tm), this is a pointer to
                  // a locked Handle
    HANDLE handle_p;
    long size;
    void grow(long new_size);
    long ub() { return (size - 1); }
  public:
    char_vect(void);
    char_vect (long n);
    char_vect(char_vect &v);
    char_vect(char a[], long n);
    ~char_vect() { GlobalFree(handle_p); }
    char FAR & operator [] (long i);  // range check safeguards
    int save(char * /*filename*/ ) { return 0; };
    int restore(char * /*filename*/ ) { return 0;  };
};
#endif
```

File double_v.h

```
// File: double_v.h
//
// Description: This file contains the clas definition for the
//              double smart vector class
//
// Copyright 1992 by Mark Watson Associates
//
//        No binary rights reserved: this software library may be used in
//        compiled form without restrictions.  All source rights
//        reserved: Source code to the GUI library can not be distributed
//        (on bulletin boards, or as part of shareware or commercial
//        products)
//        without written permission.
//
//        This software is provided "as is". The user accepts all
//        responsibility for its use.
//

#ifndef __double_vect
#define __double_vect

#include <iostream.h>

#ifndef __WINDOWS_H
#include "Windows.h"
#endif

class double_vect {
    double FAR *p;  // For Microsoft Windows (tm), this is a pointer to
                    // a locked Handle
    HANDLE handle_p;
    int size;
```

```
      void grow(int new_size);
      int ub() { return (size - 1); }
   public:
      double_vect(void);
      double_vect (int n);
      double_vect(double_vect &v);
      double_vect(double a[], int n);
     ~double_vect() { GlobalFree(handle_p); }
      double FAR & operator [] (int i);  // range check safeguards
      int save(char * /*filename*/ ) { return 0; };
      int restore(char * /*filename*/ ) { return 0;  };
};

#endif
```

File int_vect.h

```
// File: int_vect.h
//
// Description: Class definition of the int smart vector class
//
// Copyright 1992 by Mark Watson Associates
//
//        No binary rights reserved: this software library may be used in
//        compiled form without restrictions.  All source rights
//        reserved: Source code to the GUI library can not be distributed
//        (on bulletin boards, or as part of shareware or commercial
//        products)
//        without written permission.
//
//        This software is provided "as is". The user accepts all
//        responsibility for its use.
//

#ifndef __int_vect
#define __int_vect

#ifndef __WINDOWS_H
#include "Windows.h"
#endif

class int_vect {
    int FAR *p;  // For Microsoft Windows (tm), this is a pointer to
                 // a locked Handle.
    HANDLE handle_p;
    int size;
    void grow(int new_size);
    int ub() { return (size - 1); }
  public:
    int num_elements;
    int_vect(void);
    int_vect (int n);
    int_vect(int_vect &v);
    int_vect(int a[], int n);
   ~int_vect() { GlobalFree(handle_p); }
    int FAR & operator [] (int i);  // range check safeguards
    void save(char *filename);
    void restore(char *filename);
};

#endif
```

B.5   Windows-Specific Smart Vector C++
Source Files

File char_v.cp

```
// File: char_v.cp
//
// Description: smart vector implementation for chars
//
// Copyright 1992 by Mark Watson Associates
//
//          No binary rights reserved: this software library may be used in
//          compiled form without restrictions.  All source rights
//          reserved: Source code to the GUI library can not be distributed
//          (on bulletin boards, or as part of shareware or commercial
//          products)
//          without written permission.
//
//          This software is provided "as is". The user accepts all
//          responsibility for its use.
//

#include "char_v.h"

extern "C" { void exit(int); void sprintf(...); };

void Warning(char *);

// Define constants for the dynamic grow rate for char_vect data types
// and
// the maximum number of elements that a smart char_vect can have:

const long GROW_RATE = 8192;
const long MAX_SIZE = 256000;

char_vect::char_vect(void)
{
    size = (long)65336L;
    Warning("Creating a smart char vector of size 65336");
    handle_p = GlobalAlloc(GMEM_FIXED, size * sizeof(char));
    p = (char FAR *)GlobalLock(handle_p);
    if (p == 0) {
        Warning("Error allocating a char_vect.");
        exit(1);
    }
}

char_vect::char_vect(long n)
{
    if (n<= 0) {
        char buf[64];
        sprintf(buf,"Illegal size for for char_vect constructor=%d",n);
        Warning(buf);
        exit(1);
    }
    size = n;
    handle_p = GlobalAlloc(GMEM_FIXED, size * sizeof(char));
    p = (char FAR *)GlobalLock(handle_p);
    if (p == 0) {
```

```
            Warning("Error allocating a char_vect.");
            exit(1);
        }
}

char_vect::char_vect(char a[], long n)
{
    if (n<= 0) {
        Warning("illegal size for a char_vect");
         exit(1);
    }
    size = n;
    handle_p = GlobalAlloc(GMEM_FIXED, size * sizeof(char));
    p = (char FAR *)GlobalLock(handle_p);
     for (long i=0; i<size; i++)  p[i] = a[i];
}

char_vect::char_vect(char_vect &v)
{
    size = v.size;
    handle_p = GlobalAlloc(GMEM_FIXED, size * sizeof(char));
    p = (char FAR *)GlobalLock(handle_p);
     for (long i=0; i<size; i++)  p[i] = v.p[i];
}

char FAR & char_vect::operator [] (long i)
{
    if (i < 0) {
        char buf[64];
        sprintf(buf,"Illegal size for char_vect [] operator=%l",i);
        Warning(buf);
        exit(1);
    }
    if (i > ub()) {
        grow(i);
    }
    return (p[i]);
}

void char_vect::grow(long new_size)
{
    if ((new_size + GROW_RATE) >= MAX_SIZE) {
        char buf[256];
         sprintf(buf,"Error in dynamic resizing of a smart vector. New
size=%d",
                    (new_size + GROW_RATE));
        Warning(buf);
        exit(1);
    }
    size = (new_size + GROW_RATE);
    handle_p = GlobalReAlloc(handle_p, size * sizeof(char), GMEM_FIXED);
    p = (char FAR *)GlobalLock(handle_p);
}
#if 0

// test code:

main()
{
    cerr << "Start of char_vect test:\n\n";
```

```
    char_vect vv(10);
    vv[2] = 2;
    vv[220] = vv[2];   // illegal index !!
    cerr << "Done with test.\n";
}

#endif
```

File double_v.cp

```
// File: double_v.cp
//
// Description: This file contains the implementation of the double
//              smart vector class
//
// Copyright 1992 by Mark Watson Associates
//
//         No binary rights reserved: this software library may be used in
//         compiled form without restrictions.  All source rights
//         reserved: Source code to the GUI library can not be distributed
//         (on bulletin boards, or as part of shareware or commercial
//         products)
//         without written permission.
//
//         This software is provided "as is". The user accepts all
//         responsibility for its use.
//

#include "double_vect.h"

extern "C" { void exit(int); };

// Define constants for the dynamic grow rate for double_vect data types
// and the maximum number of elements that a smart double_vect can have:


const int GROW_RATE = 256;
const int MAX_SIZE = 8192;

double_vect::double_vect(void)
{
    size = 2048;
    handle_p = GlobalAlloc(GMEM_FIXED, size * sizeof(double));
    p = (double FAR *)GlobalLock(handle_p);
}

double_vect::double_vect(int n)
{
    if (n<= 0) {
        cerr << "illeagl size for a double_vect = " << n << "\n";
        exit(1);
    }
    size = n;
    handle_p = GlobalAlloc(GMEM_FIXED, size * sizeof(double));
    p = (double FAR *)GlobalLock(handle_p);
}

double_vect::double_vect(double a[], int n)
{
    if (n<= 0) {
```

```
            cerr << "illeagl size for a double_vect = " << n << "\n";
            exit(1);
    }
    size = n;
    handle_p = GlobalAlloc(GMEM_FIXED, size * sizeof(double));
    p = (double FAR *)GlobalLock(handle_p);
    for (int i=0; i<size; i++)  p[i] = a[i];
}

double_vect::double_vect(double_vect &v)
{
    size = v.size;
    handle_p = GlobalAlloc(GMEM_FIXED, size * sizeof(double));
    p = (double FAR *)GlobalLock(handle_p);
    for (int i=0; i<size; i++)  p[i] = v.p[i];
}

double FAR & double_vect::operator [] (int i)
{
    if (i < 0) {
        cerr << "illegal index for double_vect = " << i << "\n";
        exit(1);
    }
    if (i > ub()) {
        grow(i);
    }
    return (p[i]);
}

void double_vect::grow(int new_size)
{
    if ((new_size + GROW_RATE) >= MAX_SIZE) {
        cerr << "error in dynamic resizing of a smart double_vect, new
size = "
                << (new_size + GROW_RATE) << "\n";
        exit(1);
    }
    size = (new_size + GROW_RATE);
     handle_p = GlobalReAlloc(handle_p, size * sizeof(double),
GMEM_FIXED);
    p = (double FAR *)GlobalLock(handle_p);
}
#if 0

// test code:
main()
{
    cerr << "Start of double_vect test:\n\n";
    double_vect vv(10);
    vv[2] = 2;
    vv[220] = vv[2];  // illegal index !!
    cerr << "Done with test.\n";
}

#endif
```

File int_vect.cp

```
// File: int_vect.cp
//
// Description: Implementation of the int smart vector class
//
// Copyright 1992 by Mark Watson Associates
//
//          No binary rights reserved: this software library may be used in
//          compiled form without restrictions.  All source rights
//          reserved: Source code to the GUI library can not be distributed
//          (on bulletin boards, or as part of shareware or commercial
//          products)
//          without written permission.
//
//          This software is provided "as is". The user accepts all
//          responsibility for its use.
//

#include "applib.h"
#include "int_vect.h"

extern "C" { void exit(int); };

extern void Warning(char *);

// Define constants for the dynamic grow rate for int_vect data types and
// the maximum number of elements that a smart int_vect can have:

const int GROW_RATE = 1024;
const int MAX_SIZE = 15000;

int_vect::int_vect(void)
{
    num_elements = 0;
    size = 1000;
    handle_p = GlobalAlloc(GMEM_FIXED, size * sizeof(int));
    p = (int FAR *)GlobalLock(handle_p);
}

int_vect::int_vect(int n)
{
    if (n<= 0) {
    cerr << "illegal size for a int_vect = " << n << "\n";
        exit(1);
    }
    num_elements = 0;
    size = n;
    handle_p = GlobalAlloc(GMEM_FIXED, size * sizeof(int));
    p = (int FAR *)GlobalLock(handle_p);
}

int_vect::int_vect(int a[], int n)
{
    if (n<= 0) {
        cerr << "illeagl size for a int_vect = " << n << "\n";
        exit(1);
    }
    num_elements = size = n;
    handle_p = GlobalAlloc(GMEM_FIXED, size * sizeof(int));
```

```
    p = (int FAR *)GlobalLock(handle_p);
    for (int i=0; i<size; i++)  p[i] = a[i];
}

int_vect::int_vect(int_vect &v)
{
    size = v.size;
    handle_p = GlobalAlloc(GMEM_FIXED, size * sizeof(int));
    p = (int FAR *)GlobalLock(handle_p);
    for (int i=0; i<size; i++)  p[i] = v.p[i];
    num_elements = size;
}

int FAR & int_vect::operator [] (int i)
{
    if (i < 0) {
        cerr << "illegal index for int_vect = " << i << "\n";
        exit(1);
    }
    if (i > ub()) {
        grow(i);
    }
    if ((i + 1) > num_elements) num_elements = i+1;
    return (p[i]);
}

void int_vect::grow(int new_size)
{
    if ((new_size + GROW_RATE) >= MAX_SIZE) {
    cerr << "error in dynamic resizing of a smart int_vect, new size = "
            << (new_size + GROW_RATE) << "\n";
        exit(1);
    }
    size = (new_size + GROW_RATE);
    handle_p = GlobalReAlloc(handle_p, size * sizeof(int), GMEM_FIXED);
    p = (int FAR *)GlobalLock(handle_p);
}

void int_vect::save(char *file_name)
{
    filebuf out_file;
    if (out_file.open(file_name, output) == 0) {
        Warning("Could not open file for int_vect save");
        exit(1);
    }
    ostream out_stream(&out_file);
    out_stream << size;
    for (int i=0; i<num_elements; i++)
        out_stream << p[i];
    out_file.close();
}

void int_vect::restore(char *file_name)
{
    filebuf in_file;
    if (in_file.open(file_name, input) == 0) {
        Warning("Could not open file for int_vect restore");
        exit(1);
    }
```

```
    istream in_stream(&in_file);
    in_stream >> size;
    num_elements = size;
    if (size > ub()-1)  grow(size);
    for (int i=0; i<num_elements; i++)
        in_stream >> p[i];
    in_file.close();
}


#if 0

// test code:

main()
{
    cerr << "Start of int_vect test:\n\n";
    int_vect vv(10);
    vv[2] = 2;
    vv[220] = vv[2];  // illegal index !!
    cerr << "Done with test.\n";
}

#endif
```

Macintosh Class Implementation

C.1 Macintosh Resource Files

File applib.r

```
/*
 * File: applib.r
 *
 * Description: Common resource definitons for all sample programs.
 *              Some of these definitions are derived from the example
 *              resource files supplied with the MPW C++ compiler; the
 *              rest were created by using ResEdit and the mpw tool derez.
 *
 */


#include "SysTypes.r"
#include "Types.r"

#include "applibCommon.h"


/* we use an MBAR resource to conveniently load all the menus */

resource 'MBAR' (rMenuBar, preload) {
    { mApple, mFile, mApp };    /* three menus */
};


resource 'MENU' (mApple, preload) {
    mApple, textMenuProc,
    0b111111111111111111111111111111101,
    enabled, apple,
    {
```

```
        "About C++App...",
            noicon, nokey, nomark, plain;
        "-",
            noicon, nokey, nomark, plain
    }
};
resource 'MENU' (mFile, preload) {
    mFile, textMenuProc,
    0b111111111111111111111111111111111,
    enabled, "File",
    {

        "Quit",
        noicon, "Q", nomark, plain
    }
};

resource 'vers' (1) {
    0x01, 0x00, release, 0x00,
    verUS,
    "1.00",
    "1.00, Copyright © 1991 by Mark Watson Associates"
};

resource 'SIZE' (-1) {
    dontSaveScreen,
    acceptSuspendResumeEvents,
    enableOptionSwitch,
    canBackground,
    multiFinderAware,
    backgroundAndForeground,
    dontGetFrontClicks,
    ignoreChildDiedEvents,
    is32BitCompatible,
    reserved, reserved, reserved, reserved,
    reserved, reserved, reserved,
    kPrefSize * 1024,
    kMinSize * 1024
};


type 'MLW1' as 'STR ';


resource 'MLW1' (0) {
    "GUI Library based C++ Application"
};


resource 'BNDL' (128) {
    'MLW1',
    0,
    {
        'ICN#',
        {
            0, 128
        },
        'FREF',
        {
            0, 128
```

```
        }
    }
};


resource 'FREF' (128) {
    'APPL',
    0,
    ""
};

resource 'ICN#' (128) {
    {
    $"00 00 00 00 00 00 00 00 00 00 00 00 00 01 C0 00"
    $"00 03 40 00 00 05 C0 00 00 08 00 00 00 10 00 00"
    $"00 E0 00 00 01 A0 00 00 02 E0 00 00 04 10 00 00"
    $"08 08 00 00 70 05 C1 C0 50 03 7F 40 70 01 C1 C0"
    $"08 00 00 00 04 00 00 00 02 E1 C0 00 01 BF 40 00"
    $"00 E1 C0 00 00 00 00 00 00 00 00 00 10 48 02 20"
    $"18 C8 02 50 15 44 04 50 12 44 44 88 10 42 A8 F8"
    $"10 42 A9 04 10 41 11 04 00 00 00 00 00 00 00 00"
    }
};

data 'DITL' (501, purgeable) {
    $"0003 0000 0000 00DC 0133 00FC 0186 0402"
    $"4F4B 0000 0000 00DC 0193 00FC 01EA 0406"
    $"4361 6E63 656C 0000 0000 0025 0009 00D9"
    $"01ED 101A 6E65 7720 7465 7874 2064 6573"
    $"6372 6970 7469 6F6E 2062 6C6F 636B 0000"
    $"0000 0002 0009 0019 01EA 0806 5072 6F6D"
    $"7074"
};

data 'DLOG' (501, purgeable) {
    $"0042 0008 0143 01F7 0003 0100 0000 0000"
    $"0000 01F5 1445 6E74 6572 206E 6577 206E"
    $"6F64 6520 7469 746C 65"
};

data 'DLOG' (511) {
    $"0029 0039 0148 018C 0000 0100 0100 0000"
    $"0000 01FF 00"
};

data 'DITL' (511) {
    $"0002 0000 0000 0107 0116 011B 0150 0406"
    $"4361 6E63 656C 0000 0000 0004 0005 0019"
    $"015A 8813 5072 6F6D 7074 2067 6F65 7320"
    $"6865 7265 2E2E 2E00 0000 0000 0024 0007"
    $"00F6 0138 8000"
};

data 'DLOG' (515) {
    $"0028 0028 0093 01A0 0000 0100 0100 0000"
    $"0000 0203 00"
};

data 'DITL' (515) {
```

```
    $"0001 0000 0000 000A 0008 002D 0172 040B"
    $"4F70 7469 6F6E 2031 2E2E 2E00 0000 0000"
    $"0035 0009 005A 0171 040B 4F70 7469 6F6E"
    $"2032 2E2E 2E00"
};

data 'DLOG' (128) {
    $"0041 003E 0127 01C7 0001 0100 0000 0000"
    $"0000 0080 00"
};
/* these ALRT and DITL are used for 'show info' */

resource 'ALRT' (128, purgeable) {
    {40, 20, 160, 330 }, rAboutAlert, {
        OK, visible, silent;
        OK, visible, silent;
        OK, visible, silent;
        OK, visible, silent
    };
};

resource 'DITL' (128, purgeable) {
    {
        {88, 224, 108, 304},
        Button { enabled, "OK" },
        {8, 8, 24, 304 },
        StaticText { disabled, "C++App Class" },
        {32, 8, 48, 237},
        StaticText { disabled, "Copyright © 1991 by Mark Watson" },
        {56, 8, 72, 156},
        StaticText { disabled, "    " },
        {80, 24, 112, 167},
        StaticText { disabled, "Better AI software..." }
    }
};

data 'DLOG' (129) {
    $"004B 005C 010E 01B9 0001 0100 0000 0000"
    $"0000 0081 00"
};

resource 'ALRT' (129, purgeable) {
    {40, 20, 150, 260},
    129,
    {
        OK, visible, silent,
        OK, visible, silent,
        OK, visible, silent,
        OK, visible, silent
    }
};
```

File chess3d.r

```
/*
 * File: chess3d.r
 *
 */


#include "SysTypes.r"
```

```
#include "Types.r"

#include "applibCommon.h"

/* specify the desired window type: */
resource 'WIND' (rDocWindow, preload, purgeable) {
    {64, 60, 502, 496},
    rDocProc, invisible,nogoaway, 0x0, "3D Chess Program"
};

/* specify the desired menu items: */
resource 'MENU' (mApp, preload) {
    mApp, textMenuProc,
    0b111111111111111111111111111111,   /* enable everything */
    enabled, "3D Chess",
    {
        "New game (play white)", noIcon, "W", noMark, plain;
        "New game (play black)", noIcon, "B", noMark, plain;
        "Save current game position", noIcon, "S", noMark, plain;
        "Reload old board position", noIcon, "L", noMark, plain;
        "Quit", noIcon, "Q", noMark, plain;
    }
};
```

File draw.r

```
/*
 *  File: draw.r
 *
 *  Description: Resource definitons for program 'draw'
 */



#include "SysTypes.r"
#include "Types.r"

#include "applibCommon.h"

/* specify the desired window type: */
resource 'WIND' (rDocWindow, preload, purgeable) {
    {64, 60, 520, 520},
    rDocProc, invisible,nogoaway, 0x0, "C++ GUI Library Draw Program"
};

/* specify the desired menu items: */
resource 'MENU' (mApp, preload) {
    mApp, textMenuProc,
    0b111111111111111111111111111111,   /* enable everything */
    enabled, "Draw",
    {
        "Delete current drawing", noIcon, "G", noMark, plain;
        "Save drawing to a file", noIcon, "T", noMark, plain;
        "Restore from file", noIcon, "A", noMark, plain
    }
};
```

File hand.r

```
/*
 *  File: hand.r
```

```
*
*   Description: Resource definitons for program 'hand'
*/


#include "SysTypes.r"
#include "Types.r"

#include "applibCommon.h"

/* specify the desired window type: */
resource 'WIND' (rDocWindow, preload, purgeable) {
    {64, 60, 520, 520},
    rDocProc, invisible,nogoaway, 0x0, "Neural Net Example"
};

/* specify the desired menu items: */
resource 'MENU' (mApp, preload) {
    mApp, textMenuProc,
    0b111111111111111111111111111111111,   /* enable everything */
    enabled, "Handwriting",
    {   /* array: 1 elements */
        /* [1] */
        "Record training examples", noIcon, "G", noMark, plain;
        "Train and save weights to disk", noIcon, "T", noMark, plain;
        "Reload old weights", noIcon, "A", noMark, plain;
        "Test character recognition", noIcon, "T", noMark, plain
    }
};
```

File hib.r

```
/*
*   File: hib.r
*
*   Description: Resource definitons for program 'hib'
*/


#include "SysTypes.r"
#include "Types.r"

#include "applibCommon.h"
/* specify the desired window type: */
resource 'WIND' (rDocWindow, preload, purgeable) {
    {64, 60, 520, 520},
    rDocProc, invisible,nogoaway, 0x0, "C++ GUI Library Test Program"
};

/* specify the desired menu items: */
resource 'MENU' (mApp, preload) {
    mApp, textMenuProc,
    0b111111111111111111111111111111111,   /* enable everything */
    enabled, "H.I.B.",
    {
        "Load an ASCII file", noIcon, "L", noMark, plain;
        "Save in memory database to ASCII file", noIcon, "S", noMark,
         plain;
        "Clear in memory database", noIcon, "Z", noMark, plain;
        "Redraw from selected node", noIcon, "R", noMark, plain;
```

```
        "Redraw from tree root", noIcon, "T", noMark, plain;
        "Search mode", noIcon, "F", noMark, plain;
        "Edit selected node", noIcon, "E", noMark, plain;
        "Delete selected node", noIcon, "D", noMark, plain;
        "Create a new node", noIcon, "C", noMark, plain;
        "Quit", noIcon, "Q", noMark, plain
    }
};
```

File test.r

```
/*
 *  File: test.r
 *
 *  Description: Resource definitons for program 'test'
 */


#include "SysTypes.r"
#include "Types.r"

#include "applibCommon.h"

/* specify the desired window type: */
resource 'WIND' (rDocWindow, preload, purgeable) {
    {64, 60, 520, 520},
    rDocProc, invisible,nogoaway, 0x0, "C++ GUI Library Test Program"
};

/* specify the desired menu items: */
resource 'MENU' (mApp, preload) {
    mApp, textMenuProc,
    0b11111111111111111111111111111111,    /* enable everything */
    enabled, "Test App",
    {
        "Test Grapher Class", noIcon, "G", noMark, plain;
        "Test Edit Dialog", noIcon, "T", noMark, plain;
        "Test About box", noIcon, "A", noMark, plain;
        "Test Single List Selection", noIcon, "S", noMark, plain;
        "Test choose one of 2 choices", noIcon, "D", noMark, plain;
        "Test scrolling text", noIcon, "F", noMark, plain;
        "Test data plotting", noIcon, "P", noMark, plain
    }
};
```

File textbr.r

```
/*
 *  File: textbr.r
 *
 *  Description: Resource definitons for program 'textbr'
 */


#include "SysTypes.r"
#include "Types.r"

#include "applibCommon.h"

/* specify the desired window type: */
```

```
resource 'WIND' (rDocWindow, preload, purgeable) {
    {64, 60, 520, 520},
    rDocProc, invisible,nogoaway, 0x0, "Text Browser"
};

/* specify the desired menu items: */
resource 'MENU' (mApp, preload) {
    mApp, textMenuProc,
    0b111111111111111111111111111111111,   /* enable everything */
    enabled, "Text Browser",
    {
        "Load index", noIcon, "L", noMark, plain;
        "Add a text file to current index", noIcon, "A", noMark, plain;
        "Save current index", noIcon, "S", noMark, plain;
        "Word Search", noIcon, "W", noMark, plain
    }
};
```

C.2   Macintosh-Specific GUI Include Files

File applib.h

```
// File: applib.h
//
// Description: C++ header file for the Macintosh implementation of the
//              GUI library.
//                  Parts of this file were modeled after sample programs
written by
//                  Engineers at Apple Computer.
//
// Copyright 1992 by Mark Watson Associates
//
//         No binary rights reserved: this software library may be used in
//         compiled form without restrictions.  All source rights
//         reserved: Source code to the GUI library can not be distributed
//          (on bulletin boards, or as part of shareware or commercial
products)
//         without written permission.
//
//         This software is provided "as is". The user accepts all
//         responsibility for its use.
//


#ifndef __applib
#define __applib

// We want to minimize the number of Mac specific include files in
'applib.h' to speed
// up compilation of application programs.

#include <Types.h>
#include <QuickDraw.h>
#include <Events.h>

#include "apptypes.h"
#include <String.h>
#include <StdIO.h>

#include <iostream.h>
#include <stream.h>
```

```
#include "applibCommon.h"

extern "C" {
    void exit(int);
};

class TAppWindow;   // forward reference for the compiler


//
//                                        Class definition for TAppAPP
application class
//

class TAppApp : public HandleObject {
public:
    TAppApp(void);
    void EventLoop(void);
    TAppWindow *fWindow; // The active window
    void DoMenuCommand(short menuID, short menuItem);   // Handle menu
                                                        // actions

};

#define TopLeft(aRect)    (* (Point *) &(aRect).top)
#define BotRight(aRect)   (* (Point *) &(aRect).bottom)
#define HiWrd(aLong)   ((short) (((aLong) >> 16) & 0xFFFF))
#define LoWrd(aLong)   ((short) ((aLong) & 0xFFFF))

const int MAX_TEXT_LINES = 32;        // Increase this for large windows
(> 32 lines of text)
const int MAX_TEXT_LINE_SIZE = 100;  // Increase this for large windows
(> 100 characters per line)


//
//                                        Class definition for TAppWindow
//

class TAppWindow : public HandleObject {
 protected:
    WindowPtr fDocWindow;

    // For scrolling text output:
    short   top_text_clip,   right_text_clip,   bottom_text_clip,
left_text_clip;
    char *saved_text[MAX_TEXT_LINES]; // This is a ring-buffer
    int number_of_saved_lines;
    int current_ring_buffer_start;
    // We only allow either text or graphics to be active in a document
    // window.
    // The following flag is non-zero if we are using the document window
    // for
    // scrolling text.  Note that this mode changes automatically when
    // either
    // plotting or scrolling text output methods are called.
    int in_scrolling_text_mode;
    // The following flag indicates that a small scrolling text field is
    // being used
    // so we want to update both graphics and text. Note that this only
    // looks good if
```

```
    // the application program is careful to not draw in the scrolling
    // text area.
    int redraw_both_text_and_graphics;

private:
    void draw_update_contents(void);

public:
    TAppWindow(short resID);
    ~TAppWindow(void);
    void DoContent(EventRecord* theEvent);
    void DoUpdate(void);

    void do_about();
    void do_edit(char *, char *);
    void show_info(char *);
    int choose_one(char *prompt1, char *prompt2);
    int choose_one_from_list(char *prompt, char **list_items,
                                        int number_of_items);
    int choose_file_to_read(char *prompt, char * extension, char
*returned_filename);
    int choose_file_to_write(char *prompt, char *returned_filename);

    void init_scrolling_text(int top, int right, int bottom, int left);
    void init_scrolling_text();
    void put_scrolling_text(char *str);
    void reset_scrolling_text();

    // Utility methods for application access:
    void plot_line(int, int, int, int);
    void plot_string(int, int, char *);
    void plot_rect(int top, int right, int bottom, int left);
    void plot_oval(int top, int right, int bottom, int left);
    void erase_rect(int top, int right, int bottom, int left);
    int  string_height(char *str);
    int  string_width(char *str);
    void clear_display();
    // User specified methods:
    void update_display();
    void mouse_down(int, int);
    void mouse_up(int, int);
    void mouse_move(int, int);
    void do_menu_action(int);

    void idle_proc();
};


void Warning(char *);

// File selection utilities:
int choose_file_to_read(char *returned_filename, char *extension);  // 0
return -> OK, 1 return -> Failure
int choose_file_to_write(char *returned_filename); // 0 return -> OK, 1
return -> Failure

TAppWindow *current_window;

//
//                                          Macro definition for program
```

```
initialization and startup
//

#define INIT_PROGRAM \
TAppApp *gTheApplication;\
int main(void)\
{ gTheApplication = new TAppApp;\
  if (gTheApplication == nil)\
     return 0;\
\
  current_window = (TAppWindow *)(gTheApplication->fWindow);


//
//                               Macro definition for program execution
//

#define RUN_PROGRAM \
    gTheApplication->EventLoop();\
    return 0

#endif
```

File applibCommon.h

```
/*
 *  File: applibCommon.h
 *
 *  Description: As per the Apple sample programs, we break out
 *               common definitions needed in both resource (.r)
 *               and C++ (.cp) source files.
 */

#ifndef _applibCommon
#define _applibCommon


#define kPrefSize          700
#define kMinSize           600

#define     eWrongMachine    1
#define     eSmallSize       2

#define     kMinHeap         (512 * 1024)
#define     kMinSpace        (70 * 1024)

#define     eNoMemory        1
#define     eNoWindow        2

#define     rMenuBar    128
#define     rAboutAlert    128
#define     rDocWindow 128

#define     mApple           128     /* Apple menu */
#define     iAbout           1

#define     mFile            129     /* File menu */
#define     iNew             1
#define     iClose           4
#define     iQuit            12
```

```
#define    mApp                131    /* App menu */
#define    iGraph              1
```

```
#endif _applibCommon
```

File apptypes.h

```
// File: apptypes.h
//
// Description: Define macros for intrinsic data types. This is useful
//              for portability to machines with a segmented memory
//              architecture.
//
// Copyright 1992 by Mark Watson Associates
//
// Copyright 1992 by Mark Watson Associates
//
//        No binary rights reserved: this software library may be used in
//        compiled form without restrictions.  All source rights
//        reserved: Source code to the GUI library can not be distributed
//          (on bulletin boards, or as part of shareware or commercial
//          products)
//        without written permission.
//
//        This software is provided "as is". The user accepts all
//        responsibility for its use.
//
```

```
#define Char char
#define Int int   // this can be either 16 or 32 bits
#define Long long // this needs to be 32 bits
#define Short short // this needs to be 16 bits
#define Double double
#define Float float
```

C.3 Macintosh-Specific GUI C++ Source Files

File applib.cp

```
// File: applib.cp
//
// Description: Application specific code for the Macintosh
//              version of the Generic GUI toolkit. Many of
//              the "tricks" used here for interfacing C++
//              with the Mac toolbox are modeled after the
//              excellent example programs provided with the
//              MPW C++ compiler.
//
//
// Copyright 1992 by Mark Watson Associates
//
//        No binary rights reserved: this software library may be used in
//        compiled form without restrictions.  All source rights
//        reserved: Source code to the GUI library can not be distributed
//          (on bulletin boards, or as part of shareware or commercial
//          products)
//        without written permission.
//
//        This software is provided "as is". The user accepts all
//        responsibility for its use.
```

```
//

// #include <Types.h>          // must be included in applib.h
// #include <QuickDraw.h>      // must be included in applib.h
// #include <Events.h>         // must be included in applib.h
#include <Fonts.h>
#include <Controls.h>
#include <Windows.h>
#include <Menus.h>
#include <TextEdit.h>
#include <Dialogs.h>
#include <Desk.h>
#include <Scrap.h>
#include <ToolUtils.h>
#include <Memory.h>
#include <SegLoad.h>
#include <Files.h>
#include <Lists.h>
#include <OSUtils.h>
#include <StandardFile.h>
#include <Traps.h>

#include "applib.h"

// Define HiWrd and LoWrd macros for efficiency.
#define HiWrd(aLong)   (((aLong) >> 16) & 0xFFFF)
#define LoWrd(aLong)   ((aLong) & 0xFFFF)


// Constants defined in MPW C++ examples:
const short kOsEvent = app4Evt;             // event used by MultiFinder
const short kSuspendResumeMessage = 0x01;   // high byte of suspend/resume
                                            // event message
const short kClipConvertMask = 0x02;        // bit of message field clip
                                            // conversion
const short kResumeMask = 0x01;             // bit of message field for
                                            // resume vs. suspend
const short kMouseMovedMessage = 0xFA;      // high byte of mouse-moved
                                            // event message

// I define these as static local instead of in the TAppApp class to
// avoid extra
// Mac specific include files in 'applib'h'.  This sppeds up compilation
// of application
// programs considerably.

static Boolean          fHaveWaitNextEvent;
static Boolean          fDone;
static RgnHandle        fMouseRgn;
static EventRecord      fTheEvent;
static WindowPtr        fWhichWindow;

extern TAppWindow *current_window;

// Utility from Aple MPW C++ Example Programs:
TrapAvailable(short tNumber,TrapType tType)
{
    return NGetTrapAddress (tNumber, tType)  !=
GetTrapAddress(_Unimplemented);
}
```

```
//////////////////////////////////////////////////////////////
//                                                          //
//                  TAppApp Method Definitions:             //
//                                                          //
//////////////////////////////////////////////////////////////


TAppApp::TAppApp(void)
{
    SysEnvRec envRec;

    // Initialize the Mac Toolbox components
    InitGraf((Ptr) &qd.thePort);
    InitFonts();
    InitWindows();
    InitMenus();
    TEInit();
    InitDialogs((ResumeProcPtr) nil);
    InitCursor();

    (void) SysEnvirons(curSysEnvVers, &envRec);

    // Are we running on a 128K ROM machine or better???
    if (envRec.machineType < 0) {
        Warning("This machine does not have 128K ROMs!");
        exit(1);
    }

    // Expand the heap so new code segments load at the top
    MaxApplZone();
    // check to see if WaitNextEvent is implemented
    fHaveWaitNextEvent = TrapAvailable(_WaitNextEvent, ToolTrap);

    // initialize our class variables
    fWindow = nil;
    fDone = false;
    fMouseRgn = nil;
    fWhichWindow = nil;

    Handle menuBar;
    menuBar = GetNewMBar(rMenuBar);
    SetMenuBar(menuBar);
    DisposHandle(menuBar);
    AddResMenu(GetMHandle(mApple), 'DRVR');
    DrawMenuBar();
    fMouseRgn = NewRgn();

    // Make a single document window for this application:
    fWindow = new TAppWindow(rDocWindow);

}

//
//                                                      Handle events:
//


void TAppApp::EventLoop(void)
{
    int gotEvent;
```

```
EventRecord tEvt;
short partCode;
unsigned char evType;
long mResult;
WindowPtr tWind;
char key;

current_window->idle_proc();  // do idle work

while (fDone == false) {
    // always set up fWhichWindow before doing anything
    fWhichWindow = FrontWindow();
    // make sure we always draw into correct window
    SetPort(fWhichWindow);

    current_window->idle_proc();  // application idle work callback

    if (fHaveWaitNextEvent) {
        gotEvent = WaitNextEvent(everyEvent, &tEvt, (unsigned long)0,
fMouseRgn);
    } else {
        SystemTask();
        gotEvent = GetNextEvent(everyEvent, &tEvt);
    }
}
fTheEvent = tEvt;

// make sure we got a real event
if ( gotEvent ) {
    switch (fTheEvent.what) {
        case mouseDown :
            // As per Apple program examples, make sure that we
            // dereference object field references:
            partCode = FindWindow(fTheEvent.where, &tWind);
            fWhichWindow = tWind;
            tEvt = fTheEvent;
            switch (partCode) {
                case inSysWindow :
                    break;
                case inMenuBar :
                    mResult = MenuSelect(tEvt.where);
                    if (mResult != 0)
                      DoMenuCommand((short)HiWrd(mResult),
                                    (short)LoWrd(mResult));
                    break;
                case inGoAway :
                    break;
                case inDrag :
                    DragWindow(fWhichWindow, fTheEvent.where,
                               &qd.screenBits.bounds);
                    break;
                case inGrow :
                    break;
                case inZoomIn :
                case inZoomOut :
                    break;
                case inContent :
                    // If window is not in front, make it so
                    if ( fWhichWindow != FrontWindow() )
                      SelectWindow(fWhichWindow);
```

```
                    else if (fWindow != nil)
                      fWindow->DoContent(&tEvt);

                    break;
        }
        break;
      case mouseUp :
        break;
      case keyDown :
      case autoKey :
        key = (char) (fTheEvent.message & charCodeMask);
        if ((fTheEvent.modifiers & cmdKey) &&
            (fTheEvent.what == keyDown)) {
          mResult = MenuKey(key);
          if (mResult != 0) {
            DoMenuCommand((short)HiWrd(mResult),
                          (short)LoWrd(mResult));
                return;
            }
          }
          if (fWindow != nil) {
            // no document key handling used...
          }
          break;
        case updateEvt :
          // The event record contains window ptr
          fWhichWindow = (WindowPtr) fTheEvent.message;
          SetPort(fWhichWindow);
          if (fWindow != nil)
            fWindow->DoUpdate();
          break;
        case diskEvt :
          break;
        case activateEvt :
          // The event record contains window ptr
          fWhichWindow = (WindowPtr) fTheEvent.message;
          SetPort(fWhichWindow);
          break;
        case kOsEvent :
          // MultiFinder check as per Apple example programs:
          evType = (unsigned char) (fTheEvent.message >> 24) &
0x00ff;

          switch (evType) {     // High byte of message is type
                                // of event
            case kMouseMovedMessage :
              current_window->idle_proc(); // application idle
                                           // work
              break;
            case kSuspendResumeMessage :
              break;
          }
          break;
        default :
          break;
      } // end switch (fTheEvent.what)
    }
  }
}

//
```

```
//                                               Handle menu commands:
//

void TAppApp::DoMenuCommand(short menuID, short menuItem)
{
    short       itemHit;
    Str255      daName;
    short       daRefNum;
    WindowPtr   window;
    TAppWindow* fAppCurDoc = (TAppWindow*) fWindow;
    window = FrontWindow();
    switch ( menuID )
      {
      case mApple:
          switch ( menuItem ) {
              case iAbout:
                  itemHit = Alert(rAboutAlert, nil);  // "About" box
                  break;
              default:
                  GetItem(GetMHandle(mApple), menuItem, daName);
                  daRefNum = OpenDeskAcc(daName);
                  break;
          }
          break;
      case mFile:
          fDone = true;
          break;
      case mApp:
          fAppCurDoc->do_menu_action(menuItem); // user supplied
          break;
      }
    HiliteMenu(0);                     // unhighlight menu
}


////////////////////////////////////////////////////////////////////
//                                                                  //
//                   TAppWindow Method Definitions:                 //
//                                                                  //
////////////////////////////////////////////////////////////////////

TAppWindow::TAppWindow(short resID)
{
    fDocWindow = GetNewWindow(resID,nil,(WindowPtr) -1);
    SetPort(fDocWindow);
    ShowWindow(fDocWindow);      // Make sure the window is visible
    bottom_text_clip = 0; // flag to indicate no scrolling text area is
                          // set up
    clear_display(); // new 11/26/91
    in_scrolling_text_mode = 0;
    redraw_both_text_and_graphics = 0;
}


TAppWindow::~TAppWindow(void)
{
    DisposeWindow(fDocWindow);
}

void TAppWindow::draw_update_contents(void)
```

```
{
    if (in_scrolling_text_mode == 0 || redraw_both_text_and_graphics ==
1)
        update_display();  // Defined in user code
    if (bottom_text_clip > 0 &&
        ( in_scrolling_text_mode == 1 ||
        redraw_both_text_and_graphics == 1)) {

        Rect r;
        SetRect(&r,left_text_clip,top_text_clip-2,
                right_text_clip,bottom_text_clip+2);
        EraseRect(&r);

        Rect saveVis= fDocWindow->portRect;
        SetRect(&r,left_text_clip+2,top_text_clip+2,
                right_text_clip-2,bottom_text_clip-2);
        ClipRect(&r);

        // Refresh any user scrolling text:
        int next = current_ring_buffer_start;
        for (int i=0; i<number_of_saved_lines; i++) {
            next--;
            if (next < 0)   next = number_of_saved_lines - 1;
            plot_string(left_text_clip + 3,
                        bottom_text_clip - 2 -i*(string_height(" ") + 2),
                        saved_text[next]);
        }
        ClipRect(&saveVis);
        if (redraw_both_text_and_graphics == 1) {
            r.bottom += 2; r.top -= 2;
            FrameRect(&r);
        }
    }
}

void TAppWindow::DoUpdate(void)
{
    BeginUpdate(fDocWindow);              // this sets up the visRgn
    if (EmptyRgn(fDocWindow->visRgn) == 0) {
        draw_update_contents();
    }
    EndUpdate(fDocWindow);
}


static int iabs(int val)
{
    if (val > 0)    return val;
    return -val;
}


void TAppWindow::DoContent(EventRecord* /*theEvent*/)
{
    Point where; GetMouse(&where); /* = theEvent->where;   */
    mouse_down(where.h, where.v);

    Point p1;
    while (Button()) {
        GetMouse(&p1);
```

```
        mouse_up(pl.h, pl.v);
        // update_display();      // 2/17/92: commented this out for
                                  // compatibility with Window 3.0
}

void TAppWindow::plot_line(int x1, int y1, int x2, int y2)
{
    SetPort(fDocWindow);
    MoveTo(x1, y1);
    LineTo(x2, y2);
    in_scrolling_text_mode = 0;
}

void TAppWindow::plot_string(int x1, int y1, char *cp)
{
    SetPort(fDocWindow);
    TextMode(srcCopy);
    MoveTo(x1, y1);
    char buf[255];
    int len = strlen(cp);
    if (len < 254) {
        sprintf(&(buf[1]),"%s",cp);
          buf[0] = len;
          DrawString((Str255)buf);
    }
    in_scrolling_text_mode = 0;
}

void TAppWindow::plot_rect(int top, int right, int bottom, int left)
{
    Rect r;
    SetRect(&r, left, top, right, bottom);
    FrameRect(&r);
    in_scrolling_text_mode = 0;
}

void TAppWindow::erase_rect(int top, int right, int bottom, int left)
{
    Rect r;
    SetRect(&r, left, top, right, bottom);
    EraseRect(&r);
    in_scrolling_text_mode = 0;
}

void TAppWindow::plot_oval(int top, int right, int bottom, int left)
{
    Rect r;
    SetRect(&r, left, top, right, bottom);
    FrameOval(&r);
    in_scrolling_text_mode = 0;
}


int  TAppWindow::string_height(char *)
{
    FontInfo fi;
    GetFontInfo(&fi);
```

```
        return (fi.ascent + fi.descent + fi.leading);
}


int  TAppWindow::string_width(char *str)
{
    FontInfo fi;
    GetFontInfo(&fi);
    return (fi.widMax * strlen(str) / 2) + 2;
}



void TAppWindow::clear_display()
{
    SetPort(fDocWindow);
    EraseRect(&fDocWindow->portRect);
    draw_update_contents();
}

void TAppWindow::do_about()
{
    Alert(128, nil);
}

void doNodeEdit(char *prompt, char *text);

void TAppWindow::do_edit(char * prompt, char *buf)
{
    doNodeEdit(prompt, buf);
}

void TAppWindow::show_info(char *buf)
{
    do_edit(" ", buf);
}


int TAppWindow::choose_one(char *prompt1, char *prompt2)
{
    DialogPtr dLog;
    short itemHit = 0;
    GrafPort *savePort;
    char buf1[257], buf2[257];
    Handle itemH;  Rect r;
    short itemType;
    GetPort (&savePort);

    dLog = GetNewDialog (515, (Ptr)0L, (WindowPtr) -1);

    InitCursor ();

    SetPort(dLog);

    itemHit = 0;

    // Set the prompt text field:

    GetDItem(dLog, (short)1, &itemType, &itemH, &r);
    if (itemH != (Handle) 0) {
```

```
            sprintf(&(buf1[1]),"%s",prompt1);  buf1[0] = strlen(prompt1);
            SetCTitle((ControlHandle)itemH, (Str255)buf1);
    }

    GetDItem(dLog, (short)2, &itemType, &itemH, &r);
    if (itemH != (Handle) 0) {
        sprintf(&(buf2[1]),"%s",prompt2);  buf2[0] = strlen(prompt2);
        SetCTitle((ControlHandle)itemH, (Str255)buf2);
    }

    while ((itemHit != 1) && (itemHit != 2))
            ModalDialog(nil,&itemHit);

    DisposDialog (dLog);
    SetPort (savePort);
    return itemHit - 1;  // Return 0 or 1, NOT 1 or 2
}

// Handle single list selection (like Figure 5.3):

static pascal void myItem(DialogPtr dlg, short itemNumber)
{
    Handle itemHandle;
    short itemType;
    Rect itemRect;
    GetDItem(dlg, itemNumber, &itemType, &itemHandle, &itemRect);
    if (itemNumber == 3) {  // list user item
        ListHandle myList = (ListHandle)((DialogPeek)dlg)->window.refCon;
        LUpdate(dlg->visRgn, myList);
        InsetRect(&itemRect, -2, -2);
        FrameRect(&itemRect);
    }
}
static int itemSelected;

pascal Boolean myFilter(DialogPtr dlg, EventRecord *event, short
*itemHit)
{
    itemSelected = -1;
    short itemType;
    Handle itemH;
    Rect itemR;
    if (event->what == mouseDown) {
        GetDItem(dlg, (short)3, &itemType, &itemH, &itemR);  // list box
      Point where = event->where;
      GlobalToLocal(&where);
        if (PtInRect(where, &itemR)) {
            ListHandle myList = (ListHandle)((DialogPeek)dlg)-
>window.refCon;
            if (LClick(where, event->modifiers, myList)) {
                Point cellSelected = LLastClick(myList);
                itemSelected = cellSelected.v;
                *itemHit = 1;
                return true;
            }
        }
        GetDItem(dlg, (short)1, &itemType, &itemH, &itemR);  // Cancel
button
        if (PtInRect(where, &itemR)) { *itemHit = 1;  return true; }
        *itemHit = 3;
```

```
                return true;
        }
        if (event->what == keyDown)  { *itemHit = 1;  return true; }
        return false;
}

int TAppWindow::choose_one_from_list(char *prompt, char **list_items,
                                      int number_of_items)
{
        DialogPtr dLog;
        short itemHit = 0;
        GrafPort *savePort;
        char buf[257];
        Handle itemH;   Rect r;
        short itemType;
        GetPort (&savePort);

        dLog = GetNewDialog (511, (Ptr)0L, (WindowPtr) -1);

        InitCursor ();

        // Set up data for List Manager:
        SetPort(dLog);
        Rect itemR, dataR;
        GetDItem(dLog, (short)3, &itemType, &itemH, &itemR);
        SetDItem(dLog, (short)3, itemType, (Handle)myItem, &itemR);
        itemR.right -=15;
        SetRect(&dataR, 0, 0, 1, number_of_items);
        Point cellSize; SetPt(&cellSize, 260, 18);
        ListHandle myList = LNew(&itemR,&dataR, cellSize, 0, (WindowPtr)dLog,
                                                false,  false,  true,
true);
        // As per TN example, allow dialog access to List data structures:
        ((DialogPeek)dLog)->window.refCon = (long)myList;

        // Initialize the list cell contents:
        for (int i=0; i<number_of_items; i++) {
            Point cellLocation;
            cellLocation.v = i; cellLocation.h = 0;
            LSetCell(list_items[i], strlen(list_items[i]), cellLocation,
myList);
        }
        LDoDraw(true,myList);

        itemHit = 0;
        SetRect(&r,0,0,400,400);

        // Set the prompt text field:
        GetDItem(dLog, (short)2, &itemType, &itemH, &r);
        sprintf(&(buf[1]),"%s",prompt);  buf[0] = strlen(prompt);
        SetIText(itemH, (Str255)buf);

        while ((itemHit != 1))
                ModalDialog(myFilter,&itemHit);

        if (itemHit == 1) {  // Cancel

        }

        LDispose(myList);
```

```
      DisposDialog (dLog);
      SetPort (savePort);
      return itemSelected;
}


void TAppWindow::init_scrolling_text(int top, int right, int bottom, int
left)
{
      top_text_clip    = top;
      right_text_clip  = right;
      bottom_text_clip = bottom;
      left_text_clip   = left;
      number_of_saved_lines = 1 + ((bottom_text_clip - top_text_clip) /
                                                      string_height ("
"));
      if (number_of_saved_lines > MAX_TEXT_LINES)
          number_of_saved_lines = MAX_TEXT_LINES;
      Rect r;
      SetRect(&r,left_text_clip,top_text_clip-
2,right_text_clip,bottom_text_clip+2);
      EraseRect(&r);

      current_ring_buffer_start = 0;
      // Allocate storage for saved text lines:
      for (int i=0; i<number_of_saved_lines; i++) {
          saved_text[i] = new char[MAX_TEXT_LINE_SIZE + 1];
          saved_text[i][0] = '\0';
      }
      in_scrolling_text_mode = 1;
      redraw_both_text_and_graphics = 1;
      // Set the font to a non-proportional spacing font:
      TextFont(4);    // Monoco(display looks better with a non-
                      // proportional font)
}

void TAppWindow::init_scrolling_text()
{
      // Set the text area with content rectangle of the window:
      Rect r = fDocWindow->portRect;
      top_text_clip    = r.top+5;
      right_text_clip  = r.right+11;
      bottom_text_clip = r.bottom-4;
      left_text_clip   = r.left+5;
      number_of_saved_lines = 1 + ((bottom_text_clip - top_text_clip) /
                                                      string_height ("
"));
      if (number_of_saved_lines > MAX_TEXT_LINES)
          number_of_saved_lines = MAX_TEXT_LINES;
      Rect r2;
      SetRect(&r2,left_text_clip,top_text_clip-
2,right_text_clip,bottom_text_clip+2);
      EraseRect(&r2);

      current_ring_buffer_start = 0;
      // Allocate storage for saved text lines:
      for (int i=0; i<number_of_saved_lines; i++) {
          saved_text[i] = new char[MAX_TEXT_LINE_SIZE + 1];
          saved_text[i][0] = '\0';
      }
```

```
      in_scrolling_text_mode = 1;
      redraw_both_text_and_graphics = 0;  // entire window used for
scrolling text.
      // Set the font to a non-proportional spacing font:
      TextFont(4);    // Monoco(display looks better with a non-
                      // proportional font)
}
```

```
void TAppWindow::put_scrolling_text(char *str)
{
    if (bottom_text_clip != 0)  {
        Rect saveVis= fDocWindow->portRect;
        Rect r;
        RgnHandle h = NewRgn();

    SetRect(&r,left_text_clip,top_text_clip,right_text_clip,bottom_text_c
lip);
        ClipRect(&r);
        ScrollRect(&r, 0, -string_height(str) - 2, h);
        plot_string(left_text_clip + 1, bottom_text_clip - 2, str);
        DisposeRgn(h);
        char buf[257];
        if (strlen(str) < 256) {
            sprintf(buf,"%s",str);
            buf[MAX_TEXT_LINE_SIZE] = '\0';
            sprintf(saved_text[current_ring_buffer_start],"%s",buf);
            current_ring_buffer_start++;
            if (current_ring_buffer_start > (number_of_saved_lines - 1))
                current_ring_buffer_start = 0;
        }
        ClipRect(&saveVis);
        if (redraw_both_text_and_graphics == 1) {
            r.bottom += 2; r.top -= 2;
            FrameRect(&r);
        }
    } else {
        Warning("TAppWindow:  called  put_scrolling_text  before
init_scrolling_text");
    }
    in_scrolling_text_mode = 1;
}
```

```
void TAppWindow::reset_scrolling_text()
{
    for (int i=0; i<MAX_TEXT_LINES; i++) {
        saved_text[i][0] = '\0';
    }
}
```

```
static char *fileExtension;

pascal Boolean fileFilter(ParmBlkPtr paramBlock)
{
    int size2 = strlen(fileExtension);
    StringPtr sPtr = paramBlock->fileParam.ioNamePtr;
    char * fileName = (char *)sPtr;
    int size = fileName[0];
    char buf[257];
```

```
    for (int i=0; i<size; i++) buf[i] = fileName[i+1];
    buf[size] = '\0';
    // Find the position of the first '.' character of the extension (if
any):
    if (size2 > 0) {
        for (i=0; i<size; i++)
            if (buf[i] == '.') {
                if ((size - i) >= size2) {
                    int found_match = 1;
                    for (int j=i+1; j<size; j++)
                        if (buf[j] != fileExtension[j - i - 1])
                            found_match = 0;
                    if (found_match) {
                    return false;
                    }
                }
            }
        return true; // skip this file name
    }
    return false; // no file extension specified, so return every file
}

int TAppWindow::choose_file_to_read(char * prompt, char * extension,
        char *returned_filename)   // 0 return -> OK, 1 return -> Failure
{
    fileExtension = extension;
    SFReply sf;
    Point p; p.h = 100; p.v = 100;
    char prompt_buf[256];
    for (int k=0; k<strlen(prompt); k++)
        prompt_buf[k+1] = prompt[k];
    prompt_buf[0] = strlen(prompt);
    SFGetFile(p, (Str255)prompt_buf, (FileFilterProcPtr)fileFilter, -1,
            (SFTypeList)nil, (DlgHookProcPtr)nil, &sf);

    int size = sf.fName[0];
    if (sf.good == 0)   size = 0;
    for (int i=0; i<size; i++)   returned_filename[i] = sf.fName[i+1];
    returned_filename[size] = '\0';
    if (size > 0) return 0;
     else          return 1;
}

int TAppWindow::choose_file_to_write(char *prompt,
        char *returned_filename) // 0 return -> OK, 1 return -> Failure
{
    SFReply sf;
    Point p; p.h = 100; p.v = 100;
    char prompt_buf[256];
    for (int k=0; k<strlen(prompt); k++)
        prompt_buf[k+1] = prompt[k];
    prompt_buf[0] = strlen(prompt);
    SFPutFile(p, (Str255)prompt_buf, (Str255)"", (DlgHookProcPtr)nil,
&sf);
    int size = sf.fName[0];
    for (int i=0; i<size; i++)   returned_filename[i] = sf.fName[i+1];
    returned_filename[size] = '\0';
    if (size > 0) return 0;
     else          return 1;
}
```

```
void Warning(char *message)
{
#if 0
    char buf[255];
    sprintf(buf," %s",message);
    buf[0] = strlen(buf);

    SetCursor(&qd.arrow);
    ParamText((Str255)buf, "\p", "\p", "\p");
    (void) Alert(129, (ModalFilterProcPtr) nil);   // 129 is the ALRT
                                                    // resource number
#endif
    current_window->show_info(message);
}



#define NAME_SIZE 256
#define TEXT_SIZE 256

void doNodeEdit(char *prompt, char *text)
{
    DialogPtr dLog;
    short itemHit = 0;
    GrafPort *savePort;
    char buf[257];
    /*int itemType;*/  Handle itemH;  Rect r;  int len;
    short itemType;
    GetPort (&savePort);

    dLog = GetNewDialog (501, (Ptr)OL, (WindowPtr) -1);

    InitCursor ();

    itemHit = 0;
    SetRect(&r,0,0,400,400);

    GetDItem(dLog, (short)4, &itemType, &itemH, &r);
    sprintf(&(buf[1]),"%s",prompt);  buf[0] = strlen(prompt);
    SetIText(itemH, (Str255)buf);

    GetDItem(dLog, (short)3, &itemType, &itemH, &r);
    sprintf(&(buf[1]),"%s",text);  buf[0] = strlen(text);
    SetIText(itemH, (Str255)buf);

    while ((itemHit != 2) && (itemHit != 1))
            ModalDialog(nil,&itemHit);

    if (itemHit == 1) {  // OK
       GetDItem(dLog, (short)3, &itemType, &itemH, &r);
       GetIText(itemH, (Str255)buf);
       if (TEXT_SIZE>buf[0]) len = buf[0];  else len = TEXT_SIZE - 1;
       for (int i=0; i<len; i++) text[i] = buf[i+1];
       text[len] = '\0';
    }

    DisposDialog (dLog);
    SetPort (savePort);
}
```

C.4   Macintosh-Specific Smart Vector Include Files

File char_v.h

```
// File: char_v.h
//
// Description: smart character vector
//
// Copyright 1992 by Mark Watson Associates
//
//         No binary rights reserved: this software library may be used in
//         compiled form without restrictions.  All source rights
//         reserved: Source code to the GUI library can not be distributed
//         (on bulletin boards, or as part of shareware or commercial
//         products)
//         without written permission.
//
//         This software is provided "as is". The user accepts all
//         responsibility for its use.
//


#ifndef __char_vect
#define __char_vect

#include <iostream.h>
#include <fstream.h>
#include "apptypes.h"

#define output (ios::out)
#define input (ios::in)

class char_vect {
    Long size;
    void grow(Long new_size);
        Long ub() { return (size - 1); }
  public:
    Char *p;
    char_vect(void);
    char_vect (long n);
    char_vect(char_vect &v);
    char_vect(Char a[], long n);
    ~char_vect() { delete p; }
    Char & operator [] (long i);   // range check safeguards
    void save(char *filename);
    void restore(char *filename);
};

#endif
```

File double_v.h

```
// File: double_v.h
//
// Description:  smart double vector
//
// Copyright 1992 by Mark Watson Associates
//
//         No binary rights reserved: this software library may be used in
//         compiled form without restrictions.  All source rights
```

```
//        reserved: Source code to the GUI library can not be distributed
//        (on bulletin boards, or as part of shareware or commercial
//        products)
//        without written permission.
//

#ifndef __double_vect
#define __double_vect

#include <stream.h>

class double_vect {
    double *p;
    int size;
    void grow(int new_size);
  public:
        int ub() { return (size - 1); }
    double_vect(void);
    double_vect (int n);
    double_vect(double_vect &v);
    double_vect(double a[], int n);
    ~double_vect() { delete p; }
    double & operator [] (int i);   // range check safeguards
    void save(char *filename);
    void restore(char *filename);
};

#endif
```

File int_vect.h

```
// File: int_vect.h
//
// Description:  smart int vector
//
// Copyright 1992 by Mark Watson Associates
//
//        No binary rights reserved: this software library may be used in
//        compiled form without restrictions.  All source rights
//        reserved: Source code to the GUI library can not be distributed
//        (on bulletin boards, or as part of shareware or commercial
//        products)
//        without written permission.
//

#ifndef __int_vect
#define __int_vect

#include <stream.h>

class int_vect {
    int *p;
    int size;
    void grow(int new_size);
        int ub() { return (size - 1); }
  public:
    int num_elements;
    int_vect(void);
    int_vect (int n);
    int_vect(int_vect &v);
```

```
    int_vect(int a[], int n);
    ~int_vect() { delete p; }
    int & operator [] (int i);   // range check safeguards
    void save(char *filename);
    void restore(char *filename);
};

#endif
```

C.5 Macintosh-Specific Smart Vector C++ Source Files

File char_v.cp

```
// File: char_v.cp
//
// Description: smart vector implementation for characters
//
// Copyright 1992 by Mark Watson Associates
//
//         No binary rights reserved: the GUI library may be used
//         in compiled form without restrictions. All source rights
//         reserved: Source code to the GUI library can not be
//         distributed (on bulletin boards,
//         or as part of shareware or
//         commercial products) without written permission.
//
//         This software is provided "as is". The user accepts all
//         responsibility for its use.
//


#include "char_v.h"

extern "C" { void exit(int); };

extern void Warning(char *);

// Define constants for the dynamic grow rate for char_vect data types
// and the maximum number of elements that a smart char_vect can have:

const int GROW_RATE = 4096;
const int MAX_SIZE = 1048576;

char_vect::char_vect(void)
{
    size = 32768;
    p = new char[size];
}

char_vect::char_vect(long n)
{
    if (n<= 0) {
        Warning("illegal size for a char_vect");
        exit(1);
    }
```

```
        size = n;
        p = new char[size];
}

char_vect::char_vect(Char a[], long n)
{
    if (n<= 0) {
        Warning("illegal size for a char_vect");
        exit(1);
    }
    size = n;
    p = new char[size];
    for (long i=0; i<size; i++)  p[i] = a[i];
}

char_vect::char_vect(char_vect &v)
{
    size = v.size;
    p = new char[size];
    for (long i=0; i<size; i++)  p[i] = v.p[i];
}

Char & char_vect::operator [] (long i)
{
    if (i < 0) {
        Warning("illegal index for a char_vect");
        exit(1);
    }
    if (i > ub()) {
        grow(i);
    }
    return (p[i]);
}

void char_vect::grow(long new_size)
{
    if ((new_size + GROW_RATE) >= MAX_SIZE) {
        Warning("illegal re-size for a char_vect");
        exit(1);
    }
    Char *np = new Char[(new_size + GROW_RATE)];
    for (long i=0; i<size; i++) np[i] = p[i];
    delete p;
    size = (new_size + GROW_RATE);
    p = np;
}

void char_vect::save(char *file_name)
{
    filebuf out_file;
    if (out_file.open(file_name, output)==0) {
//      cerr << "Could not open output file " << file_name << "\n";
        exit(1);
    }
    ostream out_stream(&out_file);
    out_stream << size << "\n";
    for (long i=0; i<size; i++)
        out_stream << p[i] << "\n";
    out_file.close();
}
```

```
void char_vect::restore(char *file_name)
{
    filebuf in_file;
    if (in_file.open(file_name, input)==0) {
//      cerr << "Could not open input file " << file_name << "\n";
        exit(1);
    }
    istream in_stream(&in_file);
    in_stream >> size;
    for (long i=0; i<size; i++)
        in_stream >> p[i];
    in_file.close();
}

#if 0

// test code:

void main()
{
    cerr << "Start of char_vect test:\n\n";
    char_vect vv;
    for (long l=0; l<256000; l++) vv[l] = (char)(l % 128);
    for (l=0; l<256000; l++)
        if (vv[l] != (char)((l % 128)))  cerr << "Error " << l << "\n";
    cerr << "Done with test.\n";
}

#endif
```

File double_v.cp

```
// File: double_v.cp
//
// Description: smart vector implementation for doubles
//
// File: char_v.h
//
// Description: smart character vector
//
// Copyright 1992 by Mark Watson Associates
//
//         No binary rights reserved: this software library may be used in
//         compiled form without restrictions.  All source rights
//         reserved: Source code to the GUI library can not be distributed
//         (on bulletin boards, or as part of shareware or commercial
//         products) without written permission.
//
//
//         This software is provided "as is". The user accepts all
//         responsibility for its use.
//

#include "double_v.h"

extern "C" { void exit(int); };

// Define constants for the dynamic grow rate for double_vect data types
and
```

```
// the maximum number of elements that a smart double_vect can have:

const int GROW_RATE = 1;
const int MAX_SIZE = 5000;

double_vect::double_vect(void)
{
    size = 10;
    p = new double[size];
}

double_vect::double_vect(int n)
{
    if (n<= 0) {
        cerr << "illeagl size for a double_vect = " << n << "\n";
        exit(1);
    }
    size = n;
    p = new double[size];
}

double_vect::double_vect(double a[], int n)
{
    if (n<= 0) {
        cerr << "illeagl size for a double_vect = " << n << "\n";
        exit(1);
    }
    size = n;
    p = new double[size];
    for (int i=0; i<size; i++)  p[i] = a[i];
}

double_vect::double_vect(double_vect &v)
{
    size = v.size;
    p = new double[size];
    for (int i=0; i<size; i++)  p[i] = v.p[i];
}

double & double_vect::operator [] (int i)
{
    if (i < 0) {
        cerr << "illegal index for double_vect = " << i << "\n";
        exit(1);
    }
    if (i > ub()) {
        grow(i);
    }
    return (p[i]);
}

void double_vect::grow(int new_size)
{
    if ((new_size + GROW_RATE) >= MAX_SIZE) {
        cerr << "error in dynamic resizing of a smart double_vect, new
size = "
            << (new_size + GROW_RATE) << "\n";
        exit(1);
    }
```

```
        double *np = new double[(new_size + GROW_RATE)];
        for (int i=0; i<size; i++)  np[i] = p[i];
        delete p;
        size = (new_size + GROW_RATE);
        p = np;
}

void double_vect::save(char *file_name)
{
    filebuf out_file;
    if (out_file.open(file_name, output)==0) {
//      cerr << "Could not open output file " << file_name << "\n";
        exit(1);
    }
    ostream out_stream(&out_file);
    out_stream << size << "\n";
    for (int i=0; i<size; i++)
        out_stream << p[i] << "\n";
    out_file.close();
}

void double_vect::restore(char *file_name)
{
    filebuf in_file;
    if (in_file.open(file_name, input)==0) {
//      cerr << "Could not open input file " << file_name << "\n";
        exit(1);
    }
    istream in_stream(&in_file);
    in_stream >> size;
    for (int i=0; i<size; i++)
        in_stream >> p[i];
    in_file.close();
}

#if 0

// test code:

main()
{
    cerr << "Start of double_vect test:\n\n";
    double_vect vv(10);
    vv[2] = 2;
    vv[220] = vv[2];  // illegal index !!
    cerr << "Done with test.\n";
}

#endif
```

File int_vect.cp

```
// File: int_vect.cp
//
// Description: This file implements the int smart vector class
//
// Copyright 1992 by Mark Watson Associates
//
//         No binary rights reserved: this software library may be used in
//         compiled form without restrictions.  All source rights
```

```
//          reserved: Source code to the GUI library can not be distributed
//          (on bulletin boards, or as part of shareware or commercial
//          products)without written permission.
//
//
//          This software is provided "as is". The user accepts all
//          responsibility for its use.
```

```
#include "int_vect.h"

extern "C" { void exit(int); };

// Define constants for the dynamic grow rate for int_vect data types and
// the maximum number of elements that a smart int_vect can have:

const int GROW_RATE = 1;
const int MAX_SIZE = 5000;

int_vect::int_vect(void)
{
    num_elements = 0;
    size = 10;
    p = new int[size];
}

int_vect::int_vect(int n)
{
    if (n<= 0) {
        cerr << "illeagl size for a int_vect = " << n << "\n";
        exit(1);
    }
    num_elements = 0;
    size = n;
    p = new int[size];
}

int_vect::int_vect(int a[], int n)
{
    if (n<= 0) {
        cerr << "illeagl size for a int_vect = " << n << "\n";
        exit(1);
    }
    num_elements = size = n;
    p = new int[size];
    for (int i=0; i<size; i++)  p[i] = a[i];
}

int_vect::int_vect(int_vect &v)
{
    size = v.size;
    p = new int[size];
    for (int i=0; i<size; i++)  p[i] = v.p[i];
    num_elements = size;
}

int & int_vect::operator [] (int i)
{
    if (i < 0) {
        cerr << "illegal index for int_vect = " << i << "\n";
```

```
        exit(1);
    }
    if (i > ub()) {
        grow(i);
    }
    if ((i + 1) > num_elements)  num_elements = i+1;
    return (p[i]);
}

void int_vect::grow(int new_size)
{
    if ((new_size + GROW_RATE) >= MAX_SIZE) {
        cerr << "error in dynamic resizing of a smart int_vect, new size =
"
            << (new_size + GROW_RATE) << "\n";
        exit(1);
    }
    int *np = new int[(new_size + GROW_RATE)];
    for (int i=0; i<size; i++)  np[i] = p[i];
    delete p;
    size = (new_size + GROW_RATE);
    p = np;
}

void int_vect::save(char *file_name)
{
    filebuf out_file;
    if (out_file.open(file_name, output)==0) {
//      cerr << "Could not open output file " << file_name << "\n";
        exit(1);
    }
    ostream out_stream(&out_file);
    out_stream << size << "\n";
    for (int i=0; i<size; i++)
        out_stream << p[i] << "\n";
    out_file.close();
}

void int_vect::restore(char *file_name)
{
    filebuf in_file;
    if (in_file.open(file_name, input)==0) {
//      cerr << "Could not open input file " << file_name << "\n";
        exit(1);
    }
    istream in_stream(&in_file);
    in_stream >> size;
    num_elements = size;

    if (size > ub()-1)  grow(size);
    for (int i=0; i<size; i++)
        in_stream >> p[i];
    in_file.close();
}

#if 0

// test code:

main()
```

```
{
    cerr << "Start of int_vect test:\n\n";
    int_vect vv(10);
    vv[2] = 2;
    vv[220] = vv[2];   // illegal index !!
    cerr << "Done with test.\n";
}
```

```
#endif
```

C.6   Macintosh Makefiles

File chess3d.make

```
#    File:        chess3d.make
#    Target:      chess3d


OBJECTS = ∂
        chess3d.cp.o ∂
        applib.cp.o

chess3d ƒƒ chess3d.make applib.r
    Rez applib.r -append -o chess3d
chess3d ƒƒ chess3d.make chess3d.r
    Rez chess3d.r -append -o chess3d

chess3d.cp.o ƒ chess3d.make chess3d.cp applib.h
    CPlus -sym on chess3d.cp
applib.cp.o ƒ chess3d.make applib.cp applib.h
    CPlus -sym on applib.cp

chess3d ƒƒ chess3d.make {OBJECTS}
Link -w -t APPL -c MLW1 -sym on -mf ∂
    {OBJECTS} ∂
    "{Libraries}"Runtime.o ∂
    "{Libraries}"Interface.o ∂
    "{CLibraries}"StdCLib.o ∂
    #"{CLibraries}"CSANELib.o ∂
    #"{CLibraries}"Math.o ∂
    #"{CLibraries}"CInterface.o ∂
    "{CLibraries}"CPlusLib.o ∂
    #"{CLibraries}"Complex.o ∂
    -o chess3d
```

File draw.make

```
#    File:        draw.make
#    Target:      draw

OBJECTS = ∂
        draw.cp.o int_vect.cp.o ∂
        applib.cp.o

draw ƒƒ draw.make applib.r
    Rez applib.r -append -o draw
draw ƒƒ draw.make draw.r
    Rez draw.r -append -o draw
```

```
draw.cp.o ƒ draw.make draw.cp applib.h int_vect.h
    CPlus -sym on draw.cp
applib.cp.o ƒ draw.make applib.cp applib.h
    CPlus -sym on applib.cp
int_vect.cp.o ƒ draw.make int_vect.cp int_vect.h
    CPlus -sym on int_vect.cp

draw ƒƒ draw.make {OBJECTS}
    Link -w -t APPL -c MLW1 -sym on -mf ∂
        {OBJECTS} ∂
        "{Libraries}"Runtime.o ∂
        "{Libraries}"Interface.o ∂
        "{CLibraries}"StdCLib.o ∂
        #"{CLibraries}"CSANELib.o ∂
        #"{CLibraries}"Math.o ∂
        #"{CLibraries}"CInterface.o ∂
        "{CLibraries}"CPlusLib.o ∂
        #"{CLibraries}"Complex.o ∂
        -o draw
```

File hand.make

```
#    File:        hand.make
#    Target:      hand


OBJECTS = ∂
        hand.cp.o Grapher.cp.o ∂
        applib.cp.o dialog.cp.o int_vect.cp.o double_vect.cp.o ∂
        TNeural.cp.o

hand ƒƒ hand.make applib.r
    Rez applib.r -append -o hand
hand ƒƒ hand.make hand.r
    Rez hand.r -append -o hand

hand.cp.o ƒ hand.cp applib.h
    CPlus -sym on -mc68020 -mc68881 -elems881  hand.cp
applib.cp.o ƒ applib.cp applib.h
    CPlus -sym on -mc68020 -mc68881 -elems881  applib.cp
Grapher.cp.o ƒ Grapher.cp Grapher.h AppApp.h
    CPlus -sym on -mc68020 -mc68881 -elems881  Grapher.cp
dialog.cp.o ƒ dialog.cp
    CPlus -sym on -mc68020 -mc68881 -elems881  dialog.cp
TNeural.cp.o ƒ TNeural.cp
    CPlus -sym on -mc68020 -mc68881 -elems881  TNeural.cp
int_vect.cp.o ƒ int_vect.cp
    CPlus -sym on -mc68020 -mc68881 -elems881  int_vect.cp
double_vect.cp.o ƒ double_vect.cp
    CPlus -sym on -mc68020 -mc68881 -elems881  double_vect.cp

hand ƒƒ hand.make {OBJECTS}
    Link -w -t APPL -c MLW1 -sym on -mf ∂
        {OBJECTS} ∂
        "{CLibraries}"Clib881.o ∂
        "{Libraries}"Runtime.o ∂
        "{Libraries}"Interface.o ∂
        "{CLibraries}"StdCLib.o ∂
        "{CLibraries}"CSANELib881.o ∂
```

```
            "{CLibraries}"Math881.o ∂
           #"{CLibraries}"CInterface.o ∂
            "{CLibraries}"CPlusLib881.o ∂
           #"{CLibraries}"Complex.o ∂
            -o hand
```

File hib.make

```
#    File:       hib.make
#    Target:     hib


OBJECTS = ∂
        hib.cp.o tplot.cp.o Grapher.cp.o ∂
        applib.cp.o double_v.cp.o

hib ƒƒ hib.make applib.r
    Rez applib.r -append -o hib
hib ƒƒ hib.make hib.r
    Rez hib.r -append -o hib

hib.cp.o ƒ hib.make hib.cp applib.h Grapher.h tplot.h
       CPlus -sym on hib.cp
applib.cp.o ƒ hib.make applib.cp applib.h
       CPlus -sym on applib.cp
Grapher.cp.o ƒ hib.make Grapher.cp Grapher.h applib.h
       CPlus -sym on Grapher.cp

hib ƒƒ hib.make {OBJECTS}
    Link -w -t APPL -c MLW1 -sym on -mf ∂
        {OBJECTS} ∂
        "{Libraries}"Runtime.o ∂
        "{Libraries}"Interface.o ∂
        "{CLibraries}"StdCLib.o ∂
       #"{CLibraries}"CSANELib.o ∂
       #"{CLibraries}"Math.o ∂
       #"{CLibraries}"CInterface.o ∂
        "{CLibraries}"CPlusLib.o ∂
       #"{CLibraries}"Complex.o ∂
        -o hib
```

File test.make

```
#    File:       test.make
#    Target:     test


OBJECTS = ∂
        test.cp.o applib.cp.o tplot.cp.o Grapher.cp.o ∂
        double_v.cp.o

test ƒƒ test.make applib.r
    Rez applib.r -append -o test
test ƒƒ test.make test.r
    Rez test.r -append -o test

test.cp.o ƒ test.make test.cp applib.h Grapher.h tplot.h
       CPlus -sym on test.cp
applib.cp.o ƒ test.make applib.cp applib.h
       CPlus -sym on applib.cp
```

```
double_v.cp.o ƒ test.make double_v.cp
    CPlus -sym on double_v.cp
Grapher.cp.o ƒ test.make Grapher.cp Grapher.h applib.h
    CPlus -sym on Grapher.cp

test ƒƒ test.make {OBJECTS}
    Link -w -t APPL -c MLW1 -sym on -mf ∂
        {OBJECTS} ∂
        "{Libraries}"Runtime.o ∂
        "{Libraries}"Interface.o ∂
        "{CLibraries}"StdCLib.o ∂
        #"{CLibraries}"CSANELib.o ∂
        #"{CLibraries}"Math.o ∂
        #"{CLibraries}"CInterface.o ∂
        "{CLibraries}"CPlusLib.o ∂
        #"{CLibraries}"Complex.o ∂
        -o test
```

File textbr.make

```
#   File:        textbr.make
#   Target:      textbr


OBJECTS = ∂
        textbr.cp.o Grapher.cp.o ∂
        applib.cp.o dialog.cp.o char_v.cp.o TextInd.cp.o

textbr ƒƒ textbr.make applib.r
    Rez applib.r -append -o textbr
textbr ƒƒ textbr.make textbr.r
    Rez textbr.r -append -o textbr

textbr.cp.o ƒ textbr.cp applib.h
    CPlus -sym on -mc68020 -mc68881 -elems881  textbr.cp
applib.cp.o ƒ applib.cp applib.h
    CPlus -sym on -mc68020 -mc68881 -elems881  applib.cp
TextInd.cp.o ƒ TextInd.cp TextInd.h AppApp.h
    CPlus -sym on -mc68020 -mc68881 -elems881  TextInd.cp
dialog.cp.o ƒ dialog.cp
    CPlus -sym on -mc68020 -mc68881 -elems881  dialog.cp
char_v.cp.o ƒ char_v.cp
    CPlus -sym on -mc68020 -mc68881 -elems881  char_v.cp

textbr ƒƒ textbr.make {OBJECTS}
    Link -w -t APPL -c MLW1 -sym on -mf ∂
        {OBJECTS} ∂
        "{CLibraries}"Clib881.o ∂
        "{Libraries}"Runtime.o ∂
        "{Libraries}"Interface.o ∂
        "{CLibraries}"StdCLib.o ∂
        "{CLibraries}"CSANELib881.o ∂
        "{CLibraries}"Math881.o ∂
        #"{CLibraries}"CInterface.o ∂
        "{CLibraries}"CPlusLib881.o ∂
        #"{CLibraries}"Complex.o ∂
        -o textbr
```

D

X Windows Class Implementation

D.1 X Windows Menu Definition Include Files

File br_menu.h

```
// File: br_menu.h
//
// Description: use this to define your menu entries for the X Window
//              version of the C++ GUI library. Note that the Macintosh
//              and Microsoft Windows versions of the C++ GUI library
use
//              resources to define menu items.

const int num_menu_items = 5;
static char *menu_titles[5]={"Load index file","Add text file to in-
dex",
                        "Save current index", "Word search",
                        "Quit      "};
```

File ch_menu.h

```
// File: ch_menu.h
//
// Description: use this to define your menu entries for the X Window
//              version of the C++ GUI library. Note that the Macintosh
//              and Microsoft Windows versions of the C++ GUI library
//              use
//              resources to define menu items.

const int num_menu_items = 5;
static char *menu_titles[8]={"Play white       ",
                        "Play black       ",
```

File d_menu.h

```
// File: d_menu.h
//
// Description: use this to define your menu entries for the X Window
//              version of the C++ GUI library. Note that the Macintosh
//              and Windows 3.0 versions of the C++ GUI library use
//              resources to define menu items.

const int num_menu_items = 3;
static char *menu_titles[3]={"Erase window","Save...","Load..."};
```

File h_menu.h

```
// File: h_menu.h
//
// Description: use this to define your menu entries for the X Window
//              version of the C++ GUI library. Note that the Macintosh
//              and Windows 3.0 versions of the C++ GUI library use
//              resources to define menu items.
              const int num_menu_items = 4;
              static char *menu_titles[4]={"Record training data",
                                           "Train and save weights",
                                           "Reload saved weights",
                                           "Test recognition"};
```

File t_menu.h

```
// File: t_menu.h
//
// Description: use this to define your menu entries for the X Window
//              version of the C++ GUI library. Note that the Macintosh
//              and Windows 3.0 versions of the C++ GUI library use
//              resources to define menu items.

const int num_menu_items = 8;
static char *menu_titles[8]={"Test Grapher","Test Edit box",
                             "Test Info box","Single list test",
                             "Test choose 1 of 2", "Test scrolling text",
                             "Test data plotting","Quit      "};
```

D.2 X-Windows-Specific GUI Include Files

File applib.h

```
// File: applib.h
//
// Description: Header file for X Window GUI library
//
// Copyright 1992 by Mark Watson Associates
//
//      No binary rights reserved: this software library may be used in
//      compiled form without restrictions.  All source rights
//      reserved: Source code to the GUI library can not be distributed
//        (on bulletin boards, or as part of shareware or commercial
products)
//      without written permission.
//
```

```
#ifndef __applib
#define __applib

// Need to set the pop-up menu titles:
#include "menu.h"

#include <iostream.hxx>
#include <fstream.hxx>

#ifndef DEC
extern "C" {
//#include <string.h>
    int strcpy(char *, char *);
    int strlen(char *);
    int strcmp(char *, char *);
};
#endif

#ifdef X11R4
#define FUNCPROTO 1
#ifdef SPARC
#define __cplusplus 1
#endif
#define NeedFunctionPrototypes 1
#define XTFUNCPROTO 1
#endif

extern "C" { void exit(int); };

#define class Xclass
#define type Xtype
#define new Xnew
#define altzone Xaltzone
#define XtMainLoop XXtMainLoop
#define output XXoutput
#define input XXinput

#include <Xlib.h>
#include <StringDefs.h>
#include <Intrinsic.h>
#include <cursorfont.h>
#include <X.h>
#include <Command.h>
#include <VPaned.h>
#include <List.h>
#ifndef MOTIF
#include <Form.h>
#include <Dialog.h>
#include <Shell.h>
#include <Box.h>
#include <Text.h>
#include <Label.h>
#endif
#ifdef MOTIF
#include <Xm/Xm.h>
#include <Xm/DrawingA.h>
#include <Xm/Form.h>
#include <Xm/Label.h>
#include <Xm/PushB.h>
#include <Xm/RowColumn.h>
```

```
#include <Xm/BulletinB.h>
#include <Xm/Text.h>
#endif


#undef class
#undef type
#undef new
#undef altzone
#undef XtMainLoop
#undef input
#undef output

extern "C" {
    void XtMainLoop();
#ifdef DEC
    XtListReturnStruct * XtListShowCurrent(Widget);
#endif
#ifdef X11R3
    Widget XtInitialize(...);
    Widget XtCreateWidget(...);
    Widget XtCreatePopupShell(...);
    Widget XtCreateManagedWidget(...);
    void XtManageChildren(...);
    void XtRealizeWidget(...);
    void XtDestroyWidget(Widget);
    XtListReturnStruct * XtListShowCurrent(Widget);
    void XtNextEvent(XEvent *);
    void XtDispatchEvent(XEvent *);
    Widget XmCreateMenuBar(...);
    void XtManageChild(...);
    void XtPopup(Widget);
    void XtPopdown(Widget);
    int strlen(char *);
    void free(char *);
    void XmStringFree(XmString);
    void XtAddCallback(...);
    void XtAddEventHandler(...);
    void XClearArea(Display *, Window, int, int, int, int, int);
    void XDrawLine(Display *, Window, GC, int, int, int, int);
    void XDrawString(Display *, Window, GC, int, int, char *, int);
    void XGrabButton(...);
    GC XtGetGC(...);
    GC XCreateGC(Display *, Window, int, XGCValues *);
    void XMapWindow(...);
    Font XCreateFontCursor(...);
    void XtGetValues(...);
    Display * XtDisplay(...);
    Window XtWindow(...);
    void XtAddWorkProc(...);
#endif
#ifndef DEC
    void sprintf(...);
    void fprintf(...);
    void printf(...);
#else
#include <stdio.h>
#endif
};
```

```
GC createXorGC(Widget);
GC createCopyGC(Widget);

typedef struct {
    int start_x, start_y, last_x, last_y;
    GC gc;
  } mouse_data;

void do_make_menu(Widget w, int client_data, int call_data);
void start_mouse(Widget, mouse_data *, XEvent *event);
void track_mouse(Widget, mouse_data *, XEvent *event);
void end_mouse(Widget, mouse_data *, XEvent *event);
void draw_screen(Widget, caddr_t, caddr_t);

const int MAX_TEXT_LINES = 32;
const MAX_TEXT_LINE_SIZE = 100;

class TAppWindow {
 public:

    int string_height(char *) { return 13; }
    int string_width(char *str) { return 7 * strlen(str); }
    // To support scrolling text:
            short top_text_clip, right_text_clip, bottom_text_clip,
left_text_clip;
    char *saved_text[MAX_TEXT_LINES];  // This is a ring-buffer
    int number_of_saved_lines;
    int current_ring_buffer_start;
    // We only allow either text or graphics to be active in a document
    // window.
    // The following flag is non-zero if we are using the document window
    // for scrolling text.
    // Note that this mode changes automatically when either plotting or
    // scrolling text
    // output methods are called.
    int in_scrolling_text_mode;
    // The following flag indicates that a small scrolling text field is
    // being used so we want to update both graphics and text.
    // Note that this only looks good if the application program is
    // careful to not draw in the scrolling text area.
    int redraw_both_text_and_graphics;



    void init_scrolling_text(int top, int right, int bottom, int left);
    void init_scrolling_text();
    void put_scrolling_text(char *str);
    void reset_scrolling_text();

    // Graphics support:
    void plot_line(int, int, int, int);
    void plot_string(int, int, char *);
    void plot_rect(int top, int right, int bottom, int left);
    void erase_rect(int top, int right, int bottom, int left);
    void clear_display();  // Forces a redraw of window calling user

    void do_edit(char *, char *);
    void show_info(char *);
```

```
    int choose_one(char *prompt1, char *prompt2);
    int choose_one_from_list(char *prompt, char **list_items,
                             int number_of_items);
    int choose_file_to_read(char *prompt, char *extension, char
*file_name);
    int choose_file_to_write(char *prompt, char *file_name);


    // user specified methods:
    void mouse_down(int, int);
    void mouse_up(int, int);
    void mouse_move(int, int);
    void do_menu_action(int);
    void update_display();

    // Idle work method (this method should return quickly when called)
    void idle_proc();
};

void makeMenu(Widget, char **, int);
void set_enter_widget_callback(Widget, XtActionProc );
void Warning(char *);

#ifndef MOTIF
#define LABEL labelWidgetClass
#define FORM formWidgetClass
#define COMMAND commandWidgetClass
#else
#define LABEL xmLabelWidgetClass
#define FORM xmFormWidgetClass
#define COMMAND xmPushButtonWidgetClass
#endif

#ifdef MOTIF
#define MAKE_MENU       Widget control_area;\
                        control_area=XtCreateManagedWidget("controls",\

xmBulletinBoardWidgetClass,global_form,NULL,0);\
                        Widget menubar;\
                        n = 0;\
                        menubar = XmCreateMenuBar(control_area,"menubar",\
                                                    args,n);\
                        XtManageChild(menubar);\
                        makeMenu(menubar, menu_titles, num_menu_items);\
                        XtRealizeWidget(toplevel);
#else
#define MAKE_MENU       XtRealizeWidget(toplevel);\
                        n = 0;\
                        XtSetArg(args[n],XtNy,3); n++;\
                        XtSetArg(args[n],XtNx,3); n++;\
                        XtSetArg(args[n],XtNborderWidth,3); n++;\
                        menu = XtCreateManagedWidget(" Menu ", \
                                                    commandWidgetClass, \
                                                    global_form, args,
n);\
                        XtAddCallback(menu,XtNcallback,\
                                    (XtCallbackProc)do_make_menu,\
                                    (XtPointer)NULL);

#endif
```

```
#ifdef X11R3
#define XtPointer caddr_t
#endif

#define output (ios::out)
#define input (ios::in)

int do_work();

extern TAppWindow *current_window;

#define INIT_PROGRAM \
TAppWindow currentAppWindow;\
mouse_data data;\
Widget global_form, dWidget;\
main(int argc, char **argv)\
{\
  Widget toplevel, menu;\
  Arg args[10];\
  int n;\
  toplevel = XtInitialize(argv[0], "main", NULL, 0, \
                          (Cardinal *)&argc, argv);\
  n = 0;\
  XtSetArg(args[n],XtNborderWidth,0); n++;\
  global_form = XtCreateManagedWidget("global_form", FORM, \
                          toplevel, args, n);\
  n = 0;\
  XtSetArg(args[n],XtNy,40); n++;\
  XtSetArg(args[n],XtNwidth,390); n++;\
  XtSetArg(args[n],XtNheight,350); n++;\
  XtSetArg(args[n],XtNborderWidth,0); n++;\
  dWidget = XtCreateManagedWidget("  ", \
                          LABEL, \
                          global_form, args, n);\
          XtAddEventHandler(dWidget,      ExposureMask,      1,
(XtEventHandler)draw_screen,\
                  (XtPointer)NULL);\
  XtAddEventHandler(dWidget, ButtonPressMask, FALSE,\
                  (XtEventHandler)start_mouse, (XtPointer)&data);\
  XtAddEventHandler(dWidget, ButtonMotionMask, FALSE,\
                  (XtEventHandler)track_mouse, (XtPointer)&data);\
  XtAddEventHandler(dWidget, ButtonReleaseMask,\
                  FALSE, (XtEventHandler)end_mouse, (XtPointer)&data);\
MAKE_MENU \
XGrabButton(XtDisplay(dWidget), AnyButton, AnyModifier, \
          XtWindow(dWidget), TRUE, \
          ButtonPressMask | ButtonMotionMask | \
          ButtonReleaseMask,\
          GrabModeAsync, GrabModeAsync,\
          XtWindow(dWidget), \
          XCreateFontCursor(XtDisplay(dWidget),\
                          XC_crosshair));\
  data.gc = createCopyGC((Widget)dWidget); \
  current_window = &currentAppWindow;\
  XtAddWorkProc(do_work, NULL);

#define RUN_PROGRAM \
  XtMainLoop();
#endif
```

File apptypes.h

```
// File: apptypes.h
//
// Description: Define macros for intrinsic data types. This is useful
//              for portability to machines with a segmented memory
//              architecture.
//


#define Char char
#define Int int   // this can be either 16 or 32 bits
#define Long long // this needs to be 32 bits
#define Short short // this needs to be 16 bits
#define Double double
#define Float float
```

D.3 X-Windows-Specific GUI C⁺⁺ Source Files

File applib.cxx

```
// File: applib.cxx
//
// Description: Implementation of the X Window GUI library. Both
//              the Athena and Motif toolkits are supported.
//
// Copyright 1992 by Mark Watson Associates
//
//        No binary rights reserved: this software library may be used in
//        compiled form without restrictions.  All source rights
//        reserved: Source code to the GUI library can not be distributed
//        (on bulletin boards, or as part of shareware or commercial
//        products) without written permission.
//
//

extern "C" {
#ifndef DEC
#include <sys/dirent.h>
#else
#include <dirent.h>
#endif
};

#include "applib.h"

#ifdef MOTIF
#include <Xm/Separator.h>
#include <Xm/CascadeB.h>
#include <Xm/List.h>

extern "C" {
    Widget XmCreatePulldownMenu(...);
    char * XtMalloc(...);
};
#endif

#ifndef MOTIF
const y_offset = 18; // Make room for the menu button
#else
```

```
const y_offset = 28; // Make room for the menu button
#endif

// If the following flag is set, then popup dialog boxes will
// automatically goaway (as if the user clicked the cancel
// button) if the mouse cursor leaves the popup window.  I
// usually leave this set to false.
#define POPUP_GOAWAY 0

extern "C" {
#ifdef X11R3
    char * XtMalloc(...);
    void XtOverrideTranslations(...);
    void XtAddActions(...);
    char *XtParseTranslationTable(...);
#endif
};

#ifdef X11R3
extern "C" {
    void XQueryPointer(...);
    void XtSetValues(...);
    void XWarpPointer(...);
    void XSync(Display *, int);
    void XCopyArea(...);
};
#endif

extern TAppWindow currentAppWindow;
extern Widget dWidget;
extern mouse_data data;

TAppWindow *current_window;

#define DO_IDLE_WORK

static int work_count = 0;
int do_work()
{
#ifdef DO_IDLE_WORK
    if (work_count++ >1000) {
        work_count = 0;
        current_window->idle_proc();
    }
#endif
    return 0;
}

void set_leave_widget_callback(Widget, XtActionProc);

void Warning(char *message)
{
    currentAppWindow.show_info(message);
}

void do_menu(Widget /*w*/, int client_data, int /* call_data*/ )
{
    currentAppWindow.do_menu_action((int)client_data + 1);
}
```

```
void start_mouse(Widget, mouse_data *, XEvent *event)
{
    currentAppWindow.mouse_down(event->xbutton.x, event->xbutton.y -
y_offset);
}

void track_mouse(Widget, mouse_data *, XEvent *event)
{
   currentAppWindow.mouse_move(event->xbutton.x, event->xbutton.y -
y_offset);
}

void end_mouse(Widget, mouse_data *, XEvent *event)
{
    currentAppWindow.mouse_up(event->xbutton.x, event->xbutton.y -
y_offset);
}

void draw_screen(Widget, caddr_t, caddr_t)
{
  if (currentAppWindow.bottom_text_clip > 0 &&
      (currentAppWindow.in_scrolling_text_mode == 1 ||
       currentAppWindow.redraw_both_text_and_graphics == 1)) {
      XClearArea(XtDisplay(dWidget), XtWindow(dWidget), 0, 0, 1024, 1024,
0);
      int next = currentAppWindow.current_ring_buffer_start;
      for (int i=0; i<(currentAppWindow.number_of_saved_lines-1); i++) {
          next++;
          if (next > (currentAppWindow.number_of_saved_lines - 1))   next
= 0;
          currentAppWindow.plot_string(currentAppWindow.left_text_clip +
1,
                         currentAppWindow.bottom_text_clip- 2
                          - (20*(currentAppWindow.number_of_saved_lines-
i-2)),
                         currentAppWindow.saved_text[next]);
      }
  }
  currentAppWindow.update_display();
}


// Data and code for do_edit method:

#ifndef MOTIF
extern "C" {
    char *XtDialogGetValueString(Widget);
};
#ifndef DEC
#ifdef X11R4
#define XtDialogGetValueString XawDialogGetValueString
extern "C" { XawDialogGetValueString(...); };
#endif
#endif
#endif

#ifdef DEC
extern "C" { void free(char *); };
#endif

#ifdef MOTIF
```

```
extern "C" {
    char * XmTextGetString(Widget);
    XmString XmStringCreate(...);
};
#endif

static int done_do_edit;
static char *edit_field;
static void do_edit_ok(Widget, Widget dialog, caddr_t)
{
#ifndef MOTIF
    char * cp = XtDialogGetValueString(dialog);
    sprintf(edit_field,"%s", cp);
    free(cp);
#else
    char * cp = XmTextGetString((Widget)dialog);
int len = strlen(cp);
printf("len=%d, edit_field=%s\n",len,edit_field);
    sprintf(edit_field,"%s", cp);
    free(cp);
#endif
    done_do_edit = 1;
}
static void do_edit_cancel(Widget, Widget, caddr_t)
{
    sprintf(edit_field,"          ");
    done_do_edit = 1;
}

extern WidgetClass shellWidgetClass;
#ifndef MOTIF
extern WidgetClass dialogWidgetClass;
#else
extern WidgetClass xmTextWidgetClass;
#endif

extern Widget global_form;

static int popup_active = 0;

void TAppWindow::do_edit(char * prompt, char *returned_string)
{   Arg args[5];

    if (popup_active == 1)   return;  // already using a popup
    popup_active = 1;

    edit_field = returned_string;

    int n = 0;
    XtSetArg(args[n], XtNlabel, "Popup"); n++;
    Widget p_do_edit = XtCreatePopupShell("do_edit", shellWidgetClass,
                                    global_form, args, n);

#ifdef MOTIF
    Widget form = XtCreateManagedWidget("p_do_edit", xmFormWidgetClass,
                                    p_do_edit, NULL, 0);
#else
                                    Widget          form
XtCreateManagedWidget("p_do_edit",formWidgetClass,p_do_edit,
```

```
                              NULL, 0);
#endif
    n = 0;
#ifndef MOTIF
    XtSetArg(args[n], XtNlabel, prompt); n++;
    XtSetArg(args[n], XtNvalue, returned_string); n++;
    XtSetArg(args[n], XtNwidth, 560); n++;
    Widget dialog = XtCreateManagedWidget("dialog",dialogWidgetClass,
                                    form, args, n);
    n = 0;
    Widget ok_button = XtCreateManagedWidget("      OK       ",
                                    commandWidgetClass,
                                    dialog, args, n);
    n = 0;
    Widget cancel_button = XtCreateManagedWidget("   Cancel    ",
                                       commandWidgetClass,
                                       dialog, args, n);
    XtAddCallback(ok_button,XtNcallback, (XtCallbackProc)do_edit_ok,
                (XtPointer)dialog);

    XtAddCallback(cancel_button,XtNcallback,
                (XtCallbackProc)do_edit_cancel, (XtPointer)NULL);
#else
    Widget label = XtCreateManagedWidget(prompt,xmLabelWidgetClass,
                                    form, args, n);
    n = 0;
    XtSetArg(args[n], XmNeditMode, XmMULTI_LINE_EDIT); n++;
    XtSetArg(args[n], XmNwordWrap, TRUE); n++;
    XtSetArg(args[n], XmNrows, 10); n++;
    XtSetArg(args[n], XmNcolumns, 60); n++;
    XtSetArg(args[n], XmNheight, 90); n++;
    XtSetArg(args[n], XmNy, 20); n++;
    XtSetArg(args[n], XmNvalue, returned_string); n++;
    Widget dialog = XtCreateManagedWidget("dialog",xmTextWidgetClass,
                                    form, args, n);
    n = 0;
    XtSetArg(args[n], XmNy, 120); n++;
    XtSetArg(args[n], XmNx, 10); n++;
    Widget ok_button = XtCreateManagedWidget("      OK       ",
                                    xmPushButtonWidgetClass,
                                    form, args, n);
    XtAddCallback(ok_button, XmNactivateCallback,
                (XtCallbackProc)do_edit_ok, (XtPointer)dialog);
    n = 0;
    XtSetArg(args[n], XmNy, 120); n++;
    XtSetArg(args[n], XmNx, 90); n++;
    Widget cancel_button = XtCreateManagedWidget("   Cancel    ",
                                       xmPushButtonWidgetClass,
                                       form, args, n);
    XtAddCallback(cancel_button, XmNactivateCallback,
                (XtCallbackProc)do_edit_cancel, (XtPointer)NULL);
#endif

#if POPUP_GOAWAY
        set_leave_widget_callback(p_do_edit,
(XtActionProc)do_edit_cancel);

#endif

    XtManageChild(p_do_edit);
```

```
    /* Warp pointer to edit field */
#ifndef MOTIF
    XWarpPointer(XtDisplay(dialog),None,XtWindow(dialog),
                0, 0, 0, 0, 40, 40);
    XSync(XtDisplay(p_do_edit),False);
#endif

    done_do_edit = 0;
    while (done_do_edit == 0) {
        XEvent an_event;
        XtNextEvent(&an_event);
        XtDispatchEvent(&an_event);
    }
printf("before popdown\n");
    XtPopdown(p_do_edit);
printf("after popdown\n");
    XtDestroyWidget(p_do_edit);
printf("after XtDestroyWidget\n");
    popup_active = 0; // allow other popups to be created
}


// Data and code for show_info method:

static int done_show_info;
static void show_info_ok(Widget, Widget, caddr_t)
{
    done_show_info = 1;
}

void TAppWindow::show_info(char * prompt)
{   Arg args[5];

    if (popup_active == 1)  return;
    popup_active = 1;

    int n = 0;
    XtSetArg(args[n], XtNlabel, "Popup"); n++;
        Widget  p_show_info  =  XtCreatePopupShell("show_info",
shellWidgetClass,
                                    global_form, args, n);

#ifndef MOTIF
                                Widget form =
XtCreateManagedWidget("form",formWidgetClass,p_show_info,
                                NULL, 0);
#else
    Widget form = XtCreateManagedWidget("form", xmFormWidgetClass,
                                    p_show_info, NULL, 0);
#endif

    n = 0;
    XtSetArg(args[n], XtNy, 2); n++;
    XtSetArg(args[n], XtNlabel, prompt); n++;

#ifdef MOTIF
    Widget label = XtCreateManagedWidget(prompt,xmLabelWidgetClass,
                                    form, args, n);
#else
```

```
    Widget label = XtCreateManagedWidget(prompt,labelWidgetClass,
                                          form, args, n);
#endif

#ifdef MOTIF
    n = 0;
    XtSetArg(args[n], XmNy, 40); n++;
                            W i d g e t        o k _ b u t t o n
XtCreateManagedWidget("OK",xmPushButtonWidgetClass,
                                          form, args, n);
    XtAddCallback(ok_button, XmNactivateCallback,
                  (XtCallbackProc)show_info_ok, (XtPointer)NULL);
#else
    n = 0;
    XtSetArg(args[n], XtNy, 110); n++;
    XtSetArg(args[n], XtNfromVert, label); n++;
    XtSetArg(args[n], XtNvertDistance, 20); n++;
    Widget ok_button = XtCreateManagedWidget("OK",commandWidgetClass,
                                          form, args, n);
    XtAddCallback(ok_button,XtNcallback, (XtCallbackProc)show_info_ok,
                  (XtPointer)NULL);
#endif

    XtManageChild(p_show_info);

    /* Warp pointer to edit field */
#ifndef MOTIF
    XWarpPointer(XtDisplay(ok_button),None,XtWindow(ok_button),
                 0, 0, 0, 0, 10, 10);
    XSync(XtDisplay(ok_button),False);
#endif

    done_show_info = 0;
    while (done_show_info == 0) {
        XEvent an_event;
        XtNextEvent(&an_event);
        XtDispatchEvent(&an_event);
    }
    XtPopdown(p_show_info);
    XtDestroyWidget(p_show_info);
    popup_active = 0;
}
// Choose one of two choices:

static int done_choose_one;
static void choose_one_cb(Widget, int value, caddr_t)
{
    done_choose_one = value;
}

int TAppWindow::choose_one(char * prompt1, char * prompt2)
{   Arg args[5];

    if (popup_active == 1)  return 0;
    popup_active = 1;

    int n = 0;
    XtSetArg(args[n], XtNlabel, "Popup"); n++;
        Widget p_choose_one = XtCreatePopupShell("choose_one",
shellWidgetClass,
```

```
                                    global_form, args, n);

#ifndef MOTIF
                                    Widget form =
XtCreateManagedWidget("form",formWidgetClass,p_choose_one,
                        NULL, 0);
#else
                                    Widget form =
XtCreateManagedWidget("form",xı Widget form = ıs,p_choose_one,
                        NULL, 0);
#endif

    n = 0;
#ifndef MOTIF
    XtSetArg(args[n], XtNvertDistance, 20); n++;
    Widget button_1 = XtCreateManagedWidget(prompt1,commandWidgetClass,
                                    form, args, n);
    XtAddCallback(button_1, XtNcallback, (XtCallbackProc)choose_one_cb,
                (XtPointer)1);
#else
                                    Widget button_1 =
XtCreateManagedWidget(prompt1,xmPushButtonWidgetClass,
                                    form, args, n);
    XtAddCallback(button_1, XmNactivateCallback,
                (XtCallbackProc)choose_one_cb, (XtPointer)1);
#endif

    n = 0;
#ifndef MOTIF
    XtSetArg(args[n], XtNfromVert, button_1); n++;
    XtSetArg(args[n], XtNvertDistance, 10); n++;
    Widget button_2 = XtCreateManagedWidget(prompt2,commandWidgetClass,
                                    form, args, n);
    .XtAddCallback(button_2,XtNcallback, (XtCallbackProc)choose_one_cb,
                (XtPointer)2);

#else
    XtSetArg(args[n], XmNy, 40); n++;
                                    Widget button_2 =
XtCreateManagedWidget(prompt2,xmPushButtonWidgetClass,
                                    form, args, n);
    XtAddCallback(button_2, XmNactivateCallback,
                (XtCallbackProc)choose_one_cb, (XtPointer)2);
#endif

    XtManageChild(p_choose_one);

    /* Warp pointer to edit field */
#ifndef MOTIF
    XWarpPointer(XtDisplay(button_1),None,XtWindow(button_1),
                0, 0, 0, 0, 10, 10);
    XSync(XtDisplay(button_1),False);
#endif

    done_choose_one = 0;
    while (done_choose_one == 0) {
        XEvent an_event;
        XtNextEvent(&an_event);
        XtDispatchEvent(&an_event);
    }
```

```
        XtPopdown(p_choose_one);
        XtDestroyWidget(p_choose_one);
        popup_active = 0;
        return done_choose_one;
}

// List selection:

static int done_list_choose;

static void list_cancel_cb(Widget, int, caddr_t)
{
        done_list_choose = -1;
}

#ifndef MOTIF
static void list_cb(Widget this_list, int, caddr_t)
{
        XtListReturnStruct *list_struct = XtListShowCurrent(this_list);
#ifdef X11R3
        done_list_choose = 1 + list_struct->index;
#endif
#ifdef X11R4
        done_list_choose = 1 + list_struct->list_index;
#endif
        free((char *)list_struct); // we need to give back this storage
}
#else
static void list_cb(Widget, int, XmListCallbackStruct *list)
{
        done_list_choose = 1 + list->item_position;
}
#endif

int TAppWindow::choose_one_from_list(char *prompt, char **list_items,
                                     int number_of_items)
{   Arg args[10];

        if (popup_active == 1)  return -1;
        popup_active = 1;

        int n = 0;
        XtSetArg(args[n], XtNlabel, "Popup"); n++;
            Widget p_list_choose = XtCreatePopupShell("list_choose",
shellWidgetClass,
                                     global_form, args, n);

#ifndef MOTIF
                                     Widget form =
XtCreateManagedWidget("form",formWidgetClass,p_list_choose,
                              NULL, 0);
#else
        Widget form = XtCreateWidget("form",xmFormWidgetClass,p_list_choose,
                              NULL, 0);
#endif
        n = 0;
#ifndef MOTIF
        XtSetArg(args[n], XtNy, 2); n++;
        XtSetArg(args[n], XtNlabel, prompt); n++;
        Widget label = XtCreateManagedWidget(prompt,labelWidgetClass,
```

```
                                               form, args, n);
#else
    XtSetArg(args[n], XmNy, 2); n++;
    Widget label = XtCreateManagedWidget(prompt,xmLabelWidgetClass,
                                               form, args, n);
#endif

    n = 0;

#ifndef MOTIF
    XtSetArg(args[n], XtNfromVert, label); n++;
    XtSetArg(args[n], XtNvertDistance, 10); n++;
    XtSetArg(args[n],XtNlist,list_items);   n++;
    XtSetArg(args[n],XtNnumberStrings,number_of_items);   n++;
    int num_columns = 1 + (number_of_items / 30);
    XtSetArg(args[n],XtNdefaultColumns,num_columns);   n++;
    XtSetArg(args[n],XtNforceColumns,True); n++;
    Widget
a_list=XtCreateManagedWidget("a_list",listWidgetClass,form,args,n);

XtAddCallback(a_list,XtNcallback,(XtCallbackProc)list_cb,(XtPointer)NULL)
;
#else
    XmString *string_MOTIF = (XmString *)XtMalloc(sizeof(XmString)
                                               *(number_of_items +
1));
    for (int k=0; k<number_of_items; k++)
        string_MOTIF[k] = XmStringCreate(list_items[k],
                                XmSTRING_DEFAULT_CHARSET);
printf("size of list=%d\n",number_of_items);
    XtSetArg(args[n],XmNitems,string_MOTIF);   n++;
    XtSetArg(args[n],XmNitemCount,number_of_items);   n++;
    XtSetArg(args[n],XmNvisibleItemCount,number_of_items);   n++;
    XtSetArg(args[n], XmNy, 45); n++;
    Widget a_list=XtCreateManagedWidget("a_list",xmListWidgetClass,
                                form,args,n);
    XtAddCallback(a_list,XmNbrowseSelectionCallback,
                    (XtCallbackProc)list_cb,(XtPointer)NULL);
    for (k=0; k<number_of_items; k++)
        XmStringFree(string_MOTIF[k]);
    free((char *)string_MOTIF);
#endif

    n = 0;
#ifndef MOTIF
    XtSetArg(args[n], XtNfromVert, a_list); n++;
    XtSetArg(args[n], XtNvertDistance, 10); n++;
    Widget button_2 = XtCreateManagedWidget("Cancel",commandWidgetClass,
                                               form, args, n);
    XtAddCallback(button_2,XtNcallback, (XtCallbackProc)list_cancel_cb,
                    (XtPointer)1);
#else
    XtSetArg(args[n], XmNy, 18); n++;
                                Widget button_2 =
XtCreateManagedWidget("Cancel",xmPushButtonWidgetClass,
                                               form, args, n);
    XtAddCallback(button_2, XmNactivateCallback,
                    (XtCallbackProc)list_cancel_cb, (XtPointer)1);
#endif
```

```
#ifdef MOTIF
    XtManageChild(a_list);
    XtManageChild(form);
#endif

    XtManageChild(p_list_choose);


    /* Warp pointer to edit field */
#ifndef MOTIF
    XWarpPointer(XtDisplay(a_list),None,XtWindow(a_list),
                 0, 0, 0, 0, 40, 40);
    XSync(XtDisplay(a_list),False);
#endif
    done_list_choose = 0;
    while (done_list_choose == 0) {
        XEvent an_event;
        XtNextEvent(&an_event);
        XtDispatchEvent(&an_event);
    }
    XtPopdown(p_list_choose);
    XtDestroyWidget(p_list_choose);
    if (done_list_choose>-1) done_list_choose--;
    popup_active = 0;
    return done_list_choose;
}

void TAppWindow::clear_display()
{
    // Erase area and generate a redraw/expose event:
    XClearArea(XtDisplay(dWidget), XtWindow(dWidget), 0, 0, 1024, 1024,
1);
}

void TAppWindow::plot_line(int x1, int y1, int x2, int y2)
{
  /*
   * Draw once to clear the previous line.
   */
  XDrawLine(XtDisplay(dWidget), XtWindow(dWidget), data.gc,
            x1, y1+ y_offset, x2, y2+ y_offset);
}

void TAppWindow::plot_rect(int top, int right, int bottom, int left)
{
    plot_line(left, top, left, bottom);
    plot_line(left, top, right, top);
    plot_line(right, top, right, bottom);
    plot_line(right, bottom, left, bottom);
}

void TAppWindow::erase_rect(int top, int right, int bottom, int left)
{
    // Erase area without generating a redraw/expose event:
    XClearArea(XtDisplay(dWidget), XtWindow(dWidget),
               left, top + y_offset, right, bottom + y_offset, 0);
}

void TAppWindow::plot_string(int x, int y, char *str)
{
```

```
    /*
     * Draw once to clear the previous line.
     */
    XDrawString(XtDisplay(dWidget), XtWindow(dWidget), data.gc,
            x, y+ y_offset, str, strlen(str));
}
// Utility functions for popup menus for ATHENA:

#ifndef MOTIF

static int x_location = 350;
static int y_location = 300;

static int  poped_up = 0;

#define XtPointer caddr_t

Widget popup_shell, popup_shell2;

extern "C" {
    void XtPopdown(Widget);
};

static int local_count_callbacks = 1;

#ifdef X11R3
typedef struct _dummyActionList {
    String action_name;
    XtActionProc action_proc;
}   aXtActionsRec;
#endif

#ifdef X11R4
typedef XtActionsRec aXtActionsRec;
#endif

void set_leave_widget_callback(Widget w, XtActionProc cb)
{
    static char buf[100], name[20];
    sprintf(name,"name00%d",local_count_callbacks++);
    sprintf(buf,"<LeaveNotify>: %s()",name);
    static aXtActionsRec myActions[1];
#ifdef X11R4
    myActions[0].proc = (XtActionProc)cb;
    myActions[0].string = name;
#else
    myActions[0].action_proc = (XtActionProc)cb;
    myActions[0].action_name  = (String)name;
#endif
    XtAddActions(myActions,1);
    XtOverrideTranslations(w,XtParseTranslationTable(buf));
}

void set_enter_widget_callback(Widget w, XtActionProc cb)
{
    static char buf[100], name[20];
    sprintf(name,"name00%d",local_count_callbacks++);
    sprintf(buf,"<EnterNotify>: %s()",name);
    static aXtActionsRec myActions[1];
```

```
#ifdef X11R4
    myActions[0].proc = (XtActionProc)cb;
    myActions[0].string = name;
#else
    myActions[0].action_proc = (XtActionProc)cb;
    myActions[0].action_name = (String)name;
#endif
    XtAddActions(myActions,1);
    XtOverrideTranslations(w,XtParseTranslationTable(buf));
}

void PaneChosen(Widget w, XtPointer client_data, XtPointer)
{
    int selection_number = (int) client_data;
    do_menu(w, selection_number, 0);
    XtPopdown(popup_shell);
}

void do_popdown(Widget, caddr_t, caddr_t)
{
    XtPopdown(popup_shell);
    poped_up = 0;
}

void makeMenu(Widget topLevel, char **item_names, int num_items)
{   int i;
    Widget menubox, a_form, menupane[10];
    Arg args[10];
    unsigned int key_buttons;
    int win_x, win_y;
    Window root, child;

    if (poped_up == 1)    return;
    poped_up = 1;

    XQueryPointer(XtDisplay(topLevel),XtWindow(topLevel),
                    &root, &child, &x_location, &y_location, &win_x,
&win_y,
                    &key_buttons);

    // Throw away all mouse movement events so the popup menu
    // does not popdown due to residual mouse motion:
    XSync(XtDisplay(topLevel), False);

    i=0;
    XtSetArg(args[i],XtNx,x_location-40); i++;
    XtSetArg(args[i],XtNy,y_location-40); i++;
    XtSetArg(args[i],XtNborderWidth,4); i++;

            popup_shell    = XtCreatePopupShell("popup_shell",
overrideShellWidgetClass,

                                    topLevel, args, i);
    i=0;
    XtSetArg(args[i],XtNborderWidth,1); i++;

    a_form = XtCreateManagedWidget("a_form", formWidgetClass,
                                    popup_shell, args, i);

    menubox = XtCreateManagedWidget("menubox", boxWidgetClass,
                                    a_form, args, i);
```

```
    for (i = 0; i < num_items; i++) {
        int j = 0;
        XtSetArg(args[j],XtNborderWidth,0); j++;
        XtSetValues(popup_shell,args,j);
        menupane[i] = XtCreateManagedWidget(item_names[i],
                                        commandWidgetClass, menubox,
                                        args, j);
            XtAddCallback(menupane[i], XtNcallback, PaneChosen,
(XtPointer)i);
        }
    set_leave_widget_callback(popup_shell, (XtActionProc)do_popdown);

#ifdef X11R3
    XtPopup(popup_shell);
#endif
#ifdef X11R4
    XtPopup(popup_shell,XtGrabNone);
#endif

    /* Warp pointer to edit field */
#ifndef MOTIF
    XWarpPointer(XtDisplay(popup_shell),None,XtWindow(popup_shell),
        0, 0, 0, 0, 40, 40);
    XSync(XtDisplay(topLevel),False);
#endif
}

#endif   // #ifndef MOTIF

#ifdef MOTIF

void makeMenu(Widget parent, char **item_names, int num_items)
{   Arg args[4];

    Widget the_menu =XmCreatePulldownMenu(parent,
                                    "Menu1",
                                    NULL, 0);
    XtSetArg(args[0], XmNsubMenuId, the_menu);
    Widget cascade = XtCreateWidget("Menu", xmCascadeButtonWidgetClass,
                            parent,args,1);
                            WidgetList menu_buttons =
(WidgetList)XtMalloc(num_items*sizeof(Widget));
    for(int i=0;i<num_items;i++) {
        menu_buttons[i] = XtCreateWidget(item_names[i],
                                    xmPushButtonWidgetClass,
                                    the_menu, NULL, 0);
        XtAddCallback(menu_buttons[i], XmNactivateCallback,
                    (XtCallbackProc)do_menu,i);
    }
    XtManageChildren(menu_buttons, num_items);
    XtManageChild(cascade);
}

#endif

void do_make_menu(Widget, int, int)
{
  makeMenu(global_form, menu_titles, num_menu_items);
}
```

```
// Create our standard XOR GC for drawing:

GC createXorGC(Widget w)
{
    GC        gc;
    XGCValues values;
    Arg       args[5];   // Leave room for future code modifications
    int n = 0;
    XtSetArg(args[n], XtNforeground, &values.foreground); n++;
    XtSetArg(args[n], XtNbackground, &values.background); n++;
    XtGetValues(w, args,n);
printf("foreground, background=%d
%d\n",values.foreground,values.background);
//    values.foreground = values.foreground ^ values.background;
    values.line_style = LineSolid;
    values.function   = GXxor;  // different than createCopyGC
    gc = XtGetGC(w, GCForeground | GCBackground |
                    GCFunction | GCLineStyle, &values);
    return gc;
}


// Create our COPY GC for drawing:

GC createCopyGC(Widget w)
{
    GC gc;

    XGCValues values;
    Arg       args[5];   // Leave room for future code modifications
    int n = 0;
    XtSetArg(args[n], XtNforeground, &values.foreground); n++;
    XtSetArg(args[n], XtNbackground, &values.background); n++;
    XtGetValues(w, args,n);
printf("foreground, background=%d
%d\n",values.foreground,values.background);
//    values.foreground = values.foreground ^ values.background;
    values.line_style = LineSolid;
    values.function   = GXcopy;  // different than createXorDC
    gc = XtGetGC(w, GCForeground | GCBackground |
                    GCFunction | GCLineStyle, &values);
    return gc;
}


// Support for crolling text:


void TAppWindow::init_scrolling_text(int top, int right, int bottom, int
left)
{
    top_text_clip     = top;
    right_text_clip   = right;
    bottom_text_clip  = bottom;
    left_text_clip    = left;
    number_of_saved_lines = -1 + ((bottom_text_clip - top_text_clip) /
                                    string_height(" "));
    if (number_of_saved_lines > MAX_TEXT_LINES)
        number_of_saved_lines = MAX_TEXT_LINES;
    if (number_of_saved_lines < 3) number_of_saved_lines = 3;
        XClearArea(XtDisplay(dWidget),   XtWindow(dWidget),
```

```
left,top,right,bottom, 0);

    current_ring_buffer_start = 0;
    // Allocate storage for saved text lines:
    for (int i=0; i<number_of_saved_lines; i++) {
        saved_text[i] = new char[MAX_TEXT_LINE_SIZE + 1];
        saved_text[i][0] = '\0';
    }
    in_scrolling_text_mode = 1;
    redraw_both_text_and_graphics = 1;
}

void TAppWindow::init_scrolling_text()
{
    // Set the text area with content rectangle of the window:

    top_text_clip    = 0;
    right_text_clip  = 256;
    bottom_text_clip = 310;
    left_text_clip   = 0;

    number_of_saved_lines = -1 + ((bottom_text_clip - top_text_clip) /
                                  string_height(" "));
    if (number_of_saved_lines > MAX_TEXT_LINES)
        number_of_saved_lines = MAX_TEXT_LINES;
    if (number_of_saved_lines < 3) number_of_saved_lines = 3;

    XClearArea(XtDisplay(dWidget), XtWindow(dWidget), 0, 0, 1024, 1024,
0);
    current_ring_buffer_start = 0;
    // Allocate storage for saved text lines:
    for (int i=0; i<number_of_saved_lines; i++) {
        saved_text[i] = new char[MAX_TEXT_LINE_SIZE + 1];
        saved_text[i][0] = '\0';
    }
    in_scrolling_text_mode = 1;
    redraw_both_text_and_graphics = 0; // entire window used for text.
}

void TAppWindow::put_scrolling_text(char *str)
{
    if (bottom_text_clip != 0) {
        XCopyArea(XtDisplay(dWidget),XtWindow(dWidget),XtWindow(dWidget),
                  data.gc, 0,50, // src x,y
                  256, 256, 0, 30);
        plot_string(left_text_clip + 1, bottom_text_clip - 2, str);
        char buf[257];
        if (strlen(str) < 256) {
            sprintf(buf,"%s",str);
            buf[MAX_TEXT_LINE_SIZE] = '\0';
            sprintf(saved_text[current_ring_buffer_start],"%s",buf);
            current_ring_buffer_start++;
            if (current_ring_buffer_start > (number_of_saved_lines - 1))
                current_ring_buffer_start = 0;
        }
    } else {
            Warning("Called TAppWindow::put_scrolling_text before
TAppWindow::init_scrolling_text");
    }
```

```
        in_scrolling_text_mode = 1;
}


void TAppWindow::reset_scrolling_text()
{
    for (int i=0; i<MAX_TEXT_LINES; i++) {
        saved_text[i][0] = '\0';
    }
}

#ifndef DEC
extern "C" {
    int strlen(char *);
    int strcmp(char *, char *);
};
#endif

static int find_extension_in_file_name(char *file, char *extension)
{   char buf[64];
    sprintf(buf,".%s", extension);
    int len_file = strlen((char *)file);
    int len_ext  = strlen((char *)buf);
    for (int k=0; k<(len_file - len_ext + 1); k++) {
        if (strcmp((char *)buf, (char *)(&(file[k]))) == 0)
            return 1;
    }
    return 0;
}

int TAppWindow::choose_file_to_read(char *prompt, char *extension,
                                    char *file_name)
{
    DIR *dirp;
    struct dirent *dp;
    char *fileNames[500];
    int numFiles = 0;
    dirp = opendir(".");
    if (dirp != 0) {
        while ((dp = readdir(dirp)) != 0) {
            if (strlen(extension) < 1 ||
                find_extension_in_file_name(dp->d_name,extension))
                if (numFiles < 498) {
                    // Insert the file in the correct (sorted position):
                    int inserted = 0;
                    for (int m=0; m<numFiles; m++)
                        if (strcmp((char *)dp->d_name,
                                   (char *)fileNames[m])<=0 &&
                            inserted == 0) {
                            for (int k=(numFiles-1); k>=m; k--)
                                fileNames[k+1] = fileNames[k];
                            int len = strlen((char *)(dp->d_name));
                            fileNames[m] = new char[len + 1];
                            for (k=0; k<len; k++)
                                fileNames[m][k] = dp->d_name[k];
                            fileNames[m][len] = '\0';
                            numFiles++;
                            inserted = 1;
                        }
```

```
                         if (inserted == 0) {
                             int len = strlen((char *)(dp->d_name));
                             fileNames[numFiles] = new char[len + 1];
                             for (int k=0; k<len; k++)
                                 fileNames[numFiles][k] = dp->d_name[k];
                             fileNames[numFiles][len] = '\0';
                             numFiles++;
                         }
                     }
                 }
             }
         int response = choose_one_from_list(prompt, fileNames, numFiles);
         if (response > -1) {
             sprintf(file_name,"%s",fileNames[response]);
         } else {
             file_name[0] = '\0';
         }
         for (int k=0; k<numFiles; k++) delete fileNames[k];
         if (strlen(file_name) > 0) return 0;
          else                        return 1;
}

int TAppWindow::choose_file_to_write(char *prompt, char *file_name)
{
    do_edit(prompt, file_name);
    if (strlen(file_name) > 0) return 0;
     else                       return 1;
}
```

D.4 X-Windows-Specific Smart Vector Include Files

File char_v.h

```
// File: char_v.h
//
// Description: smart character vector
//
// Copyright 1992 by Mark Watson Associates
//
//       No binary rights reserved: this software library may be used in
//       compiled form without restrictions.  All source rights
//       reserved: Source code to the GUI library can not be distributed
//         (on bulletin boards, or as part of shareware or commercial
//          products)
//       without written permission.
//

#ifndef __char_vect
#define __char_vect

#include <iostream.hxx>
#include <fstream.hxx>
#include "apptypes.h"

#define output (ios::out)
#define input (ios::in)

class char_vect {
```

```
    Long size;
    void grow(Long new_size);
    Long ub() { return (size - 1); }
  public:
    Char *p;
    char_vect(void);
    char_vect (long n);
    char_vect(char_vect &v);
    char_vect(Char a[], long n);
    ~char_vect() { delete p; }
    Char & operator [] (long i);   // range check safeguards
    void save(char *filename);
    void restore(char *filename);
};

#endif
```

File double_v.h

```
// File: double_v.h
//
// Description:  smart double vector
//
// Copyright 1992 by Mark Watson Associates
//
//        No binary rights reserved: this software library may be used in
//        compiled form without restrictions.  All source rights
//        reserved: Source code to the GUI library can not be distributed
//        (on bulletin boards, or as part of shareware or commercial
//        products) without written permission.
//
//

#ifndef __double_vect
#define __double_vect

#include <fstream.hxx>

#define input (ios::in)
#define output (ios::out)

class double_vect {
    double *p;
    int size;
    void grow(int new_size);
    int ub() { return (size - 1); }
  public:
    double_vect(void);
    double_vect (int n);
    double_vect(double_vect &v);
    double_vect(double a[], int n);
    ~double_vect() { delete p; }
    double & operator [] (int i);   // range check safeguards
    void save(char *filename);
    void restore(char *filename);
};

#endif
```

File int_vect.h

```
// File: int_vect.h
//
// Description:  smart int vector
//
// Copyright 1992 by Mark Watson Associates
//
//        No binary rights reserved: this software library may be used in
//        compiled form without restrictions.  All source rights
//        reserved: Source code to the GUI library can not be distributed
//        (on bulletin boards, or as part of shareware or commercial
//        products)without written permission.
//
//

#ifndef __int_vect
#define __int_vect

#include "applib.h"

class int_vect {
    int *p;
    int size;
    void grow(int new_size);
        int ub() { return (size - 1); }
  public:
    int num_elements;
    int_vect(void);
    int_vect (int n);
    int_vect(int_vect &v);
    int_vect(int a[], int n);
    ~int_vect() { delete p; }
    int & operator [] (int i);   // range check safeguards
    void save(char *filename);
    void restore(char *filename);
};

#endif
```

D.5 X-Windows-Specific Smart Vector C++
Source Files

File char_v.cp

```
// File: char_v.cp
//
// Description: smart vector implementation for characters
//
// Copyright 1992 by Mark Watson Associates
//
//        No binary rights reserved: this software library may be used in
//        compiled form without restrictions.  All source rights
//        reserved: Source code to the GUI library can not be distributed
//         (on bulletin boards, or as part of shareware or commercial
products)
//        without written permission.
//

#include "char_v.h"
```

```
extern "C" { void exit(int); };

// Define constants for the dynamic grow rate for char_vect data types
// and the maximum number of elements that a smart char_vect can have:
//
const int GROW_RATE = 4096;
const int MAX_SIZE = 1048576;

char_vect::char_vect(void)
{
    size = 32768;
cerr << "In Char_vect default constructor, size=" << size << "\n";
    p = new char[size];
}

char_vect::char_vect(long n)
{
    if (n<= 0) {
        cerr << "illegal size for a char_vect = " << n << "\n";
        exit(1);
    }
    size = n;
    p = new char[size];
}

char_vect::char_vect(Char a[], long n)
{
    if (n<= 0) {
        cerr << "illegal size for a char_vect = " << n << "\n";
        exit(1);
    }
    size = n;
    p = new char[size];
    for (long i=0; i<size; i++)  p[i] = a[i];
}

char_vect::char_vect(char_vect &v)
{
    size = v.size;
    p = new char[size];
    for (long i=0; i<size; i++)  p[i] = v.p[i];
}

Char & char_vect::operator [] (long i)
{
    if (i < 0) {
        cerr << "illegal index for char_vect = " << i << "\n";
        exit(1);
    }
    if (i > ub()) {
        grow(i);
    }
    return (p[i]);
}

void char_vect::grow(long new_size)
{
```

```
    if ((new_size + GROW_RATE) >= MAX_SIZE) {
        cerr << "error in dynamic resizing of a smart char_vect, new size
= "
            << (new_size + GROW_RATE) << "\n";
        exit(1);
    }
    Char *np = new Char[(new_size + GROW_RATE)];
    for (long i=0; i<size; i++)  np[i] = p[i];
    delete p;
cerr << "growing a char_vect: old size = " << size << "  new size= "
<< (new_size + GROW_RATE) << "\n";
    size = (new_size + GROW_RATE);
    p = np;
}

void char_vect::save(char *file_name)
{
    filebuf out_file;
    if (out_file.open(file_name, output)==0) {
//      cerr << "Could not open output file " << file_name << "\n";
        exit(1);
    }
    ostream out_stream(&out_file);
    out_stream << size << "\n";
    for (long i=0; i<size; i++)
        out_stream << p[i] << "\n";
    out_file.close();
}

void char_vect::restore(char *file_name)
{
    filebuf in_file;
    if (in_file.open(file_name, input)==0) {
//      cerr << "Could not open input file " << file_name << "\n";
        exit(1);
    }
    istream in_stream(&in_file);
    in_stream >> size;
    for (long i=0; i<size; i++)
        in_stream >> p[i];
    in_file.close();
}

#if 0

// test code:

void main()
{
    cerr << "Start of char_vect test:\n\n";
    char_vect vv;
    for (long l=0; l<256000; l++) vv[l] = (char)(l % 128);
    for (l=0; l<256000; l++)
        if (vv[l] != (char)((l % 128)))  cerr << "Error " << l << "\n";
    cerr << "Done with test.\n";
}

#endif
```

File double_v.cp

```
// File: double_v.cp
//
// Description: smart vector implementation for doubles
//
// Copyright 1992 by Mark Watson Associates
//
//        No binary rights reserved: this software library may be used in
//        compiled form without restrictions.  All source rights
//        reserved: Source code to the GUI library can not be distributed
//        (on bulletin boards, or as part of shareware or commercial
//        products)without written permission.
//
//

#include "double_v.h"

extern "C" { void exit(int); };

// Define constants for the dynamic grow rate for double_vect data types
// and the maximum number of elements that a smart double_vect can have:
//

const int GROW_RATE = 1;
const int MAX_SIZE = 5000;

double_vect::double_vect(void)
{
    size = 10;
    p = new double[size];
}

double_vect::double_vect(int n)
{
    if (n<= 0) {
        cerr << "illeagl size for a double_vect = " << n << "\n";
        exit(1);
    }
    size = n;
    p = new double[size];
}

double_vect::double_vect(double a[], int n)
{
    if (n<= 0) {
        cerr << "illeagl size for a double_vect = " << n << "\n";
        exit(1);
    }
    size = n;
    p = new double[size];
    for (int i=0; i<size; i++)  p[i] = a[i];
}

double_vect::double_vect(double_vect &v)
{
    size = v.size;
    p = new double[size];
    for (int i=0; i<size; i++)  p[i] = v.p[i];
}
```

```
double & double_vect::operator [] (int i)
{
    if (i < 0) {
        cerr << "illegal index for double_vect = " << i << "\n";
        exit(1);
    }
    if (i > ub()) {
        grow(i);
    }
    return (p[i]);
}

void double_vect::grow(int new_size)
{
    if ((new_size + GROW_RATE) >= MAX_SIZE) {
        cerr << "error in dynamic resizing of a smart double_vect, new
size = "
                << (new_size + GROW_RATE) << "\n";
        exit(1);
    }
    double *np = new double[(new_size + GROW_RATE)];
    for (int i=0; i<size; i++)  np[i] = p[i];
    delete p;
    size = (new_size + GROW_RATE);
    p = np;
}

void double_vect::save(char *file_name)
{
    filebuf out_file;
    if (out_file.open(file_name, output)==0) {
//      cerr << "Could not open output file " << file_name << "\n";
        exit(1);
    }
    ostream out_stream(&out_file);
    out_stream << size << "\n";
    for (int i=0; i<size; i++)
        out_stream << p[i] << "\n";
    out_file.close();
}

void double_vect::restore(char *file_name)
{
    filebuf in_file;
    if (in_file.open(file_name, input)==0) {
//      cerr << "Could not open input file " << file_name << "\n";
        exit(1);
    }
    istream in_stream(&in_file);
    in_stream >> size;
    for (int i=0; i<size; i++)
        in_stream >> p[i];
    in_file.close();
}

#if 0

// test code:

main()
```

```
{
    cerr << "Start of double_vect test:\n\n";
    double_vect vv(10);
    vv[2] = 2;
    vv[220] = vv[2];   // illegal index !!
    cerr << "Done with test.\n";
}

#endif
```

File int_vect.cp

```
// File: int_vect.cp
//
// Description: This file implements the int smart vector class
//
// Copyright 1992 by Mark Watson Associates
//
//        No binary rights reserved: this software library may be used in
//        compiled form without restrictions.  All source rights
//        reserved: Source code to the GUI library can not be distributed
//        (on bulletin boards, or as part of shareware or commercial
//        products) without written permission.
//
//
//        This software is provided "as is". The user accepts all
//        responsibility for its use.
//

#include "int_vect.h"

extern "C" { void exit(int); };

extern void Warning(char *);

// Define constants for the dynamic grow rate for int_vect data types and
// the maximum number of elements that a smart int_vect can have:

const int GROW_RATE = 1;
const int MAX_SIZE = 5000;

int_vect::int_vect(void)
{
    num_elements = 0;
    size = 10;
    p = new int[size];
}

int_vect::int_vect(int n)
{
    if (n<= 0) {
        Warning("illegal size for a int_vect");
        exit(1);
    }
    num_elements = 0;
    size = n;
    p = new int[size];
}

int_vect::int_vect(int a[], int n)
```

```
{
    if (n<= 0) {
        Warning("illegal size for a int_vect");
        exit(1);
    }
    num_elements = size = n;
    p = new int[size];
    for (int i=0; i<size; i++)  p[i] = a[i];
}

int_vect::int_vect(int_vect &v)
{
    size = v.size;
    p = new int[size];
    for (int i=0; i<size; i++)  p[i] = v.p[i];
    num_elements = size;
}
int & int_vect::operator [] (int i)
{
    if (i < 0) {
        Warning("illegal index for int_vect");
        exit(1);
    }
    if (i > ub()) {
        grow(i);
    }
    if ((i + 1) > num_elements)  num_elements = i+1;
    return (p[i]);
}

void int_vect::grow(int new_size)
{
    if ((new_size + GROW_RATE) >= MAX_SIZE) {
        Warning("error in dynamic resizing of a smart int_vect");
        exit(1);
    }
    int *np = new int[(new_size + GROW_RATE)];
    for (int i=0; i<size; i++)  np[i] = p[i];
    delete p;
    size = (new_size + GROW_RATE);
    p = np;
}

void int_vect::save(char *file_name)
{
    filebuf out_file;
    if (out_file.open(file_name, output)==0) {
        Warning("Could not open output file for int vect save");
        exit(1);
    }
    ostream out_stream(&out_file);
    out_stream << num_elements << "\n";
    for (int i=0; i<num_elements; i++)
        out_stream << p[i] << "\n";
    out_file.close();
}

void int_vect::restore(char *file_name)
{
    filebuf in_file;
```

```
    if (in_file.open(file_name, input)==0) {
        Warning("Could not open input file for int vect restore");
        exit(1);
    }
    istream in_stream(&in_file);
    in_stream >> size;
    num_elements = size;

    if (size > ub()-1)  grow(size);
    for (int i=0; i<num_elements; i++)
        in_stream >> p[i];
    in_file.close();
}

#if 0

// test code:

main()
{
    cerr << "Start of int_vect test:\n\n";
    int_vect vv(10);
    vv[2] = 2;
    vv[220] = vv[2];  // illegal index !!
    cerr << "Done with test.\n";
}

#endif
```

D.6 X Windows Makefile

File makefile

```
# File: makefile

LIBDIR =
DEBUG =

# 'Generic' Unix defines for Athena Widget version of GUI library:
CFLAGS = -DSYSV  -I$(LIBDIR) -I/usr/include/X11 -DX11R3
LIBS = -lXaw -lXt -lXext -lXmu -lX -linet   -lX11 -lPW -lm
CC = ccxx

# 'Generic' Unix defines for Motif Widget version of GUI library:
#CFLAGS = -DMOTIF -DX11R3 -DSYSV  -I$(LIBDIR) -I/usr/local/MOTIF/lib
-I/usr/include/X11
#LIBS =   -lMrm -lXm -lXtM -lXext -lXmu -lX -linet   -lX11 -lPW
#CC = ccxx -g

# Sun SPARC defines for Athena Widget version of GUI library:
#LIBDIR1 = $(OPENWINHOME)/share/include/X11/Xaw
#LIBDIR2 = $(OPENWINHOME)/share/include
#LIBDIR3 = $(OPENWINHOME)/share/include/X11
#CFLAGS = -DX11R4 -DSPARC -I$(LIBDIR1)  -I$(LIBDIR2)  -I$(LIBDIR3)
-I/usr/include/X11
#LIBS = -L$(OPENWINHOME)/lib -lXaw -lXt -lXext -lXmu -lX -lX11
#CC = CC

# Dec RISC defines for Athena Widget version of GUI library:
```

```
#CFLAGS  =  -DOBJECT  -DRECTOBJ  -DX11R4  -DDEC  -DXAW_BC
-I/usr/include/mit/X11/Xaw -I/usr/include/mit/X11 -I/usr/include/mit
#LIBS = -lXaw -lXt -lXext -lXmu -lX11 -lm
#CC = cxx
# executables:

test: test.o Grapher.o tplot.o
    cp t_menu.h menu.h
    $(CC) -c -g $(CFLAGS) applib.o applib.cxx
    $(CC) -o test test.o applib.o Grapher.o tplot.o $(LIBS)

draw: draw.o int_vect.o
    cp d_menu.h menu.h
    $(CC) -c -g $(CFLAGS) applib.o applib.cxx
    $(CC) -o draw draw.o int_vect.o applib.o $(LIBS)

chess3d: chess3d.o
    cp ch_menu.h menu.h
    $(CC) -c -g $(CFLAGS) applib.o applib.cxx
    $(CC) -o chess3d chess3d.o applib.o $(LIBS)

hand: hand.o tneural.o tplot.o double_v.o int_vect.o
    cp h_menu.h menu.h
    $(CC) -c -g $(CFLAGS) applib.o applib.cxx
    $(CC) -o hand hand.o tneural.o tplot.o double_v.o int_vect.o applib.o
$(LIBS)

textbr: textbr.o textind.o char_v.o
    cp br_menu.h menu.h
    $(CC) -c -g $(CFLAGS) applib.o applib.cxx
    $(CC) -o textbr textbr.o textind.o char_v.o applib.o $(LIBS)

# compile C++ files:

applib.o: applib.cxx applib.h
    $(CC) -c -g $(CFLAGS) $@ applib.cxx

Grapher.o: Grapher.cxx Grapher.h applib.h
    $(CC) -c -g $(CFLAGS) $@ Grapher.cxx

tplot.o: tplot.cxx tplot.h applib.h
    $(CC) -c -g $(CFLAGS) $@ tplot.cxx

test.o: test.cxx applib.h
    $(CC) -c -g $(CFLAGS) $@ test.cxx

textbr.o: textbr.cxx applib.h
    $(CC) -c -g $(CFLAGS) $@ textbr.cxx

hand.o: hand.cxx applib.h
    $(CC) -c -g $(CFLAGS) $@ hand.cxx

draw.o: draw.cxx applib.h
    $(CC) -c -g $(CFLAGS) $@ draw.cxx

chess3d.o: chess3d.cxx applib.h
    $(CC) -c -g $(CFLAGS) $@ chess3d.cxx

# test code for smart vector and ource for smrt vectors:
```

```
test_int: int_vect.o
    $(CC) -o test_int int_vect.o

int_vect.o: int_vect.cxx int_vect.h
    $(CC) -c -g $(CFLAGS) $@ int_vect.cxx

test_c: char_v.o
    $(CC) -o test_c char_v.o

char_v.o: char_v.cxx char_v.h
    $(CC) -c -g $(CFLAGS) $@ char_v.cxx

test_d: double_v.o
    $(CC) -o test_d double_v.o

double_v.o: double_v.cxx double_v.h
    $(CC) -c -g $(CFLAGS) $@ double_v.cxx

test_nn: tneural.o double_v.o
    $(CC) -o test_nn tneural.o double_v.o -lm

tneural.o: tneural.cxx
    $(CC) -c -g $(CFLAGS) $@ tneural.cxx

test_ind: textind.o char_v.o
    $(CC) -o test_ind textind.o char_v.o

textind.o: textind.cxx applib.h textind.h char_v.h
    $(CC) -c -g $(CFLAGS) $@ textind.cxx
```

Bibliography

Petzold, Charles. 1990. *Programming Windows*. Redmond, Wa.: Microsoft Press.
This book is the second edition of Charles Petzold's popular Windows programming book. If your applications need to use more Windows features than are supported by the C++ GUI library developed in this book, I recommend Petzold's book as an excellent tutorial and reference.

Watson, Mark. 1991. *Common LISP modules: artificial intelligence in the era of neural networks and chaos theory*. New York: Springer Verlag.

Young, Douglas. 1990. *X Windows systems programming and applications with Motif.* New York: Prentice Hall.
This excellent tutorial can help with writing X Windows applications using Xlib and the Xt widget set.

Young, Douglas. 1989. *X Windows systems programming and applications with Xt.* New York: Prentice Hall.
This is an excellent tutorial for writing X Windows applications using Xlib and the Motif widget set.

Index

A

activation energy, 110
AddResMenu, 34-36
API functions
  Windows, 17-24
  X Windows, 53-59
Apple Macintosh (*see* Macintosh)
Apple Program Developer's Association
  (APDA), 25
application environments
  creating using Macintosh, 32-35
  creating using Windows, 16-17
applications
  3D chess, 169-199
  classes, 62
  handwriting classifier, 155-160
  HIB, 139-154
  increasing readability, 90
  Macintosh resource files for building, 29-31
  menus, 62
  text browser, 161-167
artificial intelligence (AI), 77
ASCII, text I/O, 95-96

B

background processing, 68-69
BeginPaint, 17
BeginUpdate, 36
binary files, I/O, 96-97

C

C++ programming language, xi-xiii
classes
  application utilities, 75-138
  applications, 62
  curve plotting, 99-108
  data object, 89-94
  generic GUI reference, 203-204
  graphical tree browser, 77-87
  library, 61-73, 209-225

text browser, 210-211
TextIndex, 119-138
TNeuralNet, 109-118
vector, 89-91, 225-234
Windows implementation, 205-234
ClipRect, 36
CreateWindow, 17
curve plotting class (*see* TPlotClass)

D

data object class, 89-94
  integer vector, 91-94
  vector, 89-91
DefWindowProc, 17-18
device context (DC), 10
dialog boxes
  Macintosh, 31-32
  modal, 52-53, 64-68
  Windows, 11-13
  X Windows, 51-53
DialogBox, 18-19
DigDirList, 19
DigDirSelect, 19
DispatchMessage, 19
DisposeRgn, 36
document windows, 62
  creating Macintosh, 32
  creating using Windows, 13-16
DragWindow, 36-37
drawing, 4-6
  Macintosh makefile, 270-271
  Macintosh resource file, 239
  Windows resource file, 206-207
DrawMenuBar, 34, 37
DrawString, 37

E

EndDialog, 19-20
EndPaint, 20
EndUpdate, 37

environmental events, Windows, 9
EraseRect, 37
event handling
    Macintosh, 27-28
    Windows, 8-10
    X Windows, 46-50

F

files, I/O, 95-97
FillRect, 20
FindWindow, 38-39
FrameRect, 37
FrontWindow, 35
functions
    API, 53-59
    toolbox, 33-45
    Windows, 17-24

G

generic pattern matcher class (*see* TNeuralNet
    class)
GetDigItemText, 20
GetDItem, 39
GetFontInfo, 38
GetMessage, 20-21
GetNewDialog, 39
GetNewMBar, 34, 38
GetNewWindow, 39
GetNextEvent, 38
GetPort, 38
GetStockObject, 21
graphics
    Macintosh, 28-29
    Windows, 10-11
    X Windows, 50-51
graphics context (GC), 50
Graphics Device Interface (GDI), 10

H

handwriting classifier, 155-160
    implementation, 156-160
    Macintosh makefile, 271-272
    Macintosh resource file, 239-240
    user interface, 155
    Windows resource file, 207-209
HIB, 139-154
    data, 139-141
    functions, 142-145
    implementation, 146-154
    Macintosh makefile, 272
    Macintosh resource file, 240-241
    supported menu actions, 152-154

Hierarchical Information Browser (*see* HIB)
HiliteMenu, 39

I

I/O
    ASCII text, 95-96
    binary, 96-97
InitCursor, 34, 40
InitDialogs, 34
InitFonts, 34
InitGraf, 40
InitGraf, 33-34
input/output (*see* I/O)
interfacing
    basic user components, 61-68
    integer smart vector class, 91
    TPlotClass, 100-101
InvalidateRect, 21

K

KillTimer, 21

L

LDispose, 40
library class, 68-73
    basic user interface components, 61-68
    handling background processing, 68-69
    Macintosh header files, 242-246
    Macintosh makefiles, 272-273
    Macintosh resource files, 235-238, 241
    Macintosh source files, 246-260
    test program using abstract design, 70-73
    Windows header file, 211-214
    Windows resource file, 209-210
    Windows source file, 215-225
    X Windows header file, 276-281
    X Windows source file, 282-299
LineTo, 21, 40
LNew, 40
LSetCall, 40-41

M

Macintosh, 25-45
    application environments, 32-35
    application interface to OS, 26-27
    class implementation, 235-273
    dialog boxes, 31-32
    document windows, 32
    event handling, 27-28
    graphics operations, 28-29
    resource files for building applications, 29-31
    toolbox functions, 33-45

Macintosh include files, 242-246
  data types header file, 246
  library class header file, 242-246
  smart vector, 261-263
Macintosh makefiles, 270-273
  3D chess, 270
  drawing, 270-271
  handwriting classifier, 271-272
  HIB, 272
  test program, 272-273
  text browser, 273
Macintosh resource files, 235-242
  3D chess, 238-239
  drawing, 238-239
  handwriting classifier, 239-240
  HIB, 240-241
  test program, 241
  text browser, 241-242
Macintosh source files, 246-260
  smart vector, 263-270
MakeProcInstance, 21
MaxApplZone, 34, 41
memory
  allocation, 90-91
  nonsegmented architecture, 92-94
Microsoft Windows (see Windows)
modal dialog boxes, 64-68
  X Windows, 52-53
ModalDialog, 41
MoveTo, 21, 41

N

neural networks, rationale for using, 109 (see
  also TNeuralNet)
neurons, 110
New Technology operating system, 8
NewRgn, 41

O

operating systems
  Mac OS, 26-27
  NT, 8
  Unix, 48

P

PostQuitMessage, 21-22
programs (see source code)

R

Rectangle, 22
RegisterClass, 22

S

ScrollRect, 41
SelectObject, 22
SendDlgItemMessage, 22
SendMessage, 23
SetCTitle, 41-42
SetDlgItemText, 23
SetMenubar, 34, 42
SetPort, 42
SetRect, 23
SetTimer, 23
SFGetFile, 42-43
SFPutFile, 43
ShowWindow, 43-44
software
  faster testing, 90
  using smart vectors, 90
source code
  applib applib applib.cxx, 282-299
  applib.h, 211-214, 242-245, 276-281
  applib.r, 235-238
  applibCommon.h, 245-246
  apptypes.h, 214-215, 246, 282
  br_menu.h, 275
  char_v char_v.h, 225-227, 260, 299-300
  chess.rc, 205-206
  chess3d chess3d.make, 270
  chess3d.r, 238-239
  ch_menu.h, 275
  double_v double_v.h, 226-227, 260-262,
    300
  draw draw.make, 270-271
  draw.r, 239
  draw.rc, 206-207
  d_menu.h, 276
  grapher grapher.h, 79-80
  hand hand.make, 271-272
  hand.r, 239-240
  hand.rc, 207-209
  hello hib hib.make, 272
  hib.r, 240-241
  h_menu.h, 276
  int_vect int_vect.h, 91, 227, 262-263
  makefile, 308-310
  test test.make, 272-273
  test.r, 241
  test.rc, 209-210
  textbr textbr.make, 273
  textbr.r, 241-242
  textbr.rc, 210-211
  TextInd TextInd.h, 121-123
  TNeural TNeural.h, 111-113

source code *cont.*
  tplot   tplot.h, 100-101
  t_menu.h, 276
SysEnvirons, 34, 44

T

TAppApp, 33, 77
TAppWindow, 62-64, 69, 77, 87, 105-106, 160, 163
TEInint, 34, 44
text browser class, 161-167
  implementation, 163-167
  Macintosh makefiles, 273
  Macintosh resource file, 241-242
  user interface, 161
  Windows resource file, 210-211
text indexing class (*see* TextIndex class)
TextEdit, 34
TextFont, 44
TextIndex class, 119-138
  building index files, 137-138
  data structures, 120-121
  design, 120-121
  design requirements, 119-120
  header file, 121-123
  implementation, 121, 124-137
  reading index files, 138
  using, 137-138
TextOut, 23
TGraph, 77, 80
3D chess, 169-199
  designing C++ classes to play, 170-172
  implementation, 172-199
  Macintosh makefile, 270
  Macintosh resource file, 238-239
  rules, 169-170
  user interface design, 170
  Windows resource files, 205-206
timer events, Windows, 9-10
TNeuralNet class, 109-118
  data structure, 111
  design, 110-111
  header file, 111-113
  implementation, 113-118
  model, 110
  software modules, 111
  using, 118
toolbox functions, 33-45
TPlotClass, 99-108
  design, 99
  header file, 100-101
  implementation, 101-104
  interface, 100-101

  usage, 104-108
TranslateMessage, 23-24
TrapAvailable, 34
tree browser class
  data structure definitions, 78-80
  data structure tree layout, 80-87
  design, 77-78
  header file, 79-80
  implementation, 78-87
  using, 87

U

Unix operating system, 48
user events, Windows, 9
utilities
  curve plotting, 99-108
  handwriting classifier, 155-160
  I/O, 95-96
  information browser, 139-154
  neural networks, 109-118
  text browser, 161-167
  text indexing, 119-138
  tree browser, 77-87
  vector classes, 89-94

V

vector class
  existing software use, 90
  faster software testing, 90
  header file, 91
  implementating integer, 91-94
  increasing readability of applications programs, 90
  interface for integer, 91
  Macintosh header files, 261-263
  Macintosh source files, 263-270
  portability for special memory limitations, 90-91
  using, 89-91
  Windows header files, 225-227
  Windows source files, 228-234
  X Windows header files, 299-301
  X Windows source files, 301-308

W

WaitNextEvent, 35
WaitNextEvent, 44-45
Windows, 7-24
  API functions, 17-24
  application environments, 16-17
  application interface to DOS, 7-8
  class implementation, 205-234
  dialog boxes, 11-13

document windows, 13-16
event handling, 8-10
graphics operations, 10-11
Windows include files
data types header files, 214-215
library class header files, 211-214
smart vector class header files, 225-227
Windows resource files
3D chess, 205-206
drawing program, 206-207
handwriting classifier, 207-209
library class, 209-210
text browser, 210-211
Windows source files
library class, 215-225
smart vector class, 228-234
WM_COMMAND, 8, 9
WM_CREATE, 9
WM_LBUTTONDOWN, 9
WM_LBUTTONUP, 9
WM_MOUSE_MOVE, 9
WM_PAINT, 9
WM_TIMER, 9-10

X

X Windows, 47-59
API functions, 53-59
class implementation, 275-310
dialog boxes, 51-53
event handling, 46-50
graphics operations, 50-51
interface to Unix, 48
makefiles, 308-310
modal dialogs, 52-53

data types header files, 282
library class header files, 276-281
vector class header files, 299-301
X Windows source files, 282-299
library class, 282-299
vector class, 301-308
XClearArea, 53
XClearFontCursor, 53
XDrawLine, 53-54
XDrawString, 54
XmCreateMenubar, 54
XmCreatePulldownMenu, 54
XmStringCreate, 55
XmTextGetString, 54
XtAddCallback, 55
XtAddEventHandler, 55
XtAddWorkProc, 55
XtCreateManagedWidget, 56
XtCreatePopupShell, 55-56
XtCreateWidget, 56
XtDestroyWidget, 56
XtDispatchEvent, 49, 56
XtDisplay, 56-57
XtGetGC, 57
XtGetValues, 57
XtInitialize, 57
XtListShowCurent, 57-58
XtManagerChild, 58
XtManageChildren, 58
XtNextEvent, 58
XtPopdown, 58
XtPopup, 58
XtRealizeWidget, 59
XtWindow, 59
XtNextEvent, 49

Mark Watson is a computer scientist working with the Science Applications International Corporation and has experience with expert system tools, natural language processing, neural networks and systems programming, and programs in C++, C, LISP, Prolog, SmallTalk, and Pascal. He has been instrumental in the design and implementation of new technologies, such as the SAIC Object Programming Environment (SOPE), and in establishing the portability of these technologies.